Growing Your Own Herbs

The TIME LIFE
Complete Gardener

Growing Your Own Herbs

By the Editors of Time-Life Books
ALEXANDRIA, VIRGINIA

The Consultant

Holly Shimizu is chief horticulturist and assistant executive director of the United States Botanic Garden in Washington, D.C. She was the first curator of the National Herb Garden at the United States National Arboretum, holding this post for 8 years, and has worked at many well-known European gardens and nurseries including the Hillier Arboretum and the Garden of the Royal Horticultural Society, Wisley. In 1987 she received the Herb Society of America's Award for Outstanding Achievement in Horticulture and, as honorary president of the society, is working to set up the society's national collections of herbs. Shimizu has lectured extensively throughout North America and writes on a variety of horticultural subjects, with an emphasis on herbs, edi-

ble landscapes, environmentally responsible gardening, and roses. She was a contributor to *The American Garden Guide Book on Herb Gardening* (1994) and *Burpee's Encyclopedia of Horticulture* (1995), and served as a consultant on *Eyewitness Handbook on Herbs* (1994). She is a frequent host on the gardening television show *The Victory Garden.*

Library of Congress Cataloging-in-Publication Data
Growing your own herbs / by the editors of Time-Life Books.
p. cm.—(The Time-Life complete gardener)
Includes bibliographical references (p.) and index.
ISBN 0-7835-4114-7
1. Herb gardening. 2. Herbs. I. Time-Life Books. II. Series
SB351.H5H3718   1996   635'.7—dc20   96-12431   CIP
© 1996 Time Life Inc. All rights reserved.

This volume is one of a series of comprehensive gardening books that cover garden design, choosing plants for the garden, planting and propagating, and planting diagrams.

Time-Life Books is a Division of TIME LIFE INC.

TIME LIFE INC.

PRESIDENT and CEO: George Artandi

TIME-LIFE BOOKS

PRESIDENT: John D. Hall
PUBLISHER/MANAGING EDITOR: Neil Kagan

THE TIME-LIFE COMPLETE GARDENER

Director, New Product Development:
Quentin S. McAndrew
Marketing Director: James A. Gillespie

Editorial Staff for *Growing Your Own Herbs*

EDITOR: Janet Cave
Deputy Editors: Sarah Brash, Jane Jordan
Administrative Editor: Roxie France-Nuriddin
Art Director: Kathleen D. Mallow
Picture Editor: Jane A. Martin
Text Editors: Sarah Brash (principal),
Darcie Conner Johnston, Paul Mathless
Associate Editors/Research-Writing: Katya Sharpe,
Robert Speziale, Mary-Sherman Willis
Technical Art Assistant: Sue Pratt
Senior Copyeditor: Anne Farr
Picture Coordinator: David A. Herod
Editorial Assistant: Donna Fountain

Special Contributors: Anne Sinderman (consultant);
Cyndi Bemel, Jennifer Clark (research); Linda Bellamy,
Catriona Tudor Erler, Carole Ottesen, Ann Perry,
Margaret Stevens (research-writing); Bonnie Kreitler
(writing); Gerry Schremp (editing); John Drummond
(art); Lina B. Burton (index).

Correspondents: Christine Hinze (London), Christina
Lieberman (New York)

Vice President, Director of Finance:
Christopher Hearing
Vice President, Book Production: Marjann Caldwell
Director of Operations: Eileen Bradley
Director of Photography and Research:
John Conrad Weiser
Director of Editorial Operations: Judith W. Shanks
Production Manager: Marlene Zack
Quality Assurance Manager: Miriam P. Newton
Library: Louise D. Forstall

*Cover: Reminiscent of a wild meadow, an Oregon property sports fragrant drifts of pale pink and deep purple lavender, pink cranesbill and silvery gray Santolina chamaecyparissus. **End papers:** A North Carolina herb garden is laid out in traditional formal style with symmetrical beds of Santolina virens, 'Silver Mound' artemisia, Lavandula x intermedia 'Provence', and lemon grass; and topiary focal points of silver leaf germander, French lavender, and oak-leaved geranium. **Title page:** A bed of acid yellow lady's-mantle, purple sage gold origanum, and pink chives becomes a study in color and texture in a kitchen garden.*

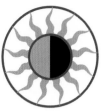

CHAPTER ONE

Herbs in Your Garden

When you plant lavender or thyme in your garden or pot up a basil seedling for your kitchen window, you're becoming part of a tradition as old as recorded history. Herbs—a class of plants distinguished by their wide range of practical uses—have been of service in the household, in commerce, and in religious life for thousands of years. Today they appear as seasoning in food, as teas, and as the active ingredients in medicines, cosmetics, perfumes, and even pesticides. All have a heritage that links them to other places and eras, imparting a sense of timelessness as well as practicality to any garden that includes them.

And yet, these hardworking plants also have a wealth of ornamental graces, as this waterside garden on Bainbridge Island, Washington, shows. Deep purple wands of lavender play against pink and cerise flower heads of yarrow and the tart yellow of curry plant. On the following pages, you'll find a number of other beautiful ways—both traditional and modern—in which to enjoy herbs in your own garden.

A. *Lavandula latifolia (spike lavender) (1)* **B.** *Lavandula angustifolia 'Munstead' (English lavender) (6)* **C.** *Phlomis fruticosa (Jerusalem sage) (1)* **D.** *Rosa 'The Fairy' (rose) (3)* **E.** *Achillea 'Sandstone' (yarrow) (3)* **F.** *Lilium 'Salmon Queen' (lily) (4)* **G.** *Erysimum 'Bowles' Mauve' (wallflower) (2)* **H.** *Perovskia atriplicifolia 'Blue Spire' (Russian sage) (2)* **I.** *Helichrysum angustifolium (curry plant) (7)* **J.** *Salvia officinalis 'Purpurascens' (garden sage) (1)* **K.** *Aster x frikartii (Frikart's aster) (1)*

The key lists each plant type and the number of plants needed to replicate the garden shown. The letters and numbers above refer to the type of plant and the number sited in an area.

Antique Plants for Garden Beauty

A GARDEN OF OLD-TIME REMEDIES
The gray-green foliage of 'Silver King' artemisia makes a soothing backdrop for hot pink catchfly and bright yellow feverfew in this Pennsylvania garden. Artemisia's leaves were used by Native Americans in fever compresses, and feverfew tea was an ancient remedy for arthritis, colds, fevers, and cramps. Today, scientists are studying feverfew for the relief of migraine.

Broadly speaking, herbs are plants associated with the practical. They are used as medicines, flavorings, fragrances, dyes, and pesticides, and in the spiritual realm have served as ceremonial offerings, as mind-altering substances for religious inspiration, and as embalming materials. Herbs are a huge group that includes not only such familiar herbaceous plants as parsley and chives but also shrub-like perennials such as lavender, evergreens such as insect-repelling santolina, and various woody shrubs and trees. For example, *Cinnamomum camphora,* the camphor tree, known for the medicinal qualities of its aromatic wood, bark, and foliage, would be considered an herb. So would laurel for its bay leaf, a much used seasoning; and so would many roses, because of their curative properties as well as their perfume. A number of vines, mosses, and cacti are also used in functional ways, earning them membership in this extensive family.

Herbal History and Lore

In bygone centuries, every part of a plant—roots, stems, bark, leaves, flowers, fruit, seeds, and the essential oils extracted from them—had a potential use. Through hundreds of years of trial and error, people the world over discovered which parts were most effective—and when. For instance, the Chinese learned that the rind of *Citrus reticulata* (tangerine) produces two different kinds of drugs, depending on whether the fruit is ripe or unripe.

Herbs are, in fact, the oldest cultivated garden species in the world. Many that are currently available have remained close to their ancient original, or common, form, as the words *communis* or *vulgaris* in their botanical names attest. Botanical names can also reflect former uses; *officinalis* designates a medicinal plant, for example. Indeed,

from the earliest times herbs have been grown for their various health-giving and healing properties, according to ancient Chinese, Ayurvedic, and Egyptian writings dating from 5,000 years ago.

As trade routes developed, herbal lore spread throughout Greece, Rome, the Arab-speaking world, and Europe. Herbal recipe books such as the first-century AD Greek *De Materia Medica*—the authority on plants and their medical applications for the next 1,500 years—served as the foundation of extensive herbal traditions that developed in medieval European monasteries.

When Europeans began immigrating to North America, they brought with them the native herbs they considered useful, pleasing, and necessary for survival: lady's-mantle *(Alchemilla),* a styptic to control bleeding; *Filipendula ulmaria,* which produces salicylic acid, the chemical base of aspirin; tasty parsley, spearmint, laurel, oregano, common sage, thyme, garlic, and fennel; sweet-scented lavender and soothing chamomile from the Mediterranean; the common hopvine *(Humulus lupulus),* used as a sedative; and many others.

They also came with exotic herbs they had imported from other lands. Onion, mustard, caraway, coriander, and the fragrant damask rose all originated in the Middle East. Cinnamon, cardamom, and basil *(Ocimum basilicum)* were originally transplants from India, *Aloe vera* and the castor bean are African natives, and ginger, licorice, ginseng, and camphor wood are Chinese.

Besides the botanical wealth the settlers carried with them, they found a Native American culture expert in the use of a whole new class of herbs. For example, they learned to use the native slippery elm *(Ulmus rubra)* for stomach ulcers, wild indigo *(Baptisia tinctoria)* as a blue dye, and witch hazel *(Hamamelis virginiana)* for irritated skin and sore muscles. Woodland plants such as red trillium *(Trillium erectum)* helped induce childbirth, and as late as the Civil War, the bark of dogwood *(Cornus florida)* was used to treat malaria.

Herbs in Garden Design

Knowing an herb's place of origin is the best starting point when planning an herb garden, because herbs bring with them the soil, moisture, and sun requirements of their native habitats. Most prefer plenty of sun and a fast-draining soil, but many are shade- and moisture-tolerant woodland plants, and scores perform well in pots. In the following pages, you'll discover how to group your plants thematically as well as visually to create a truly personal garden design.

NATIVE PLANTS WITH MANY USES
Broad leaves of bloodroot nestle among fronds of maidenhair fern in this mossy Alabama woodland. Bloodroot, which grows along the East Coast and westward to Kansas and Texas, was used by the Cherokee as a remedy for colds and cancerous growths, and as war paint and fabric dye. Some tribes also made a rinse from the foliage of maidenhair to give their hair luster and body.

Hazardous Herbs

Herbs can be harmful as well as beneficial. Used in excess, any can make you ill, but some, such as the foxglove below, require extra care. Avoid these plants if you have small children or pets:

SKIN IRRITANTS

Hydrastis canadensis
(goldenseal)
Myrica cerifera
(bayberry)
Ruta graveolens
(rue)

CARCINOGENS

Acorus calamus
(sweet flag)
Angelica archangelica
(angelica)
Symphytum officinale
(comfrey)

TOXIC TO THE HEART

Arnica montana
(arnica)
Digitalis purpurea
(foxglove)
Tanacetum vulgare
(tansy)

POISONOUS

Artemisia absinthium
(wormwood)
Cimicifuga racemosa
(black cohosh)
Colchicum autumnale

(autumn crocus)
Convallaria majalis
(lily of the valley)
Gaultheria procumbens
(wintergreen)
Hedeoma pulegioides
(pennyroyal)

Iris versicolor
(blue flag)
Ricinus communis
(castor-oil plant)
Sanguinaria canadensis
(bloodroot)

Digitalis purpurea 'Excelsior Hybrids' (foxglove)

Herbs for All Reasons

Herbs have traditionally occupied a separate and distinct place in the garden. Grouped for practical purposes, these valued plants were also often enclosed in protected spaces to keep them sheltered from the elements and performing at their best.

You can draw on the wealth of traditions and associations surrounding herbs to add meaning to your own garden design. Some herb enthusiasts create thematic arrangements drawn from literature or mythology, while others collect herbs according to their many specific uses. On the other hand, herbs can also be incorporated into the main body of your garden—mixed among grasses, say, or trimmed into hedges, or punctuating a garden path with fragrant mounds of foliage.

Inspiration from the Past

Two traditional types of herb gardens may guide you in designing a garden with historic appeal. The first is the geometric monastery garden of medieval Europe, and the other is the dooryard garden of Colonial North America, which is less formal and is oriented loosely to the exterior contours of the house. Both suit the practical nature of herb gardening and convey a sense of grace and order at the same time.

Monastery gardens reflect the life of the clergy in the Middle Ages. Monasteries were walled sanctuaries in which gardening was almost as important as prayer. In the kitchen garden the resident monks grew vegetables, fruits, and culinary herbs such as parsley, thyme, sage, mint, fennel, lovage, rue, and lemon balm. And in what was called the physic garden, they developed herbal medicines, supplying curative herbs during plague years. The first rose known to be cultivated for its medicinal value—*Rosa gallica* 'Officinalis', or apothecary's rose—was a staple in these walled gardens.

Medieval herb gardens were laid out in formal rows of rectangular beds, an arrangement that was deemed the most efficient for cultivating and keeping track of the plants. These beds were usually raised and contained within wooden boards. The kitchen herbs were organized according to use: leafy culinary herbs in one bed, for example, and onions, garlic, and shallots in another. Medicinal herbs were segregated from the culinary to avoid the danger of picking the wrong plants.

The garden enclosed within the cloister walls was a kind of outdoor chapel, a place to meditate and pray. Surrounded by a covered walkway, the space was divided into quarters by pathways that intersected at a central focal point—a fountain or a well, for instance. These paths represented the four rivers of Paradise as described in the book of Genesis and were typically configured with a north-south and an east-west axis. Ornamental flowers were scarce, so monks sometimes constructed the paths in decorative patterns on the ground, curved in a maze or knot shape.

Later, in the 16th century, the knot design would be traced out with low-growing herbal hedges, planted to weave together in intricate patterns like those woven into carpets and fabrics of the day. Gardeners of the English Renaissance

A CLUSTER OF CULINARY HERBS
In this New Jersey garden, kitchen herbs create a feast for the eyes as well as the palate. Curving blades of lemon grass arch over spiky rosemary, while broad-leaved borage elbows for space with neat mounds of lemon basil and orange mint. Brightening the scene is white-flowering cilantro, whose seeds make the spice cardamom.

planted knots of evergreen herbs such as lavender, santolina, and germander; boxwood too was often used. Besides adding beauty to the garden, the hedging probably served as a place to dry laundry. Spread over hedges in the sun, the wet cloth would absorb the herbs' refreshing fragrance.

While many gardeners honor herbal history by recreating the graceful layout of a knot garden *(page 22)*, others prefer to put together collections of plants on the basis of historical associations. A garden of biblical herbs would be likely to include wormwood, rue, hyssop, anise, mint, dill, coriander, saffron, cumin, and roses. Shakespeare lovers might plant cowslip, primrose, and dianthus; cooking herbs such as marjoram and oregano; low shrubs of lavender and germander; and the antique *Rosa gallica* and *Rosa* 'Alba Semi-Plena'.

Herbs in the Dooryard

The more modest dooryard garden is a descendant of the peasant cottage garden, where indispensable herbs were kept close at hand. These were among the first gardens to appear in Colonial America. Tucked against the walls of the house and lining pathways, such gardens contained the household's herbs, organized according to their purpose. While modern dooryard gardens are not as vital to the household as they were in the past, valued herbs are still kept near at hand.

Foremost are flavorings and garnishes for the kitchen. Your dooryard garden might include herbs for salads and soups, colorful and strong-flavored herbs to enliven bland dishes, and herbs that ease digestion, such as fennel, dill, and caraway. In addition, certain culinary herbs offer benefits besides seasoning. Garlic, for instance, acts as an intestinal disinfectant, and parsley is often used as a breath freshener and is valued as a rich source of iron and vitamin A.

Near your culinary plants you might also grow herbs for the teapot. Infusions of chamomile *(Matricaria recutita)* and mint make soothing after-

A Walled Garden Paradise

The tradition of a high-walled or fenced herb garden is an ancient one. Indeed, the word *paradise* comes from the Greek word for the walled gardens of Persia. Secluded and secure, the enclosures contain the heady scents of blossoms such as roses—as well as the buzz of insects busily working over their blooms.

More than just property markers, walls and fences have always been used to keep out roving animals, screen utilitarian gardens from view, and shelter plants from buffeting winds. They also come in handy as supports for climbing plants, such as the bright pink swamp rose *(Rosa palustris)* growing in the southeast Texas herb

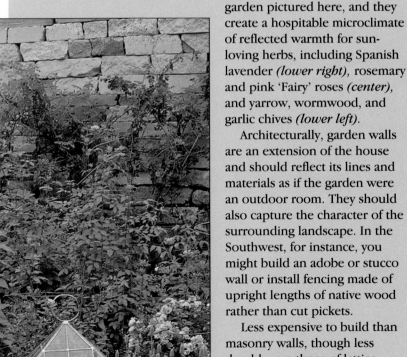

garden pictured here, and they create a hospitable microclimate of reflected warmth for sun-loving herbs, including Spanish lavender *(lower right)*, rosemary and pink 'Fairy' roses *(center)*, and yarrow, wormwood, and garlic chives *(lower left)*.

Architecturally, garden walls are an extension of the house and should reflect its lines and materials as if the garden were an outdoor room. They should also capture the character of the surrounding landscape. In the Southwest, for instance, you might build an adobe or stucco wall or install fencing made of upright lengths of native wood rather than cut pickets.

Less expensive to build than masonry walls, though less durable, are those of lattice. These let in light and breezes and provide climbing support for roses and vining herbs.

Evergreen Herbs

Arctostaphylos uva-ursi (bearberry)	*Poterium sanguisorba* (salad burnet)
Artemisia x *'Powis Castle'* (artemisia)	*Salvia officinalis 'Berggarten'* (sage)
Chamaemelum nobile (Roman chamomile)	*Santolina chamaecyparissus* (lavender cotton)
Dianthus caryophyllus (clove pink)	*Satureja montana* (winter savory)
Equisetum hyemale (rough horsetail)	*Teucrium chamaedrys* (germander)
Gaultheria hispida (snowberry)	*Thymus* x *citriodorus 'Aureus'* (golden lemon thyme)
Gaultheria procumbens (wintergreen)	*Thymus herba-barona* (caraway thyme)
Hyssopus officinalis ssp. *aristatus* (hyssop)	*Thymus pulegioides* (broad-leaved thyme)
Lavandula angustifolia (English lavender)	*Thymus vulgaris* (common thyme)

Bands of dwarf lavender cotton and germander wind through loops of barberry in this California knot garden. A clipped ball of myrtle centers the composition.

dinner beverages, and the steeped hips of *Rosa canina* or *R. rugosa* provide a healthy dose of vitamin C. Herbal teas can be stimulating or relaxing: Those made with thyme, elecampane, hyssop, lovage, and mint can perk you up, while catmint, chamomile, chicory root, lemon balm, and mugwort are soothing before bedtime.

In another section of the Colonial dooryard garden were the herbs that served as the household's medicine cabinet. From them were made "simples"—remedies containing a single healing ingredient—to cure anything from snakebite to depression. In the present day, a collection of curative plants would be mostly for show, because self-medication with herbs is risky for a number of reasons— dosages are often inexact and unpredictable, and many plants are poisonous. Among historical herbal remedies were valerian root as a painkiller, horehound tea as a cough remedy, and comfrey to help heal broken bones. Arnica was used to treat bruises and inflammation, eucalyptus oil killed germs and relieved chest colds, and clove oil eased toothache.

Herbs served the family's cosmetic needs as well. Skin-healing herbs included calendula, rose, witch hazel, elderflower, and comfrey. Today, chamomile and rosemary are often added to hair rinses, and peppermint, spearmint, bloodroot, and thyme are natural antiseptics used in toothpastes and mouthwashes.

Weavers and spinners found yet another use for this versatile group of plants, growing herbs for fabric dyes. Shades of yellow are produced by comfrey leaves, certain chamomile flowers, and marigold and tansy petals. The leaves of woad *(Isatis tinctoria)* produce a blue dye, while elderberries yield violet-purple, and elder leaves pro-

FLANKING A GARDEN PATH *Encroaching upon the gravel path in this Seattle property, aromatic 'Hopley's Purple' oregano (Origanum laevigatum) (lower left) froths over with wine red flowers, while across the way powder-green leaves of 'Berggarten' sage send up clouds of fragrance when stepped on.*

duce green. The roots of meadowsweet *(Filipendula ulmaria)* yield black, and red can be produced from madder, rue, and alkanet.

A Garden of Scented Herbs

Usefulness is but one appealing property of herbs. Another—and one that heightens their sensual impact—is the fragrance of their volatile oils, flowers, fruits, roots, and resins. Many herbs are commercial sources of perfume. The best modern perfumes and colognes consist of sharp scents like lime, basil, coriander, bergamot, and lavender, mixed with flowers and spices like rose, jasmine, nutmeg, clove, and ginger. A third, woody, scent is added for balance: usually cedarwood, sandalwood, vetiver, or vanilla.

The ancient and recently revived practice of aromatherapy draws on the pungent power of herbs and their oils to achieve desired mental states and physical effects. For example, specific aromas are reputed to soothe or stimulate the mind, energize the body, induce a positive mood, or help cure insomnia. Commercially available aromatherapy preparations include massage oils and bath salts as well as distilled essences.

When dried, certain fragrant herbs are used in sachets and potpourris. Herbal potpourri is a decorative mix of chopped-up plants, twigs, and bits of fruit set out in open bowls to scent a room *(page 81)*. Sachets, on the other hand, consist of dried herbs such as lavender or rose petals packaged in fabric pouches and placed in a drawer or a closet to keep its contents fresh. Known as strewing herbs, plants used for this purpose are those that smell delicious even after they've been dried.

A number of strewing herbs pleasing to the human nose are repellent to insects. As a result, such herbs can help protect fabrics from damage by certain pests. Dry the leaves of sweet woodruff, Indian tobacco *(Nicotiana rustica)*, tansy, Euro-

SILVERY HERBS IN A POOL OF LIGHT
United by similar silver tones, the foliage in this Connecticut garden also provides a pleasing variety of forms. Lance-shaped leaves of 'Silver King' artemisia, growing in front of pink-blooming bee balm, contrast with the feathery wands of fringed wormwood (Artemisia frigida) to the right and the furry round lamb's ears surrounding it. Blooms of lavender cotton, yarrow, and a single elecampane flower add spots of yellow.

pean and American pennyroyal, and the flower heads of painted daisy *(Chrysanthemum coccineum)*, then crumble them into sachets. Or try patchouli *(Pogostemon cablin)*, lavender, mint, and rosemary, the sharp camphor scent of camphor basil or eucalyptus, and the woody perfume of vetiver and sweet flag roots. The sachets should keep their potency for about 3 months.

The deterrent properties of certain herbs can be used in other ways as well. The essential oils of lemon balm, black cohosh *(Cimicifuga racemosa)*, European pennyroyal, and spicebush all keep insects away. Citronella, made from oil grass *(Cymbopogon nardus)*, is a mosquito repellent available in candles to be lit and placed around your patio or deck. More than merely repelling pests, both the nicotine in tobacco and the pyrethrum derived from *Tanacetum cinerariifolium* are effective insecticides.

When planting a garden of these herbs, the trick is knowing where to place them for best effect. Herbs with fragrant foliage—such as thymes, sages, rosemary, lemon verbena, lavender, santolina, and the many scented geraniums—need the sun to release their volatile oils. Others release them only when their foliage is lightly crushed by being stepped on or brushed against. Plant low-growing chamomile, thyme, and pennyroyal among steppingstones, and taller mint, anise, catmint, and artemisia along a border's edge. Or keep any of them in a pot to pinch as you pass by.

Fragrant herbs that bloom—including almond-scented meadowsweet, violets, lemony bee balm, lavender, garlic chives, spicy nasturtiums, rosemary, nicotiana, dianthus, and roses—can be best appreciated when they are grown in raised beds or large planters that elevate them so that their scents waft nearer your nose. You may also want to situate your blooming herbs near windows so you can enjoy their perfume inside as well as out.

A LURE FOR BUTTERFLIES
The rusty pink flowers of Joe-Pye weed (above) are a common summer sight in meadows and thickets from New Hampshire to Florida and across the Great Plains to western Nebraska. A decorative herb for the back of the flower bed, domesticated cultivars can grow as high as 12 feet. Native Americans made a diuretic tea from the plant, named for a 19th-century settler who promoted the root as a cure for typhus.

Growing among a profusion of ornamental flowers in the Washington State garden below, flat disks of yarrow and frothy lady's-mantle bloom in yellows that complement the violet scabiosa and purple 'Red Fox' veronica around them. When paired with blues and violets, yellow heats up the color scheme—and here it also picks up the gold deep in the throats of the pink trumpet lilies that tower over the bed.

A Garden of Wild Herbs

Some of the most popular herbs are those that grow in the wild *(list, page 19),* but many of these are becoming scarce. For example, American ginseng *(Panax quinquefolius),* native to eastern North America, has been collected almost to extinction since it began to be exported in the 1700s as a substitute for Chinese ginseng, which is thought to protect against the effects of stress.

Consider providing a haven for some of these species in your garden. Be aware, though, that certain native and naturalized plants can become invasive where conditions are especially to their liking. European woad *(Isatis tinctoria),* for example, can take over a garden in California. The list of native and naturalized herbs on page 19 contains those that are the least invasive.

For a shady woodland garden, choose naturalized woodland species such as mountain mint, lily of the valley, sweet woodruff, and periwinkle, and natives such as wild ginger, bloodroot, maidenhair fern, bunchberry *(Cornus canadensis),* black cohosh, and frost-tender yerba buena *(Satureja douglasii),* which can adapt to sun or shade. Place them among a collection of medicinal shrubs and small trees that might include witch hazel, dogwood, sassafras, and Carolina allspice.

If your garden is open and sunny, plant butterfly weed, fragrant goldenrod, yarrow, purple coneflower *(Echinacea purpurea),* artemisia, sage, bearberry, bayberry, and rugosa roses. In moist areas, try marsh mallow, blue flag iris, New England aster *(Aster novae-angliae),* alumroot, and sweet violets among aromatic spicebushes and tall American sweetgum *(Liquidambar styraciflua),* an old-fashioned source of antiseptic.

A note of caution: Never take plants from the wild unless they are about to be destroyed by development. Instead, look for them in nurseries, garden centers, and catalogs. Catalogs specific to your region often offer the best selection of well-suited natives. If you do purchase nursery plants, make sure they are identified as "nursery propagated." The terms "nursery raised" or "nursery grown" may denote plants that have been collected illegally and grown in the nursery for a season.

The Ornamental Herb

Herbs are not usually the first plants to come to mind if the purpose of your garden is purely ornamental. But they can supply colors, textures, and forms to rival the best ornamentals, and they can be tough in the bargain. Some, such as lady's-mantle, carnations, daisies, lily of the valley, crocuses, and roses, have been garden flowers for so long that they're hardly considered herbs anymore.

A number of the showiest flowers in the garden belong to herbs. Clary sage produces 12-inch stems covered with white or pale blue flowers backed by pink bracts. Foxgloves, mulleins, hollyhocks *(Alcea rosea),* and giant alliums send up flower spires that reach considerable heights. *Cimicifuga racemosa,* with its tall white blooms, is a late-summer showstopper. And cultivars of native American bee balm produce curious spider-like flowers in hues of red, pink, or white that are a lure to hummingbirds.

And yet, as decorative as the flowers of herbs can be, it is the colors and textures of their foliage that are their greatest glory. The varieties of leaf patterns and colors within even a single species—such as species of mint, thyme, marjoram, and salvia—can make handsome collections on their own. For example, the various cultivars of *Salvia officinalis* could furnish a beautiful garden: 'Aurea' has leaves variegated gold and green; those of 'Berggarten' are wide and woolly; 'Tricolor' is mottled green, white, and maroon; 'Purpurea' foliage is solid burgundy; and the original species has narrow leaves of bluish gray.

If you're looking for interesting tones and shades of yellow, try the warm foliage of *Laurus nobilis* 'Aurea', lemon balm, variegated ginger mint, golden oregano *(Origanum vulgare* 'Aureum'), lemony *Thymus* x *citriodorus* 'Aureus', and golden hops *(Humulus lupulus* 'Aureus'). For variegated green-and-white foliage, plant pineapple mint, scented geraniums, variegated sweet myrtle, lungwort, silver thyme, and blue-green variegated rue. And if it's purple foliage you want, 'Purple Ruffles' and 'Dark Opal' basil, as well as purple perilla, should satisfy your desire.

The blue-gray part of the herbal spectrum is especially beautiful. Woolly thyme, artemisia, lavender, sage, catmint, santolina, dittany-of-Crete, and the ghostly gray of lamb's ears *(Stachys byzantina)* tone down hot colors and add an exquisite counterpoint to dusty pinks, lavenders, and blues. Dittany-of-Crete and lamb's ears are fuzzy and soft, contrasting well with shiny- and leathery-leaved plants like roses and rosemary.

Herbal Edging and Hedging

An herb planting or a vegetable bed, so often composed of a medley of diverse plants, needs the strong line of a hedge or a planted edging to define its contours. A hedge or an edging also unifies the structure of the whole garden by drawing lines that lead the eye from one part to the other. The plant or plants you choose for this purpose are typically dictated by the style of your garden.

Formal arrangements require frequent trimmings throughout the season to keep the lines sharp and neat. Select compact herbs for formal gardens that need a low sculpted hedge or edging. Dwarf cultivars of curry plant, germander, hyssop, and lavender are well suited to form hedges up to 2 feet high, and *Santolina chamaecyparissus* can be trimmed to 32 inches.

Taller hedges make a beautiful and fragrant backdrop for plants in the foreground. Lavender cotton and southernwood can be shaped into a neat hedge almost 3 feet tall to make a gray background. *Lavandula spica*, a rough gray-green, can reach 4 feet; *Rosmarinus officinalis* 'Miss Jessup's Upright' can reach as high as 6 feet in Zone 8. Even with the repeated trimming throughout the season that these shrubs need to keep looking their dignified best, they will bloom in summer.

An informal border edge can be looser and more billowy, fashioned of slightly unruly plants like *Nepeta mussinii* 'Blue Wonder' (dwarf catmint), unclipped artemisia, sage, lady's-mantle, and lavender. The silvery colors of these plants al-

low the bed's more dramatic elements to take center stage. Or, if you'd like blooms along the periphery of your herb garden, primulas, dianthus, and English daisies make pretty, cheerful edgings.

Many shrubby herbs are evergreens, invaluable for maintaining the shape of your design throughout the seasons *(list, page 12)*. However, in the North even these hardy plants take a beating, so in these regions a border of annual herbs is probably the best solution. Try dwarf basil, in particular *Ocimum basilicum* 'Bush' and 6-inch-tall *O. b.* 'Spicy Globe'. The basil cultivar 'Purple Ruffles' grows only to 18 inches and makes a stunning border. Marjoram, parsley, and chervil also serve admirably as edging plants, with the advantage that any trimmings go straight to the kitchen.

Two shrubs not technically classified as herbs have traditionally been included in herb gardens. The first, boxwood *(Buxus)*, is a staple for hedging and topiary in formal gardens, and when used as a backdrop its lustrous dark green foliage seems to bring out the best in other plants. *Buxus microphylla* (littleleaf box) is lower growing and hardier than *B. sempervirens* (common box), although the cultivars *B. s.* 'Suffruticosa' (dwarf English box) and the lighter-colored *B. s.* 'Compacta' have compact, rounded forms that are good for shaping into low hedges and globes. These boxwoods will

STEP IN THYME
This soft-textured lawn of caraway thyme (Thymus herba-barona) thrives under the hot California sun, becoming a carpet of lavender flowers in summer. Growing only 2 to 5 inches tall, the lawn needs no mowing, but any trimmings can be added to meat and poultry dishes. Along the front of the yard, a low hedge of catmint (Nepeta x faassenii) emits a minty smell when brushed against. It too produces a bounty of flowers in summer, the blue-violet blooms set off by the grayish foliage.

stay under 2 feet. Other varieties, left unclipped, grow into tall, spreading shrubs.

The second companion shrub is the rugged barberry *(Berberis thunbergii)*, whose dangling berries appear in colors of red, yellow, blue, or black in the fall. *B. t.* 'Atropurpurea' has reddish leaves that contrast beautifully with the silvers and greens of other herbs; 'Crimson Pygmy' is the dwarf variety, reaching 2 feet after 8 years. 'Erecta' has an upright habit ideal for taller hedges, while 'Globe' is rounded in form. For multicolored foliage look for 'Variegata', which is mottled with spots of white, light gray, and yellow.

Herbs with Other Plants

A number of ornamental plants make congenial partners with herbs in beds and borders. Many, including peonies, hellebores, irises, and lilies, appeared in the ancient herbals. Others, with a rough, easy vigor, simply *look* like herbs. Lupines, columbines, and poppies, for example, are perennials with colorful flowers that mingle especially well with herbs.

Many herbs thrive in sunny, even dry, locations. Attractive companions that are drought tolerant—mixing well with like-minded yarrow, artemisia, or lavender—include Mexican evening primrose *(Oenothera berlandieri)*, Shasta daisy *(Chrysanthemum* x *superbum)*, yellow- and pink-flowered sun roses *(Helianthemum nummularium)*, sedum, the papery blossoms of bellflower *(Campanula)*, sea thrift *(Armeria maritima)*, and toadflax *(Linaria purpurea)*. And to add the drama of spiky leaves to your garden, plant sea holly *(Eryngium maritimum)*, cardoon *(Cynara cardunculus)*, yucca, globe thistle *(Echinops)*, or the rhubarb relative *Rheum palmatum*—all of which also prefer quick-draining, sunny conditions.

Grasses also pair well with herbs. Their arching, upright forms interweave with the herbs' sprawling or clumping foliage and pick up their subtle colors. Try Bowles' golden grass *(Milium effussum* 'Aureum') or moisture-tolerant Bowles' golden sedge *(Carex elata* 'Aurea') to augment the warm hues in lemon balm and the flowers of lady's-mantle. In a silver-blue or silver-green scheme, add blue fescue *(Festuca ovina* var. *glauca)*, blue oat grass *(Helictotrichon sempervirens)*, or 5-foot-tall *Stipa gigantea* (feather grass). For tinges of red, use red fescue, Japanese blood grass *(Imperata cylindrica* 'Red Baron'), or the stunning *Hakonechloa macra* 'Aureola', with green-striped yellow leaves and reddish flower spikes in fall. If you've planted herbs with variegated

An Herb Garden to Please Bees

Bees are some of the best pollinators in the garden. Without them, your hollies and apple trees would produce fewer fruits, and many annual flowers would go unpollinated, failing to develop seeds. Luckily, you can attract bees to your garden by planting their favorite herbs, as the owner of the New Jersey herb garden pictured above has done. Bees seek out yellow, blue, and purple flowers to feed on the nectar, and in the process they distribute pollen from plant to plant. In spring, they begin their task on early primroses and crocuses, as well as on annuals such as these yellow and orange marigolds.

With the arrival of summer's bonanza of flowers, bees seek out lavender, sage, basil, and thyme. Your garden might also include bee balm, one of the few red flowers they are drawn to. Catmint, hyssop, marjoram, dill, lemon balm, borage, melilot *(Melilotus officinalis)*, and viper's bugloss *(Echium vulgare)* are all rich in nectar and attractive to bees. In fall, winter savory and roses provide forage until the season ends.

In addition to food, bees need shelter. A bee skep—the hive-shaped basket pictured above—is purely ornamental. It harks back to Colonial days, when a similar type of basket with a hole in its bottom served as a primitive hive. Even without housing, bees will come to your garden if you just choose a quiet, sunny spot protected from the wind. Provide a sheltering hedge of rosemary or lavender, or a taller privet with its heavily scented flowers, or build a trellis for a climbing rose. Then listen for the telltale drone of bees at work.

HERBS TO
TAKE THE HEAT
Drought tolerant and sun loving, a swath of lavender cotton, set to open its buttonlike sulfur yellow flowers, wraps around a boulder in a Santa Barbara, California, rock-garden terrace. Nestled beside the lavender cotton, a prostrate juniper, along with various succulents, seems to cascade between the stones,

Native and Naturalized Herbs

Acorus calamus *** (sweet flag)

Adiantum capillus-veneris *** (maidenhair fern)

Anthemis tinctoria *** (dyer's chamomile)

Arctostaphylos uva-ursi (bearberry)

Artemisia ludoviciana *** (white sage)

Asarum canadense *** (wild ginger)

Asclepias tuberosa *** (butterfly weed)

Calendula officinalis (calendula)

Cimicifuga racemosa *** (black cohosh)

Digitalis lanata (foxglove)

Eupatorium purpureum *** (Joe-Pye weed)

Filipendula ulmaria (queen-of-the-meadow)

Gaultheria procumbens *** (wintergreen)

Geranium maculatum *** (wild geranium)

Heuchera americana *** (alumroot)

Iris versicolor *** (blue flag)

Matricaria recutita (German chamomile)

Melissa officinalis (lemon balm)

Monarda fistulosa *** (wild bergamot)

Papaver rhoeas (corn poppy)

Salvia clevelandii *** (blue sage)

Sanguinaria canadensis *** (bloodroot)

Santolina chamaecyparissus (lavender cotton)

Saponaria officinalis (soapwort)

Solidago odora *** (fragrant goldenrod)

Symphytum officinale (comfrey)

Tanacetum parthenium (feverfew)

Verbascum thapsus (mullein)

Viola tricolor (Johnny-jump-up)

*This plant is native to North America.

Anthemis tinctoria (dyer's chamomile)

foliage, echo the pattern with white-striped zebra grass (*Miscanthus sinensis* 'Zebrinus') or manna grass (*Glyceria maxima* 'Variegata').

In mixed beds and borders, ornamental shrubs can add height and mass—and more color. The 5-foot-tall *Caryopteris* 'Heavenly Blue' produces a haze of small blue flowers in August that matches the violet-blue of catmint, while *Spiraea japonica* (Japanese spirea) has flat clusters of scented pink or scarlet flowers. *S.* x *bumalda* is smaller, about 2 feet high compared with the 4 feet of its cousin, and sports new foliage that is tinged pink. The spirea accentuates the pinks and reds of bee balm, saxifrage, pink cultivars of *Achillea millefolium* (yarrow), foxglove, chives, pink meadowsweet (*Filipendula rubra*), and pink roses. Viburnums, buddleias, mock orange, lilac, and even a small fig tree also make lovely companions. Balance their loose-formed habits and anchor the composition with a juniper, a yew, or a clipped boxwood.

Vegetable and rose gardeners have long de-pended on fragrant herbs to protect and improve their plants. Garlic and rue, for example, enjoy an enduring reputation for keeping aphids away from roses, and wormwood and southernwood seem to deter moths and beetles. Chamomile has been called the plant doctor because of its apparent health-giving effects on anything growing nearby. On the other hand, beans are said to grow poorly in the company of fennel, and basil to languish next to rue.

Unfortunately, much of the evidence for the beneficial effects of companion planting is anecdotal. For example, an old axiom has it that plants that go together in cooking grow well together—tomatoes and basil, cabbages and dill, carrots and sage—and many gardeners routinely combine these plants without knowing why. The explanation may simply be that one provides the other with necessary cooling shade. Or the herb may attract beneficial insects such as bees to the area, offering them nectar, pollen, and shelter for laying eggs *(page 17)*. For instance, the helpful ladybug likes to congregate on tansy and yarrow, and daisy and marigold pollen attract hover flies, which produce aphid-eating larvae. Whatever the reasons for their success, combinations involving herbs are worth experimenting with to find which work best for you. The potential of these powerful plants is still being explored.

Designing Your Herb Garden

For all their traditional appeal, herbs lend themselves well to gardening in modern landscapes. Most garden settings today are similar to the compartmentalized gardens of the past in that each area of a home landscape tends to have its own purpose. Some gardens within the overall scheme may be purely decorative, while others may be used for recreation, escape, or the cultivation of special plants. Some open to a distant vista, while others offer shelter and repose. Whatever the nature of the garden, herbs have a place.

Understanding some simple design principles will help simplify the work of planning a visually appealing herb garden. At the same time, you'll need to factor in such practicalities as finding the right site, situating pathways, and selecting plants for year-round interest. Once you've considered all of these variables, you'll be ready to put your plan into action.

Even if you're only designing a small herb-filled niche, it should be unified with the rest of the setting. You can accomplish this by using materials for edging that are similar to those used for other features in the landscape. For example, if you have a brick terrace, outline a nearby garden with a row of the same bricks set on end. Also, make the outline of the garden follow or repeat the lines of the house, the garden walls, the patio, or some primary feature within the garden itself, such as a pond.

The size of your garden in relation to the landscape around it and to the objects within it is another critical consideration. An herb garden can be a small, densely packed planting nestled in a corner, or a patterned expanse such as a knot garden, or a free-ranging ground cover. Whatever the configuration, it should neither overpower nor be diminished by the objects around it.

The most important measuring rod to establish scale is the human body. An herb bed too wide to reach across can't be tended, and a plant that car-

A FORMAL GARDEN IN WINTER DRESS
Snow cloaks the simple yet beautiful forms in this Connecticut herb display. A plain knot garden made of squares of germander and rue sits at the point where an alley of bare 'Seckel' pears and evergreen 'Wichita Blue' junipers intersects with two short rows of 100-year-old boxwood hedges. A trellised fence with an arched gateway separates the orderly refuge from the woods beyond.

At the same time, keep in mind that a bit of color contrast will prevent the monotony that can result from reliance on a narrow palette. Pink or lavender nicely accents a white garden, for instance, and yellow pops out among blue or purple flowers. Especially pure yellows are found in the buttons of 'E. C. Buxton' dyer's chamomile, yellow foxglove *(Digitalis lutea),* French marigolds, the yarrow cultivar 'Moonshine', and the wide, daisylike disks of elecampane. For delicate yellow flowers tinged with green, plant lady's-mantle, angelica, mustard, and rue. Calendulas in shades of orange-yellow, or red-flowered pineapple sage and bee balm can also warm up a blue garden.

Foliage size, shape, and texture create another source of contrast. The feathery leaves of dill, fennel, and French marigold create a misty filigree, while fine-toothed santolina, caraway, artemisia, fringed lavender *(Lavandula dentata),* parsley, tansy, and yarrow contrast with the bold foliage of comfrey or castor bean, the spires of foxglove, or the flat-faced leaves of lady's-mantle.

Finally, a plant's overall form makes an important statement. Spiky iris or towering cardoon add vertical movement and dramatic contrast when placed next to mounding plants like dwarf basil, rue, lavender, or artemisia. Mat-forming or clumping ground huggers such as thyme, chamomile, creeping savory, dwarf santolina, pinks, and lady's-mantle link taller plants to each other visually and to the landscape, as well as softening craggy slopes and rounding off the sharp edges of retaining walls, stone steps, and rock edging.

Choosing a Style and Making a Plan

If your taste leans toward the formal, consider planting a knot garden, composed of intertwined bands laid out like a bas-relief carpet in a mirroring symmetry. Achieved with careful planning *(page 22),* it is beautiful even in winter, embossed with a blanket of snow. Herbs for each band of the knot garden should be of markedly different foliage colors to create a strong contrast between the intertwining areas of the design.

Choose plants that are roughly the same height at maturity—less than 24 inches tall and wide—and dense enough to create a seamless and solid design when pruned. Some naturally compact herbs are dwarf basil, curly chives, 'Blue Mound' rue, 'Twikel' English lavender, and burnet *(Poterium sanguisorba),* as well as the more traditional knot-garden members like germander, santolina, hyssop, low-growing artemisias, lemon thyme, and

A DOORYARD DISPLAY *An informal garden suits this rustic Texas home and provides the kitchen with herbs. Fennel and bay laurel grace the front of the bed, while silver artemisia and a border of lavender-flowered onion chives lead the eye toward the house. Mexican oregano, growing behind the fennel, is a native herb used in Southwest cuisine.*

ries its flowers too high to see or smell can't be enjoyed. Similarly, you'll want to choose plants that aren't wildly different in scale. In addition, keep the height of the tallest plants in a border to less than half the distance from front to back.

You can also unify your herb garden by repeating the same plant at regular intervals. Or you can establish a color theme. For example, a blue-and-lavender garden would group catmint, bachelor's-buttons, lavender, spiderwort, and blue flag irises. A white garden would include angelica, artemisia, sweet woodruff, and the white-flowering cultivars of hyssop, bee balm, and creeping thyme *(Thymus praecox* ssp. *arcticus* 'Albus'). For pink, look for pink-flowering allium *(Allium neapolitanum),* marsh mallow, dittany-of-Crete, summer and winter savory, clary sage, and pink creeping thymes.

How to Construct and Plant a Knot Garden

The 10-by-10-foot closed knot garden described below consists of three bands of contrasting plants that make interlocking rectangles with a circle weaving through them. Site your knot garden in full sun on level ground; shade may cause the plants to grow unevenly.

To obtain true 90° square corners, lay out your bed using a process known as triangulation, as shown below. Materials you will need include wooden stakes and pegs; string; and sand, bone meal, or powdered lime to mark lines on the soil. After marking the bed's perimeter, prepare the soil (pages 58-59), and install a brick or wooden edging to keep the look neat and trim.

Space the plants closely, and buy several extra plants in case you need replacements during the season. You will also need to mulch the ground between the bands with woodchips or gravel, or, alternatively, plant a low-growing ground-cover herb such as caraway thyme. Install a dwarf boxwood near each corner to finish the design.

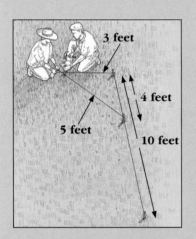

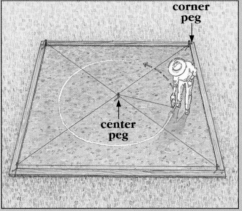

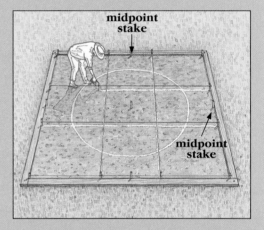

1. To create square corners, mark off one 10-foot side of the bed with stakes and string. Then, with a helper, set a peg 4 feet from the first stake and tie a string to it; mark the string at a point 5 feet from the peg. Tie a string to the first stake and mark it 3 feet from the stake. Cross the strings at the marks and set a new peg at that point. To stake off the next side, run a string from the first stake out to a length of 10 feet; repeat the squaring process. Repeat for remaining corners. Install edging along the string line and prepare the soil for planting.

2. Run string to link opposite corners; set a peg where the strings intersect at the center of the square. Next, to mark a circle at the garden's center, tie a string to a nail in the top of the center peg. Mark your string at a point that is half the distance from the center peg to a corner stake. Tie a sand- or lime-filled bottle to the string at the mark and, keeping the string pulled taut, walk around the peg with the bottle inverted so the sand pours out and marks a circle.

3. To outline the two interlocking rectangles, set stakes at the midpoint of each side of the bed. Then set two pegs on either side of each midpoint stake, 1½ feet away, so that the pegs are 3 feet apart. Run string between each of the opposite pegs to make two sets of parallel lines. Then mark the lines on the ground by dribbling sand or lime along the string lines. Remove the string, but keep the stakes and pegs in place.

4. Working outward from the center, space the plants 3 to 6 inches apart along the sand lines, adding a dose of slow-release fertilizer for each plant, following package directions. Plant a same-sized dwarf box at each corner, as shown in the diagram. In the spaces between the bands of plants, spread gravel or woodchips, or plant a ground cover. As the garden matures, trim the herbs every few weeks so that the bands appear to go under or over each other, like a lattice piecrust (inset).

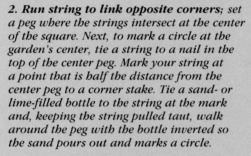

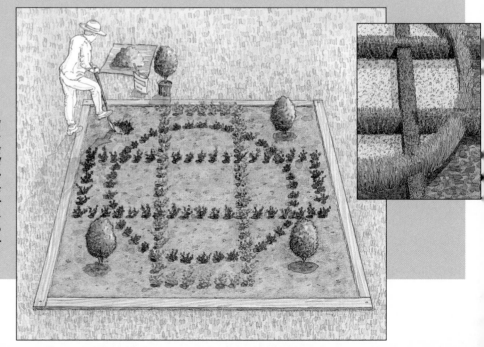

dwarf sage. Fill in the ground between the bands with low-growing flowers or herbal ground covers such as creeping thyme, pennyroyal, or curly parsley, which makes an interesting ground cover when mass-planted. Or spread woodchip mulch, crushed brick, tile, slate, seashells, or colored sand.

If you prefer an informal garden, remember that it will still need careful planning. Although such gardens don't contain any strict geometric lines, they take on a satisfying sense of balance with sinuous lines of beds and paths that lead you to a focal point. Without this focal point, the garden will appear jumbled and formless. Consider a garden bench or an ornament to draw the eye and create atmosphere. Traditionally, a sundial, a stone or iron urn, or a small statue appear at a central focal point in a formal garden—whereas a birdhouse, a birdbath, or a bee skep can transform an informal setting into a homey and inviting sanctuary.

Once you have decided on the ideal place for your herb garden, you're ready to lay it out. Either plot your design on paper, or plan your garden at the site itself. Mark the outer corners of the garden with stakes, and tie string from one stake to the other to approximate the garden's perimeter.

This will allow you to "see" the finished garden from all angles and to determine the best location for your plants. At the same time, mark features such as benches, ornaments, and pathways, keeping in mind that for two people to walk side by side—or to accommodate a wheelbarrow—your paths will need to be at least 4 feet wide.

Plan for a sheltering enclosure to keep out the wind and hold in the herbs' scents. Even one wall or hedge can make a difference. A trimmed boxwood hedge nicely complements formal architecture, while lattice or low walls of wattle—vines woven between stout branches driven into the earth—are especially well suited to informal or naturalistic settings.

Once you have planned the layout and the hard structures of your garden, draw up your list of herbs, noting their heights so that you can assign their positions in the garden. Also take into account their bloom times; with a little planning you can have flowers all season long. Last, plan for a generous proportion of the herbs to be evergreen. Plants in the list on page 12 will maintain a presence all through the winter when the rest of the garden is bare.

A PROFUSION OF HERBS— WITHIN BOUNDS
The billowing herbs in this Mobile, Alabama, garden are contained within the formal straight lines of brick-edged garden beds. Laid out in a traditional quartered design, the garden features a sundial at its center, surrounded by low-growing hollies and culinary herbs, including yellow-flowering dill and fennel, in the four outer sections. White blooms of flowering tobacco at the edge of the lawn perfume the evening air.

CHAPTER TWO

The Portable Herb Garden

Indoors or outdoors, container-grown herbs can transform even the smallest space into a garden. You can locate the garden wherever the plants will thrive and look their best, and rearrange or move it as you wish. Depending on the season, you may set containers inside on a window sill or outside on a porch or patio.

With a bit of pampering, most herbs adapt well to containers. And—in addition to providing handsome greenery—some offer delicious fragrances, while others can be used in cooking. In the California patio garden shown here, pots of pineapple mint (Mentha suaveolens 'Variegata') at far left and sage and cilantro at far right will delight the senses for months to come.

Herbs can be displayed in any type of container—pots of clay or glazed terra cotta, steel buckets, and hanging baskets are just a few you can choose from. On the following pages you will find the basics of designing container gardens and caring for them year round.

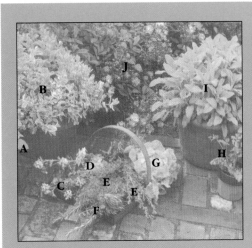

A. *Melissa officinalis (lemon balm)* **B.** *Mentha suaveolens 'Variegata' (pineapple mint)* **C.** *Pelargonium graveolens (rose geranium)* **D.** *Dianthus barbatus (sweet William)* **E.** *Origanum vulgare (oregano)* **F.** *Rosmarinus officinalis 'Miss Jessup's Upright' (rosemary)* **G.** *Lactuca hybrid (butterhead lettuce)* **H.** *Coriandrum sativum (coriander)* **I.** *Salvia officinalis (garden sage)* **J.** *Rosa 'Belinda' (rose)*

Please refer to the key at right to identify the plants in the garden shown.

Designing Container Gardens with Herbs

Planting herbs in pots allows you to grow a lavish garden where—and when—you choose. If your in-ground growing space is small, containers can expand it by incorporating surrounding areas—such as a walkway or a set of stairs—into your overall scheme. And if you have a roomy garden, you can use container-grown herbs to embellish a design or to emphasize special plantings.

Whether you allow them to develop their natural form or train them as espaliers or topiaries, herbs in containers are excellent accents in a garden. A pair of large containers filled with tall herbs can become a dramatic way to flank the entrance to a garden path. And matching topiaries can be set up to march in a rhythmic geometric pattern across a bare wall or along a stockade fence.

A Portable Visual Feast

The simplest way to create a lovely display of container-grown herbs is to cluster together small pots holding different plants. The herbs for this type of arrangement may be chosen for appearance' sake alone or may be related by a theme of color, scent, or use—a grouping of culinary herbs, for example, can be situated right outside your kitchen door. A more ambitious design technique is to plant a large container with a variety of complementary herbs to form what will amount to a movable garden. You can take the container to any part of the property or—if it suits you—take it into your home or greenhouse. Using a dolly to transport your pots makes even heavy concrete containers portable.

Inside, the kitchen is a logical setting for a grouping of culinary herbs. Scented and decorative herbs would be worthwhile additions to any part of your living quarters, and bathrooms are humid quarters for plants that thrive on moisture. In cold climates you can grow long-lived tender herbs such as sweet bay laurel, camphor tree, and lemon grass outdoors in pots during the summer months and move them indoors when temperatures drop and nights grow cold.

Containers also allow you to bring herbs that are at the peak of their season and are looking their best into prominent spots in the garden for viewing. If you want to dress up a shady spot for a

A Victorian-style urn, bursting with Aloe vera, becomes the focal point of this Pennsylvania garden. Standing the urn on a concrete pedestal—painted to match—adds extra height while balancing the proportions of the bowl to the base. The blades of iris foliage at the foot of the pedestal mimic the spiky aloe, while the velvety silver lamb's ears lining the walk pick up the pale color of the urn.

Cinnamomum camphora (camphor tree)

Long-Lived Container Herbs

Aloe vera
(aloe)
Aloysia triphylla
(lemon verbena)
Cinnamomum camphora
(camphor tree)
Cinnamomum zeylanicum
(cinnamon tree)
Citrus aurantium
(bitter orange)
Citrus limon
(lemon)
Cymbopogon citratus
(lemon grass)
Elettaria cardamomum
(cardamom)
Eucalyptus citriodora
(lemon-scented gum)
Laurus nobilis

(bay laurel)
Myrtus communis
(myrtle)
Pelargonium spp.
(scented geranium)
Punica granatum var. nana
(pomegranate)
Rosmarinus officinalis
(rosemary)
Tulbaghia violacea
(society garlic)

Note: The abbreviation "spp." stands for the plural of "species"; where used in lists it means that many, but not all, of the species in a genus meet the criterion of the list.

Herbs for Kitchen Gardens

Agastache foeniculum
(anise hyssop)
Allium schoenoprasum
(chives)
Allium tuberosum
(Chinese or garlic chives)
Aloysia triphylla
(lemon verbena)
Artemisia dracunculus
var. *sativa*
(French tarragon)
Cymbopogon citratus
(lemon grass)
Foeniculum vulgare
(fennel)
Foeniculum vulgare
'Purpurascens'
(copper fennel)
Levisticum officinale
(lovage)
Melissa officinalis
(lemon balm)
Mentha x piperita
(peppermint)
Mentha spicata
(spearmint)
Ocimum basilicum
(sweet basil)
Origanum majorana
(sweet marjoram)
Origanum onites
(Greek oregano)
Petroselinum crispum
(parsley)
Rosmarinus officinalis
(rosemary)
Rumex acetosa
(sorrel)
Salvia officinalis
(sage)
Satureja hortensis
(summer savory)
Thymus x citriodorus
(lemon thyme)
Thymus vulgaris
(thyme)
Tropaeolum majus
(nasturtium)

CONVENIENT HARVEST OF FLAVOR
Culinary herbs are kept close at hand on a New Jersey deck (above) and outside a Washington State kitchen door (below). The rustic planter filled with thyme and the clay pots containing mint, oregano, and other herbs also create different design effects.

party, for instance, you can move in containers planted with sun-loving herbs, display them there for the few hours they are needed, and then whisk them back to their more hospitable location.

Selecting Plants for Containers

Choosing different herbs to mix in a container can be as much of a creative challenge as designing a garden bed or border. Keep in mind the growth habits of the plants as well as which ones look good together. As a starting point, perennials are logical companions for other perennials, annuals for other annuals. For best success, combine plants with similar needs. Mediterranean herbs such as sage, lavender, and rosemary require well-drained soil and can tolerate a degree of drought. Don't mix them with plants like parsley, pennyroyal, valerian, or lady's-mantle, which prefer rich, moist conditions.

Also consider the mature shape and size of each herb so the finished effect will show off all of the plants to best advantage. Be careful not to set a slow-growing or naturally small plant next to one that will quickly envelop its smaller companion in foliage. Lemon verbena and lovage, for example, reach heights of 6 feet or more if left to grow unchecked. Marjoram, nasturtium, French tarragon, and parsley tend to get choked out by that sort of vigorous plant.

Most herbs need a minimum of 6 hours of sunlight to flourish. When you plan your containers, make sure sun-loving plants aren't shaded by taller neighbors. One likely trio for a sunny site would feature sweet basil, lemon basil, and sweet marjoram. Herbs that tolerate some shade include angelica, costmary, lovage, mint, and tarragon. Chervil, coriander, and parsley all enjoy a cool, moist environment.

Designing Plant Combinations

As you work out what plants will mix well because of similar growing requirements, use your imagination to create displays that are beautiful as well as functional.

Plant herbs with trailing habits on the edges of pots, where they can cascade down over the sides. Among your choices might be silver or golden lemon thyme, marjoram, and prostrate rosemary. To cover bare soil in a container planted with a tall-growing plant or a standard, use low-growing herbs such as creeping thymes or Roman chamomile (*Chamaemelum nobile*).

Pairings for Color and Texture

Consider planting a container with a color theme, combining—for example—the variegated pink, green, and cream foliage of tricolor sage with pink-flowering chives. Tricolor sage would also look stunning against the deep purple foliage of purple basil. For a golden motif, you might choose gold-leaved forms of sage (*Salvia officinalis* 'Icterina'), feverfew (*Tanacetum parthenium* 'Aureum'), marjoram (*Origanum vulgare* 'Aureum'), and thyme (*Thymus* x *citriodorus* 'Aureus'). Herbs with gray or silver foliage include lamb's ears, southernwood, silver thyme, santolina, and French lavender (*Lavandula dentata* var. *candicans*). For a large container, consider silver horehound (*Marrubium incanum*), which can grow 2 feet or more in height.

To create a look that is subtle but no less striking, combine herbs that have contrasting leaf textures. Allow the lacy gray-green foliage of southernwood to intermingle with the wrinkled, bumpy leaves of tricolor sage (*Salvia officinalis* 'Tricolor'), or contrast the large leaves of purple sage (*S. o.* 'Purpurea') with delicate thyme foliage.

Perfuming the Air with Geraniums

Scented geraniums, tender perennials native to Africa's Cape of Good Hope, were introduced in England around 1795. Growers soon found that the plants would thrive indoors in winter if given ample light. The geraniums were an instant success because of their diverse, fascinating leaf forms—the herb mutates readily, and bee-crossed hybrids are common—and distinctive scents: Victorian women would brush their skirts against large pots of geranium to release its fragrance into a room. Ardent collectors amassed hundreds of varieties.

Today, although nursery catalogs may claim scents as diverse as clove, apricot, and coconut, most experts agree that the possibilities for perfume are limited to variations of lemon, mixed citrus (combining lemon, lime, and orange), mint, rose, rose-lemon, apple, pepper, and a pungent odor—more or less pleasant depending on the cultivar—that can only be described as spicy.

Fragrant geraniums boast leaf forms to satisfy just about any gardener. Size varies from the crinkly ½-inch-diameter leaf of lemon-scented *Pelargonium crispum* 'Minor' to the pungent *P. hispidum*, with leaves that measure 4 to 5 inches across. Leaf shapes range from the ruffled round of apple geranium (*P. odoratissimum*) to the deeply indented of rose geranium (*P. graveolens*). Leaves come in many shades of green, some with a light brush of velvet, as well as in variegated mixtures of green with cream, white, brown, and even maroon.

With so many cultivars available, choosing scented geraniums for your garden can seem overwhelming. If your growing space is limited, opt for a citrus-, rose-, or mint-scented plant since these are the most useful for cooking and for making sachets and potpourri.

Pelargonium quercifolium 'Fair Ellen' (oak-leaved geranium)

WINTER HARVEST INDOORS
*Comely clay pots on a Virginia kitchen window sill
keep dill (left), parsley, lemon balm, purple basil,
sage, thyme, and rosemary (far right) convenient for
flavoring a winter dinner. An unshaded south-facing
window is ideal for growing them; just remember to
rotate the pots weekly so the herbs will grow evenly.*

Herbs with Good Taste

If you'd like to make flavor your theme, create a
lemon-scented garden in a large container. Plant
lemon-scented gum *(Eucalyptus citriodora)* at
the center, then surround it with a selection of
smaller edible herbs such as lemon grass *(Cymbopogon citratus),* golden lemon thyme (*Thymus* x
citriodorus 'Aureus'), lemon basil (*Ocimum basilicum* 'Citriodorum'), and lemon-scented geraniums (*Pelargonium crispum* 'Prince Rupert' and
P. c. 'Mabel Grey').

Many herbs are delicious brewed as tea, and
some are said to have health-giving properties
as well. To add to your pleasure, grow a tea garden in containers planted with bee balm, chamomile, mint (peppermint, apple mint, and orange
mint have distinctive flavors), lemon balm, and
sweet woodruff.

Herbs to Start from Seed Indoors

Allium schoenoprasum
(chives)
Allium tuberosum
(Chinese or garlic chives)
Anthriscus cerefolium
(chervil)
Capsicum
(pepper)
Lavandula
(lavender)

Melissa officinalis
(lemon balm)
Nepeta cataria
(catnip)
*Ocimum basilicum
cultivars*
(basil)
Origanum majorana
(sweet marjoram)

Melissa officinalis (lemon balm)

Enjoying Rosemary Year Round

Pine-scented rosemary lives for years if it is planted in gardens as temperate as those of its native Mediterranean. In summer, it will flourish in any sunny garden in well-drained soil, if given a modicum of water. Though most rosemaries succumb to prolonged freezes, some varieties such as *Rosmarinus officinalis* 'Arp', 'Hill Hardy', 'Salem', 'Dutch Mill', and 'White Flowered' can survive winter temperatures as low as -10° F.

Indoors, potted rosemary does best in a cool, sunny spot. Dry indoor heat in winter will cause the plant to desiccate and die. Rosemary plants are under the greatest stress in late January, when the stronger sun begins to draw moisture out of plants more quickly. But too much moisture in the air can promote powdery mildew.

To give your rosemary a fighting chance under such trying conditions, begin by potting the plant in a light growing medium of peat moss mixed with perlite and vermiculite. Then water your plant only when the mix is dried out—the pot will feel light and the mix will have turned a pale brown; make sure to let all the excess water drain out. Brown leaves at the plant's base is a sign that your rosemary has been overwatered, whereas wilted terminal shoots indicate a thirsty plant.

As the plant grows, pinch off long shoots and branches to use in cooking and to promote bushiness. Flowers in lavender-blue, pink, or white will appear from winter through spring. Among the earliest bloomers are 'Beneden Blue' and 'Tuscan Blue', flowering in late winter; prostrate rosemary can bloom almost continually, if it is given enough light.

Root-bound plants should be transplanted in spring to a next-size-larger pot. Too large a pot prevents the plant from using up the moisture in the soil and encourages rot. Fertilize your plant once every 2 weeks during the growing season with a balanced fertilizer. Stop fertilizing in autumn, a few weeks before you bring the plant indoors.

Annual Herbs in Winter

Many annuals that are valued for seasoning food germinate quickly from seed and are thus well suited for growing indoors *(list, opposite)*. Although the plants won't last as long as they would outdoors—about 6 weeks is the maximum life span, even under the best conditions—you will be able to harvest a steady supply of fresh herbs throughout the winter by scheduling three or four successive sowings, spaced about 3 weeks apart. That way new plants will be mature enough to use at about the time you're ready to throw the old ones away.

A top-quality homemade soilless potting mix *(recipe, page 67)* should contain enough nutrients to satisfy the plants. If you want to supplement the mix, use an organic houseplant fertilizer, applying it at only half the recommended rate. A fertilizer with a low nutrient analysis of 3-6-4 or 5-5-5 will suffice; giving the plants more fertilizer than that may cause them to produce excess foliage and lose flavor.

Once the plants sprout, they will need the same light conditions as would any herb grown indoors. *(For instructions on growing herbs from seed, see pages 66-67.)*

Potting and Caring for Herbs

Once you have decided on the type of herbs to grow, your next step is to choose the containers in which to grow them. Almost any container will do as long as it is clean and has one or more holes in the bottom for ample drainage. However, there are some differences worth considering between the two main container types, plastic and clay.

Plastic pots hold moisture well, but plants in them must be monitored carefully—especially if they are in the shade—to make sure the soil doesn't stay too wet. By contrast, clay containers are porous, providing plants with good air circulation and drainage. For just these reasons, however, plants in clay pots need to be watered frequently, especially in hot weather, so that the soil doesn't dry out.

Cleaning and Reusing Clay Pots

Before using an old clay pot for a new plant, first check the pot for chips or cracks that would allow moisture to seep away. Then give the pot a good cleaning. To remove algae and fungi as well as the possibility of any lurking disease, scour the pot under cold running water with a nylon scrubbing pad, then soak it for several hours in a solution of 1 part bleach to 5 parts water. Rinse the pot thoroughly. If you won't be using the container right away, let it dry completely before storing it.

Even this good a cleaning may not remove the white salts—residue from alkaline water—that sometimes streak clay pots. Soak these pots in undiluted vinegar (buy it in gallon jugs to save money) for a day or two. Rinse them under cold water and scrub with a nylon pad. If salt streaks persist, repeat the process, using fresh vinegar. Gardeners with time to spare can set the salt-streaked containers outside; rain will have them fresh and clean within a few months.

CHIMNEY-FLUE HERB GARDEN
The square tiles used to line the inside of a chimney are imaginatively employed as containers, planted with parsley, purple basil, peppers, marigold, and scented geranium, in this Georgia garden. Other possibilities for unusual containers include decorative watering cans, discarded wheelbarrows, large shells such as those of giant clams or conchs, and weather-beaten, hollowed-out logs.

Ideal Potting Soil Mixtures

Soil collected directly from the garden should not be used in containers. In most cases it is too heavy, and it often harbors harmful insects and diseases. Soilless, commercially packed container mixes, on the other hand, tend to be so light that fast-growing roots soon make herbs potbound. These mixes also dry out very quickly.

To give a packaged potting mix more substance, boost its consistency by blending it with sterilized compost (available in bags at most nurseries) at a ratio of 2 parts potting mix to 1 part compost.

Or, if you have access to top-quality loam soil from a mulch or landscape company, you can prepare a container mix by blending 1 part loam soil and 1 part soilless potting medium such as a peat/perlite mix. Moisten with fish emulsion diluted at the rate of ¼ cup per gallon of water.

TIPS FROM THE PROS
Tricks to Retain Moisture in Containers

During the hot months of summer, container-grown plants dry out quickly and may need watering once—even twice—a day. Here are some ways to escape the tyranny of tending pots:

• Choose a container that retains moisture. The materials with the lowest evaporation rate are plastic, fiberglass, metal, and glazed ceramic, often called terra cotta. The most porous materials are clay (unglazed ceramic), wood, and concrete. Generally, plants in porous pots need watering three times more often than those in plastic or metal containers.

• Pick white containers, which tend to reflect heat, thus somewhat reducing the rate of evaporation. Dark-colored pots, on the other hand, absorb heat, causing the soil to dry out faster.

• Find a pot that is slightly larger than the plant requires. The extra soil will hold more moisture.

• Blend soil polymers—available at most garden centers—which hold moisture, into your container mix.

• Place decorative bark or pebbles on top of the soil to slow surface evaporation. Or cover the soil with an organic mulch of compost or grass clippings and top with the bark or pebbles.

• Group containers together to shade and humidify each other. Place the small pots, which are likely to dry out first, in the center of the cluster.

• Shelter pots from desiccating wind.

• Install an automatic irrigation system with a line running to each container. The initial effort may seem great, but so will the rewards.

Planting the Containers

Before you plant a new clay pot, soak it in water overnight. Then, for any type of container, cover the drainage hole with a piece of mesh screen, a large pebble, or a pottery shard. Fill the bottom of the container with potting medium and position the plant in the pot so that the soil level of the rootball will be below the pot's rim. Fill the pot with soil and tamp firmly to remove air pockets. Water thoroughly.

If you are replanting a container of mixed herbs in the spring, first remove any perennials so you can work the soil without interference. Replenish the potting mix by adding a 1-inch layer of well-rotted chicken manure; mix it in thoroughly, aerating the soil at the same time. Replant the perennials and add new annual herbs.

Feeding Hungry Container-Grown Herbs

Herbs planted in the ground typically have a more intense flavor and a more pungent aroma if they are fertilized with a light hand. By contrast, those planted in containers require extra nourishment. Frequent watering leaches nutrients from the soil, and the problem is compounded when several plants are grown in one pot and they are all competing for food.

During the growing season, feed herbs in containers every 2 weeks with an organic fertilizer that is high in nitrogen; seaweed and fish emulsion are two good choices. Follow the directions on the package to measure out and dilute the fertilizer. At the end of summer, cut back on the feeding, and stop altogether in late fall.

Grooming Potted Herbs

Plants will grow bushier and be more attractive if stem tips are pinched off regularly to encourage more branching. In the case of container-grown herbs, this care is especially important to control plants like sage and lemon verbena that tend to grow large and sprawl. Even less vigorous herbs benefit from being trimmed when they occupy a container with other plants.

Make it a habit to carry clippers with you when you check on your container-grown herbs, and take a few moments to snip and shape the plants. Use the pieces you harvest in the evening meal, for potpourri, or in flower arrangements.

Repotting Root-Bound Perennials

Over time, perennial herbs outgrow their containers. If roots protrude from the bottom of the pot, or if you notice that water doesn't soak through the soil properly, the plant has become root bound and needs to be repotted. If possible, do the job in spring, when the plant is ready to begin a growth spurt. The least desirable time to repot is late autumn or winter, when the plant is dormant and will be slow to generate new roots.

Increase the container size gradually rather than in big jumps. Choose a pot 2 inches larger in diameter than the old one, and prepare it for

HIGH-DENSITY LIVING
These long wooden planters take little space yet drape this Maryland deck with a lush curtain of herbs. The planters brim with (from left) lovage, redmint (Mentha x gracilis), madonna lily, nasturtium, lavender, lemon balm, Jerusalem sage, rose-lemon-scented geranium, lemon-scented geranium, and comfrey. Swags of wild yam (Dioscorea bulbifera) festoon the railing.

The Well-Watered Strawberry Pot

To obtain even moisture throughout a large strawberry pot with six or more pockets, turn PVC (polyvinyl chloride) pipe into a watering tube. Choose pipe 2 to 4 inches in diameter and 4 inches less in length than the pot's height. Place the pipe upright in the pot and mark the location of each pocket on the pipe. This ensures that water will reach the roots of every plant directly. Drill ½-inch holes at those marks. Cover the bottom of the pipe with a square of plastic mesh and secure it by wrapping wire around the pipe. Fill the pipe with pebbles, tamping them as you go, then cap the top of the pipe with mesh. Next, put a mesh square over the pot's drainage hole, and center the pipe on the hole. Align the drilled holes with the pockets. Add soil to the pot to the level of the first pockets.

With a chopstick or screwdriver, gently push the first plant's rootball into the lowest pocket, roots pointed down. Keep the crown of the plant level with the lip of the pocket to allow for settling; add more soil to the level of the next pocket. Repeat until all the pockets are full and soil reaches to within 1 inch of the rim. Then center a plant over the pipe and fill in the rest of the pot with soil.

Set the container in a pan of water to soak up moisture. Then water the top and pockets with a fine spray.

Herbs for Strawberry Pots

ON TOP

Lavandula dentata
(French lavender)
Lavandula stoechas
(Spanish lavender)
Pelargonium graveolens
(rose geranium)
Petroselinum crispum
(parsley)
Salvia officinalis 'Nana'
(dwarf sage)
Tropaeolum minus
(dwarf nasturtium)

IN POCKETS

Allium schoenoprasum
(chives)
Mentha pulegium
(pennyroyal)
Mentha requienii
(Corsican mint)
Ocimum basilicum 'Minimum'
(bush basil)
Origanum dictamnus
(dittany-of-Crete)
Origanum majorana
(sweet marjoram)
Pelargonium odoratissimum
(apple geranium)
Petroselinum crispum
(parsley)
Santolina chamaecyparissus 'Nana'
(dwarf lavender cotton)
Thymus caespititius
(tufted thyme)
Thymus x citriodorus
(lemon thyme)
Thymus x citriodorus 'Silver Queen'
(silver lemon thyme)
Thymus herba-barona
(caraway thyme)
Thymus praecox
(creeping thyme)
Viola tricolor
(Johnny-jump-up)

planting by covering the drainage hole and spreading a layer of container mix in the bottom. Remove your plant from its old pot and gently loosen the roots. Position it so it will sit at the same level in the pot as before. Fill in the gaps with soil, and water well.

Some herbs—tender perennials, trees, and shrubs such as jasmine, eucalyptus, and myrtle—can live in a container for years. However, you'll need to refresh and replenish the soil annually. This can be as simple as carefully removing the top layer and replacing it with fresh potting mix enriched with a slow-release fertilizer. However, some experts recommend lifting the plant out of its pot and carefully scraping soil from the sides and bottom of the rootball as well, then replenishing with fresh soil mix as you replant the herb.

For a severely root-bound plant, lift the herb from the pot, slice off the outer layer of roots, and loosen the rootball before replacing the plant in its original container. Add fresh potting mix to fill the extra space, then trim back the foliage to compensate for the loss of roots.

Winter Care for Outdoor Containers

In the northern climate zones, even hardy herbs will need winter protection if they are grown above ground. If you prefer to overwinter your hardy perennials outdoors, one choice is to replant them in the ground in autumn or to bury the containers so that the roots are better insulated.

Tropaeolum majus 'Double Gleam' (nasturtium)

Herbs for Hanging Baskets

Alchemilla mollis
(lady's-mantle)
Centella asiatica
(gotu kola)
Nepeta mussinii
(catmint)
**Ocimum basilicum
'Minimum'**
(bush basil)
Ocimum basilicum 'Minimum Purpurascens'
(purple bush basil)

Origanum dictamnus
(dittany-of-Crete)
Origanum majorana
(sweet marjoram)
Origanum onites
(Greek oregano)
**Petroselinum crispum
var. crispum**
(curly parsley)
**Rosmarinus officinalis
'Prostratus'**
(prostrate rosemary)

Satureja spicigera
(creeping savory)
**Thymus praecox ssp.
arcticus cultivars**
(creeping thyme)
Tropaeolum majus
(nasturtium)

Alternatively, you can cluster the pots together in a sheltered spot away from the wind and pile mulch around them. Otherwise, even the containers will be at the mercy of the vagaries of winter: Unglazed clay pots crack and flake when they freeze and thaw.

If you want to bring your container-grown herbs indoors, start getting them ready in early autumn. Cut back the plants by about half their new growth, trim back the roots if the plant is root bound, and repot with fresh soil. Then move the plants to a sheltered area such as a patio or terrace to help them make the transition to their new environment. When the weather begins to turn cold, carry the pots indoors.

You can also pot up tender perennials growing in the garden—rosemary, lemon verbena, lemon grass, and the like. If a plant is too large for the pot you want to use or the indoor space you have, trim the foliage back to a manageable size before you dig it up. Then, a few weeks before you put them into pots, trim the roots of the plants: Use a shovel to slice through the earth all around the rootball, cutting off the outer edge of the roots. This pruning will encourage the growth of new feeder roots that will help the plant cope with the transition indoors.

Overwintering Pots Indoors

Once indoors, your herbs will still need their 6 hours minimum of direct sunlight; a sunny, south-facing window is best. If you don't have a location with adequate natural light, purchase special growing lights or use ordinary fluorescents. (Incandescent lights give off too much heat.) Hang two to four light tubes 5 to 6 inches above the plants. If you mount the lights on chains, you can easily adjust the height as the plants grow. Ideally the lights should be color balanced to replicate natural light, but you can simulate sun by pairing cool-white and warm-white tubes. To meet the equivalent of 6 hours of sun, turn the lights on for 14 to 16 hours a day.

The air inside your home during the winter is likely to be very dry and can take a toll on plants. Set each pot on top of pebbles in a water-filled tray or dish, making sure that the pot itself isn't sitting in the water. As the water evaporates, it will humidify the air. If the humidity level indoors drops below 40 percent, give the herbs a misting.

Because the plants are dormant, you won't need to water as frequently as during the growing season; however, take care not to allow the soil to dry out completely.

Topiaries and Espaliers

Like trees and shrubs, dozens of sturdy herbs can be grown in marvelous shapes and forms using the techniques developed for producing topiaries and espaliers. The training process is creative and fun, and with fast-growing herbs you get the quick gratification of a product finished in months rather than years.

There are many advantages to growing trained herbs in containers rather than in the ground. Since they are portable, you can move these accent plants to create special effects in different garden spots at different times, and any tender herbs can be taken indoors for the winter. In addition, most herbs have shorter lives than trees or shrubs. As older trained plants begin to decline, replacement plants can be trained behind the scenes and positioned in the garden when they are at their peak.

Tied Topiaries

Topiaries are simple to make; the process just involves bending supple new plant growth and tying it onto a wire frame. Shapes suitable for training plants include spirals, globes, hearts, teardrops, wreaths, and animals or birds with simple outlines. You can buy these wire forms or make your own using No. 8 or No. 9 gauge wire.

Tied topiaries make ideal tabletop decorations, but remember that most herbs require a lot of light (full sun for 6 hours a day is a minimum) and benefit from good air circulation. After use, carry them back outside as soon as possible.

Ornamental Standards

An easy topiary to create is the so-called standard, which doesn't require a wire frame. Resembling a stylized miniature tree, the simplest standard has one globe-like crown of foliage atop a single stem. The "poodle" variation has two or three balls of foliage growing on branches out of the straight, central stem at regular intervals.

Either type is easy to train (pages 38-39) and makes a striking garden accent. Put a pair of standards at the entrance to your home or garden for dramatic effect. If they are placed against a building, turn the pots regularly to ensure that all sides are exposed to the light. Or

consider featuring a standard topiary instead of a birdbath, statue, or sundial as the focal point in the center of a low-growing flower bed.

Standard topiaries tend to be top-heavy. You can provide counterbalance by adding an attractive top dressing of pebbles to the soil in the container. (This will also help maintain moisture.) Or place the pot inside a larger container and fill in the gap with pebbles. Make sure the size of the outer container is in pleasing proportion to the plant.

Training a Tied Topiary

Using your topiary frame as a reference, plant one young herb for every leg of the frame. Place the frame in the pot with its legs next to the plants; remove any leaves that rub against the frame. Then gently bend the plants' stems to follow the wire. Taking care not to crush the leaves, tie the stems at about 1-inch intervals with ½-inch strips of nylon hose, cut horizontally. Continue to tie new growth until the frame is covered, and replace ties as they get too tight. When the plant becomes woody, it will keep its shape on its own and you can remove the ties. Prune regularly to accentuate the desired form, and pinch off the tip, or leader, of the central stem when it reaches the length you need.

Herbs Suitable for Training

AS STANDARDS

Aloysia triphylla
(lemon verbena)
Helichrysum angustifolium
(curry plant)
Laurus nobilis
(bay laurel)
Lavandula dentata
(French lavender)
Lavandula x intermedia
(lavandin)
Lavandula stoechas
(Spanish lavender)
Myrtus communis
(myrtle)
Pelargonium crispum
(lemon geranium)
Pelargonium graveolens
(rose geranium)

Prostanthera rotundifolia
(Australian mint bush)
Rosmarinus officinalis 'Arp', 'Tuscan Blue'
(rosemary)
Salvia officinalis
(sage)
Santolina chamaecyparissus
(lavender cotton)
Thymus vulgaris (upright form)
(thyme)

AS TIED TOPIARIES AND ESPALIERS

Myrtus communis
(myrtle)
Rosmarinus officinalis
(rosemary)

Rosmarinus officinalis (rosemary)

Decorative Espaliers

Because they are grown flat against a support, espaliered herbs make appealing decorations for a wall, fence, or trellis. Like a tied topiary, the plant is trained on a frame; the pattern can be casual and free-form or symmetrical and formal. Among the classic designs are the fan pattern known as palmette oblique; and the cordon, in which the plant is trained into several tiers of parallel horizontal rows. Other popular patterns include the candelabra, diamond, V-shape, U-shape, and triangle.

Pruning Trained Herbs

Some gardeners prune their trained herbal topiaries and standards every day—using nail scissors—to ensure absolutely perfect specimens with no leaf or branch out of place. Such commitment is hardly essential, although these plants do require frequent grooming. Any time you notice branches growing long enough to distort the desired shape of the topiary, get out your scissors or clippers and do some trimming.

Don't shear plants, lest you end up with ugly, blunt edges and maimed leaves. Rather, trim back each branchlet to a leaf node, cutting at a 45° angle just above a bud or node. Every time you cut back a branch to a bud, two new shoots will develop, eventually creating a beautiful, bushy plant.

In addition to maintaining a standard's shape, you must periodically clean out the inside of the foliage globe. Remove dead twigs and thin the crown so that light and air can penetrate.

New Pots for Topiary

To keep your topiary's root system from outgrowing its container, repot it annually—preferably in autumn or spring, when weather conditions are optimum for new root growth. Remove the plant from the container and gently loosen the rootball, shaking away the released soil. Trim back any extra long roots. If the rootball has grown very tight, cut off the outer edge of the roots, on the sides and the bottom, with scissors or a knife, reducing the rootball by about one-third. Use fresh soil to replant the herb in the same pot.

Water repotted herbs immediately. You can water from the top as usual, but you also should set the pot in a pan of water so it can draw up moisture from the bottom. That way any loose soil around the roots will settle, preventing air pockets.

How to Train a Standard Topiary

Herbs amenable to training as standards have central stems that grow straight up until the plant reaches its full height. However, pinching off the tip, or leader, at any time encourages lateral buds along the stem to sprout branches and form a crown.

To create a standard, find a young plant with a stem that has never been pinched. Start in early spring so that the plant has a long season of favorable weather to grow tall and strong.

Before pinching the stem tip, consider the proportions you eventually want to have. The final height should be in balance with the size of the pot as well as the crown.

1. Insert an 8- to 10-inch long stake next to the plant in the pot. Remove side shoots along the plant's stem but leave in place the primary leaves; remove any leaves that rub against the stake. Tie the stem to the stake at 1- to 1½-inch intervals, taking care not to damage the stem. As the plant grows, continue to tie the stem to the stake; when the plant outgrows the stake, replace it with a taller one. Also replace ties that have tightened as the stem has grown.

2. As the plant approaches the desired height, pinch off the tip of the central stem. Allow the side branches near the top of the plant to continue growing; when they are about 4 inches long, pinch each of these just above a node (right) to encourage vigorous growth. Continue pinching as needed to keep the head of the plant bushy and well branched.

Two rosemary stand-ards flank a tiered ivy topiary in this formal planting. Perfect as focal points or standing sentry at the entrance to a home or garden, standards add a regal air to a setting. The upright form of rosemary is particularly suited to growing as a standard, and its narrow, needle-like leaves give off an assertive fragrance reminiscent of pine.

3. Once the top growth has filled in and you are happy with the way the topiary looks, remove the primary leaves growing along its central stem. Repot the plant, if necessary, in a container appropriate for its size. Pinch as needed to maintain the plant's shape. If you like, you can underplant the topiary with small herbs.

Versatile Herbs

The usefulness of herbs has inspired gardeners to cultivate them for centuries. Hardworking and adaptable, these plants fit in obligingly with any garden style, from the formally geometric wheel garden shown here to the loose amplitude of the cottage garden on pages 46-47. They thrive where other plants falter—on dry, rocky slopes like the one on pages 42-43, or wedged in the cracks of the slate terrace on page 49.

But their utilitarian character does not mean herbs are drudges. Whether they adorn a pathway with the beauty of their flowers or release their captivating scents as you finger their foliage, herbs are the sensualist's definition of the perfect plant.

HERBS AT THE HUB
Pink sweet William, a drift of lavender-flowered English thyme, and chartreuse-leaved lemon thyme revolve at the hub of this wheel garden in northern California. Spokes of blue star creeper radiate from the birdbath.

**OLD WORLD PLANTS
IN THE NEW WORLD**
*A Berkeley, California,
garden is home to a col-
lection of Mediterrane-
an herbs that flourish
in the poor, dry hillside
soil. Dwarf santolina at
left and dittany-of-Crete
at right make a silvery
counterpoint to the fine
dark green foliage of
woolly thyme flowing
around chunks of bro-
ken concrete used as
steppingstones. Laven-
der (far right) grows
side by side with a
bright pink heron's-bill
(Erodium absinthoi-
des), and Lebanese
oregano tumbles down
from above. The rem-
nant of a stone column
gives the garden the
mystery of an old ruin.*

A MOVABLE FEAST IN MARYLAND
A pot of sweet basil flanked by two sages—furry-leaved 'Berggarten' sage on the right and purple sage on the left—occupy a place of honor on the deck outside this Maryland gardener's kitchen door. Under the purple sage, lemon thyme cascades over its container, jockeying for space with silvery lavender and bright green sweet marjoram. A pot on the deck holds oregano, Italian parsley, and more purple sage.

BRINGING HERBS INDOORS
A winter garden provides a palette of fresh tastes for the Virginia cook who tends these herbs. At far left are slim-leaved garlic chives and thyme. Two kinds of oregano crown the strawberry pot at center, and a small variegated sage is tucked in its side pocket. A pot of catnip for the household feline and a basket with curly parsley and dwarf basil complete the garden.

**A FLOWERY
HERBAL OASIS**
*Only a stone's throw
from the busy Pennsyl-
vania Turnpike, this
cottage herb garden is
an ornamental Eden
full of vibrant colors,
fragrances, butterflies,
and bees. A low stone
wall holds back the
overflow of creeping
alyssum 'Basket of Gold'
(right foreground),
bright yellow Greek
yarrow bracketed by
spiky purple salvia, and
a cascade of lavender
catmint. Behind the
yarrow a drift of san-
tolina is sprinkled with
tiny yellow buttonlike
flowers. The tall fox-
gloves rising at the back
of the garden and the
'Gourmet Popcorn' rose
next to a handsome
iron urn add harmo-
nizing touches of pink.*

HERBS UNDERFOOT

A bluestone terrace in Greenwich, Connecticut, is studded with cushions of drought-tolerant thymes— among them pink-blooming creeping thyme, white mother-of-thyme at right, and a single ghostly white upright silver thyme at left. Two rounded yellow-blooming santolinas contrast with the long, low hedge of 'Munstead' and 'Jean Davis' lavender bordering the terrace. In the background, a 'New Dawn' rose and 'Jackmanii' clematis garland the trellis and gray picket fence that define the garden's perimeter.

AN ISLAND OF SCENTS

Solid as a coastal outcrop, a bright red bench resists the tide of woolly thyme lapping at its feet in this garden on Bainbridge Island, Washington. A wave of lavender rises up behind the bench, while beside it a sturdy pot containing small sages and a yellow-tinged lemon thyme complete the elegant composition. A visitor to the bench would be surrounded by spicy scents and perfumes wafting from head to toe.

48

WITHIN GARDEN WALLS

High walls and a bright blue gate enclose this Santa Barbara, California, garden, making a private haven and an enchanting transition from the outside world to the house. The long-stemmed fragrant flowers of English lavender (left foreground) lean over a Mexican evening primrose, whose pale pink petals surround bright yellow stamens. Spilling onto the tile walk is a drift of Mexican fleabane sprinkled with dainty pink-and-white daisylike flowers. Enormous upward-branching rosemaries flank the gate in the wall, which is adorned with a brilliant red trumpet creeper.

A Guide to the Gardens

HERBS AT THE HUB

pages 40-41

A. *Laurentia fluviatilis* (54)
B. *Pelargonium x hortum 'Rio'* (4)
C. *Allium schoenoprasum* (1)
D. *Thymus vulgaris 'Argenteus'* (1)
E. *Thymus x citriodorus* (1)
F. *Dianthus barbatus 'Wee Willy'* (5)

G. *Thymus vulgaris* (1)
H. *Thymus vulgaris 'Lime'* (1)
I. *Thymus praecox ssp. arcticus* (1)
J. *Chrysanthemum paludosum* (1)
K. *Spinacia oleracea* (4)
L. *Origanum vulgare 'Variegated Golden'* (5)

M. *Lavandula angustifolia 'Rosea'* (1)
N. *Consolida ambigua* (8)
O. *Polygonum odoratum* (1)
P. *Alstroemeria 'Ligtu Hybrids'* (2)
Q. *Levisticum officinale* (1)

OLD WORLD PLANTS IN THE NEW WORLD

pages 42-43

A. *Thymus pseudolanuginosus* (12)
B. *Santolina chamaecyparissus* (1)
C. *Narcissus bulbocodium*

var. conspicuus (1)
D. *Origanum dictamnus* (2)
E. *Eschscholzia lobbii* (1)
F. *Thymus mastichina* (1)
G. *Thymus caespititius* (1)

H. *Lavandula latifolia* (1)
I. *Origanum libanoticum* (2)
J. *Origanum calcaratum* (3)
K. *Dudleya edulis* (1)
L. *Erodium absinthoides* (1)

NOTE: The key lists each plant and the total quantity needed to replicate the garden shown. The diagram's letters and numbers refer to the type of plant and the number sited in an area.

BRINGING HERBS INDOORS

pages 44-45

A. *Allium schoenoprasum* (1)
B. *Thymus vulgaris* (6)
C. *Origanum dictamnus* (1)
D. *Origanum vulgare ssp. vulgare* (1)

E. *Salvia officinalis 'Variegata'* (1)
F. *Nepeta cataria* (1)
G. *Petroselinum crispum* (2)
H. *Ocimum basilicum 'Minimum'* (2)

A MOVABLE FEAST IN MARYLAND

page 45

A. *Lavandula x intermedia* (1)
B. *Thymus x citriodorus* (3)
C. *Origanum majorana* (2)
D. *Origanum vulgare* (1)
E. *Lavandula angustifolia* (1)
F. *Petroselinum crispum 'Italian'* (1)
G. *Salvia officinalis* (1)
H. *Rumex acetosa* (1)
I. *Lavandula x intermedia 'Dutch'* (1)
J. *Ocimum basilicum 'Genovese'* (2)
K. *Salvia officinalis 'Berggarten'* (1)

A FLOWERY
HERBAL OASIS

pages 46-47

A. *Nepeta sibirica hybrids* (6)
B. *Iberis sempervirens* (1)
C. *Salvia x superba* (2)
D. *Aurinia saxatilis 'Basket of Gold'* (3)
E. *Hypericum frondosum* (1)
F. *Achillea taygetea* (15)

G. *Santolina virens* (2)
H. *Satureja montana* (1)
I. *Stachys officinalis* (3)
J. *Geranium pratense* (2)
K. *Salvia dominica* (1)
L. *Lavandula angustifolia 'Croxton's Wild'* (4)

M. *Santolina 'Bowles' Form'* (1)
N. *Rosmarinus officinalis* (1)
O. *Dianthus spp.* (2)
P. *Agastache cana* (1)
Q. *Rosa 'Gourmet Popcorn'* (1)
R. *Tanacetum parthenium* (1)
S. *Digitalis purpurea* (4)

AN ISLAND OF SCENTS

page 48

A. *Thymus pseudolanuginosus* (5)
B. *Carex glauca* (1)
C. *Salvia leucantha* (1)

D. *Arctotis x hybrida* (3)
E. *Salvia officinalis 'Tricolor'* (1)
F. *Thymus x citriodorus 'Aureus'* (1)

G. *Lavandula x intermedia 'Grosso'* (1)
H. *Lavandula x intermedia 'Provence'* (1)

NOTE: *The key lists each plant type and the total quantity needed to replicate the garden shown. The diagram's letters and numbers refer to the type of plant and the number sited in an area.*

HERBS UNDERFOOT
pages 48-49

A. *Lavandula angustifolia 'Munstead' and 'Jean Davis'* (16)
B. *Santolina chamaecyparissus* (3)
C. *Rosa 'Summer Snow'* (1)

D. *Clematis x jackmanii* (2)
E. *Lilium hybrid* (1)
F. *Rosa 'New Dawn' and 'White Dawn'* (4)
G. *Santolina virens* (1)

H. *Thymus praecox ssp. arcticus* (5)
I. *Thymus 'Hall's Woolly'* (4)
J. *Thymus x citriodorus 'Silver Queen'* (1)

WITHIN GARDEN WALLS
pages 50-51

A. *Lavandula angustifolia 'Hidcote Giant'* (7)
B. *Oenothera berlandieri* (9)
C. *Erigeron karvinskianus* (5)
D. *Alyssum spp.* (many)

E. *Salvia leucantha* (2)
F. *Rosmarinus officinalis* (6)

CHAPTER THREE

Growing and Propagating Herbs

Herbs flourish in a wide range of habitats, and the knowledgeable gardener can find varieties adapted to almost any growing environment. For example, sweet flag (Acorus calamus) is a natural for a waterside planting, while caraway thyme (Thymus herba-barona) will thrive in a bit of sand between paving stones. The garden shown here blends herbs that have widely diverse textures, colors, and growing habits; the attractive design provides niches to satisfy the different needs of various plants. Bright pink dianthus, woolly lamb's ears, and lavender thrive in the heat radiated by paving stones in the garden's sunny center. A different set of herbs, including tall pink and white foxgloves, has been sited in the cooler semishade at the woodland edge beyond.

Although you may be content to plant only nursery-grown herbs, starting plants yourself from cuttings or from seed is not difficult. The techniques presented in this chapter may prompt you to try this economical and satisfying way to furnish your garden.

A. Stachys byzantina (3) B. Thymus praecox ssp. arcticus 'Pink Chintz' (2) C. Nepeta x hybrida (5) D. Lavandula angustifolia 'Munstead' (3) E. Geranium himalayense (2) F. Dianthus sp. (3) G. Rosa 'Gourmet Popcorn' (1) H. Anemone pulsatilla (2) I. Lavandula dentata (1) J. Origanum 'Hardy Greek' (1) K. Lavandula angustifolia 'Hidcote' (2) L. Thymus praecox ssp. arcticus 'Albus' (1) M. Artemisia splendens (2) N. Allium sp. (1) O. Rosmarinus officinalis 'Mrs. Reed's Blue' (1) P. Santolina chamaecyparissus 'Bowles' Form' (3) Q. Achillea taygetea (6) R. Tanacetum parthenium (3) S. Digitalis spp. (many)

The key lists each plant type and the number of plants needed to replicate the garden shown. The letters and numbers above refer to the type of plant and the number sited in an area.

Taking Stock of Your Garden

The first step in successful herb gardening is to assess the growing conditions in your garden. Variations in soil, microclimate, and light exposure will produce several different habitats that are congenial to different kinds of herbs. Although some herbs are very choosy about their soil requirements, most will grow vigorously in an open, loamy, well-drained soil. If drainage is too slow—usually because the soil is clayey—the oxygen that is vital for normal growth will be replaced by water. Plants may suffocate or, in less extreme conditions, produce weak shoots that tend to wilt or die back at the tips.

Only a few herbs tolerate waterlogged soil. If you have a drainage problem in a spot where you want to plant a wide variety of herbs, you'll need to loosen the soil. Begin by laying out your bed in the fall and digging the soil to a depth of 12 to 18

inches. In early spring, work in a 1- to 2-inch layer of builder's sand or poultry grit and about 1 inch of organic matter such as compost or leaf mold. Let the bed settle for several weeks before planting. If amending the existing soil is too big a job, you may prefer to build a raised bed *(pages 62-63)*.

Some Like It Sandy

If your garden has a coarse, sandy soil, it will provide the fast drainage some herbs demand, notably those that are native to the Mediterranean region. These include such favorites as lavender, rosemary, thyme, and oregano. To accommodate herbs that prefer moist, fertile soil, incorporate about 2 inches of organic matter. This will enhance the soil's ability to hold water and will pre-

A PLACE IN THE SUN
The yellow blooms and bright green foliage of Santolina virens tumble cheerfully around a dark drift of 'Crimson Pygmy' bayberry and a birdbath adorned with a sundial in this Oregon garden. A pungently scented Mediterranean native, santolina is tolerant of both drought and heat.

vent nutrients from running off too quickly to be absorbed. Be diligent about watering, and periodically replenish the supply of organic matter.

Picky Eaters

Restraint is called for when you fertilize perennial and woody herbs, which will respond to small doses of organic fertilizer with increased vigor and health. Bone meal, blood meal, fish emulsion, and kelp are all excellent choices. Working compost into the soil at the beginning of the growing season will also boost the level of nutrients.

Fast-growing annuals that are harvested repeatedly for their leaves and stems need higher levels of nutrients to continue producing new growth. They should be fed with liquid fertilizer every 2 weeks. You can make your own fertilizer from the potassium-rich foliage of comfrey *(Symphytum officinale),* a perennial herb. Pour 4 cups of boiling water over a handful of fresh comfrey leaves. Steep them for at least 10 minutes, then strain the liquid through cheesecloth and let it cool before using. Along with potassium, this infusion will provide phosphorus, nitrogen, trace elements, and minerals. The leaves of a number of other herbs, such as tansy, goosefoot, nettle, yarrow, dill, and coltsfoot, can also be made into liquid fertilizer.

Testing the Soil's pH

Before planting herbs, it's prudent to determine the soil's pH, which is a measure of its acidity or alkalinity. You can do it yourself with a kit bought at a garden center, or you can send a soil sample to your Cooperative Extension Service for testing. Most soils in the eastern half of the country are acidic because of high rainfall levels that leach alkaline elements from the soil. Conversely, alkaline soils are common in the drier West.

The majority of herbs will grow well in soils ranging from 6, which is slightly acid, to 7.5, which is mildly alkaline. If the pH falls outside this range, nutrients in the soil may not be available to plants. To raise the pH level, dust the soil with dolomitic limestone at least 1 month before planting, following the directions on the package. An application of sulfur will lower the pH level if your soil is too alkaline. For gardeners in the eastern part of the country who want to grow any of the Mediterranean herbs, soil testing is essential. Although they will grow in slightly acid soil, their preference is for a pH range of 7 to 8.2.

Light and Climate

Most herbs are sun worshipers, requiring at least 6 hours of direct light each day. Ideally, an herb bed has a southern exposure. When assessing how much light a site receives, factor in shade cast from structures such as sheds, trellises, and walls as well as hedges, shrubs, and trees. Luckily, several culinary herbs, among them parsley, chives, chervil, and hot peppers, can be planted in partial shade (4 to 6 hours of sun a day). And a number of herbs native to American woodlands, such as wild ginger and bloodroot, are at home in the dappled light beneath a canopy of trees.

The intensity of light is as important as the

Herbs for Shade

Alchemilla mollis (lady's-mantle)
Angelica archangelica (angelica)
Anthriscus cerefolium (chervil)
Asarum canadense (wild ginger)
Galium odoratum (sweet woodruff)
Gaultheria procumbens (wintergreen)
Hydrastis canadensis (goldenseal)
Mentha requienii (Corsican mint)
Myrrhis odorata (sweet cicely)
Panax spp. (ginseng)
Sanguinaria canadensis (bloodroot)
Viola odorata (sweet violet)

Note: The abbreviation "spp." stands for the plural of "species"; where used in lists it means that many, but not all, of the species in a genus meet the criterion of the list.

Viola odorata (sweet violet)

number of hours of sunshine. Herbs that prefer fewer than 6 hours of sun will grow best with direct morning light and dappled light or shade during the afternoon. Bright afternoon sun may be filtered by planting herbs on the northeast side of a trellis covered with a quick-growing vine.

Climate is another consideration. Winter cold presents special challenges to the gardener who wants to grow an herb that isn't reliably hardy in his or her zone. To greatly increase the prospects for winter survival:

• Locate your herb bed near a wall or an evergreen hedge for protection from winter winds.

• Avoid fertilizing or pruning borderline-hardy herbs late in the season; the new growth this stimulates will be more susceptible to winter injury than growth that has had time to mature.

• Use an antidesiccant foliar spray on evergreen herbs that are grown as ornamentals only and are not for culinary use.

• Mulch the bed with evergreen boughs after the ground has frozen.

• Pot up tender plants in the fall for overwintering indoors. Shrubby herbs like rosemary are good candidates for this treatment *(page 31)*.

Gardeners in the South have the advantage of a long growing season. There are, however, a few cultural practices that are critical for healthy herbs in the typically hot, steamy southern summers.

Improving air circulation is important for all herbs cultivated in high humidity, which favors fungal diseases such as powdery mildew. Allow plenty of growing space between plants and thin them to keep the interior airy.

Herbs with gray or silver leaves are difficult to grow in muggy climates; the little hairs that give the leaves their grayish cast also slow evaporation. This trait is a boon in hot, dry climates but a drawback where the moisture level is high. Give these plants a sunny site and mulch them with a 2-inch layer of light-colored sand or gravel, which will reflect light and heat onto them.

Herbs that cannot tolerate the intense heat of midsummer can be planted in early spring and harvested as long as temperatures remain moderate. After a midsummer break, a second planting can be made in early fall. Remember, too, that an herb that thrives in full sun in the North may perform well in the South only if it is sheltered from the blazing afternoon sun.

Herbs for Hot, Humid Climates

Allium ampeloprasum **var.** ***ampeloprasum***
(elephant garlic)
Artemisia **spp.**
(wormwood)
Centella asiatica
(gotu kola)
Cymbopogon citratus
(lemon grass)
Eupatorium purpureum
(Joe-Pye weed)
Foeniculum vulgare
(fennel)
Ocimum **spp.**
(basil)
Rosmarinus officinalis
(rosemary)
Salvia coccinea
(Texas sage)

Salvia elegans
(pineapple sage)
Salvia officinalis **'Berggarten'**
(sage)
Tagetes lucida
(sweet marigold)
Thymus **spp.**
(thyme)

Note: The abbreviation "spp." stands for the plural of "species"; where used in lists it means that many, but not all, of the species in a genus meet the criterion of the list.

Ocimum basilicum 'Dark Opal' (basil)

Planting and Cultivating Your Herb Garden

Herbs—adaptable, undemanding, and forgiving of mistakes—are perfectly suited to beginning and busy gardeners. Just be sure there's a good match between the herbs you choose and your garden's growing conditions and that you get them off to a good start with proper planting. After that, you'll find them remarkably easy to care for.

Planning before Planting

Most successful herb gardens use a combination of annuals, biennials, perennials, and woody subshrubs. Because perennials and subshrubs give an herb garden its structure, it's especially important to satisfy their cultural needs so that you can count on their long-term presence.

The short life span and rapid growth of annuals and biennals make them ideal subjects for experimenting with different looks for a planting or for sampling unfamiliar culinary herbs and new ingredients for potpourri. Some annuals and biennials can be more or less permanent residents if they are allowed to sow themselves. But they don't necessarily stay put: Between the wind and birds scattering the seeds, sometimes the plants pop up in surprising places from year to year. Also, you can't count on the offspring of a hybrid to be assets in an ornamental planting; very often they are disappointingly different from the parent.

Making the Right Choices

It's best to start small when deciding how many herbs to grow for the first time, especially in the case of culinary herbs. One or two plants of any one kind are usually enough, though you'll want to make room for more if you develop a taste for a specialty such as pesto, which calls for large quantities of fresh basil.

Don't overbuy. Plants pinched for space are likely to grow tall and spindly, and the lack of air circulation may result in disease. Remember to factor in a particular variety's mature height and spread, growth rate, and any tendency to invasiveness. Lovage, a perennial herb that takes its time reaching maturity, may surprise—or dismay—the unwary gardener when, about four summers after

planting, it shoots up to a dizzying 6 or even 8 feet.

Herbs purchased at a local nursery or from a mail-order nursery in your region will often be better suited to your climate than plants raised farther afield. This is especially true for cultivars, which may not be quite as vigorous, hardy, or disease resistant as their parents. When purchasing container-grown herbs, look for plants that have brightly colored foliage, undamaged leaves, and bushy, full growth with no signs of insect infestation or disease. Check that no more than a few roots are growing out of the bottom of the pot. A root-bound plant is often weaker because it has depleted the nutrients in its container.

Planting Primer

If your schedule and the weather give you a choice, a cool, cloudy day is ideal for planting herbs. And it's best to wait a few weeks after the

Easy-to-Grow Ornamental Herbs

Achillea millefolium (yarrow)
Artemisia abrotanum (southernwood)
Chamaemelum nobile (Roman chamomile)
Dianthus caryophyllus (clove pink)
Galium odoratum (sweet woodruff)
Mentha pulegium (pennyroyal)
Monarda didyma (bee balm)
Nepeta mussinii (catmint)
Ruta graveolens (rue)
Santolina chamaecyparissus (lavender cotton)
Stachys officinalis (betony)
Tanacetum parthenium (feverfew)

Monarda didyma (bee balm)

last frost date to minimize the chance that an un-usually late cold snap could damage the young plants. Before removing the herbs from their pots, arrange them in the bed according to your garden plan to see whether you want to make any last-minute adjustments. Once the herbs are placed to your satisfaction, you are ready to begin planting.

Dig each planting hole several inches wider and deeper than the container. Fill the hole with water, allow it to drain, then add a few inches of soil, tamping lightly to prevent excessive settling.

Next, gently ease your herbs from their containers. Using a garden knife or your fingers, loosen compacted soil around the roots of large container-grown herbs. Seedlings in large flats should be divided into fist-sized clumps with a trowel; leave as much soil around the roots as possible. If the seedlings were grown in peat pots, they can be planted, pot and all, directly in the garden. Just be sure to tear off the top half-inch or so of the peat pot, since any portion of the rim that is exposed above the surface of the soil will soak up water and nutrients, to the seedling's disadvantage.

Place each plant in the prepared hole and add enough soil to fill it. Firm the soil around the plant, and water thoroughly with a fine spray.

A number of popular herbs, including basil and chives, are very easy to grow from seed sown directly in the garden. And direct-sowing is the preferred method for herbs with fleshy, sparse roots or long taproots that make them difficult to transplant, such as coriander, chervil, dill, parsley, German chamomile, nasturtium, and summer savory.

Sow seeds according to the packet instructions for spacing and depth. If no instructions exist, a good rule of thumb is to plant in shallow trenches at a depth of twice the seed's diameter. Cover the seeds lightly with soil, and water well with a fine spray. To keep birds, insects, and other pests from feasting on your herbs-to-be, consider covering your seedbed with a floating row cover, which will let in rain, light, and air while protecting the seeds.

Building a Raised Bed of Stone

The raised bed shown here can be planted from the side as well as the top, since a soil mixture fills the spaces between the stones. The stone walls rest on footings and are further stabilized by being stepped. Use large, flat stones 12 inches or more across for the footings; smaller or more rounded stones are fine for the rest of the structure. This bed stands 18 inches above grade. For a higher bed, seek the advice of a mason.

2. Lay the second row of stones on top of the first, stepping their outer edges in slightly from the outer edge of the footing stones. Pack the gaps with soil. Continue laying stones in this manner until they are a maximum of 18 inches above ground level. Fill the gaps in the aboveground portion of the walls with a planting mix of equal parts of soil, leaf mold, and sand or poultry grit.

1. Mark off the outline of the bed with lime. Dig a trench about 15 inches deep and as wide as the footing stones. Next, put 10 inches of crushed stone into the trench. Lay the footing stones on this base so that they slope at a slight angle toward the bed's center; the ends of the stones should touch one another. Pack soil tightly into any spaces between and around the stones.

3. To plant in the wall pockets, remove each seedling or cutting from its container just before planting and wrap its tiny soil ball in damp sphagnum moss to protect the roots. Make a planting hole in the pocket with a widger—the spatula-shaped tool shown at left—or a tongue depressor. Lay the plant on the tool, ease it into place, and gently tamp soil mix around its roots.

The soil must remain moist for the seeds to germinate, so check the seedbed frequently. When the seedlings emerge, thin them according to the directions on the seed packet. Don't allow the soil to dry out, and apply a water-soluble fertilizer every other week for approximately 6 weeks.

Thriving between a Rock and a Hard Place

Many herbs will flourish in the nooks and crannies of your garden where other plants might not survive. Try tucking small thyme plants in gaps between the paving stones of a garden path or a terrace. The crimson-flowered creeping thyme (*Thymus praecox* ssp. *arcticus* 'Coccineus'), the caraway-scented *T. herba-barona,* and the half-inch-tall gray-leaved woolly thyme (*T. pseudolanuginosus)* are all low-growing varieties that will

withstand an occasional footfall. One caution—woolly thyme may decline and even disappear if the climate is too humid.

For most gardeners, steep inclines are troublesome areas to cultivate. Turn hot, dry banks into an asset by planting them with drought-resistant herbs such as lavender, creeping savory (*Satureja spicigera*), winter savory, costmary (*Chrysanthemum balsamita*), mountain mint (*Pycnanthemum virginianum*), mullein (*Verbascum thapsus*), santolina, and soapwort (*Saponaria officinalis*). Easy-care herbs with fibrous, spreading roots such as calamint (*Calamintha grandiflora*), wild marjoram (*Origanum vulgare*), and Our-Lady's bedstraw (*Galium verum*) will clothe a bank with foliage and flowers as they slow erosion.

A gravel path can also be enlivened with an informal planting of herbs. Self-sowers such as feverfew (*Tanacetum parthenium*), borage (*Borago officinalis*), fennel, apple-scented German cham-

4. *To prepare the interior of the bed for herbs that prefer light, fast-draining soil, add garden soil to a depth of 6 to 8 inches. Then fill the bed to within 3 inches of the top with a mixture of 1 part each of gravel, loam, and sand or grit. After planting, mulch the herbs with a 2-inch layer of sand or pea-sized gravel to help keep their crowns dry, retain soil moisture, and thwart weeds.*

Herbs for Crevice Planting

Alchemilla alpina
(dwarf lady's-mantle)
Crocus sativus
(saffron)
Gaultheria procumbens
(wintergreen)
Mentha pulegium
(pennyroyal)
Origanum dictamnus
(dittany-of-Crete)
Origanum vulgare 'Aureum'
(golden oregano)
Rosmarinus officinalis

'Prostratus'
(prostrate rosemary)
Sanguinaria canadensis
(bloodroot)
Teucrium chamaedrys 'Prostratum'
(wall germander)
Thymus herba-barona
(caraway thyme)
Thymus praecox ssp. *arcticus* 'Coccineus'
(red-flowering thyme)
Thymus pulegioides
(broad-leaved thyme)

A raised bed overflowing with catmint is home to creeping thyme rooted between stones (right, center). The yellow-tinted shrub at far left is a dwarf false cypress.

Herbs for Ground Cover

Arctostaphylos uva-ursi
(bearberry)
Asarum canadense
(wild ginger)
Chamaemelum nobile
'Treneague'
(Roman chamomile)
Galium odoratum
(sweet woodruff)
Gaultheria procumbens

(wintergreen)
Mentha pulegium
(pennyroyal)
Mentha requienii
(Corsican mint)
Rosmarinus officinalis
'Prostratus'
(prostrate rosemary)
Satureja spicigera
(creeping savory)

Teucrium chamaedrys
'Prostatum'
(germander)
Thymus praecox ssp.
arcticus 'Coccineus'
(red-flowering thyme)
Thymus serpyllum
(creeping thyme)
Viola odorata
(sweet violet)

A fragrant green carpet of creeping thyme (Thymus serpyllum) softens a contemplative nook in this Washington State garden.

omile *(Matricaria recutita),* and love-in-a-mist *(Nigella damascena)* will eventually spread onto a path if they are growing alongside it, but you can hasten the process by sowing the path with seed yourself. In each area that you want to plant, mix compost into the gravel, using 1 part compost to 3 parts gravel. The mixture should be at least 2 inches deep, so if the existing gravel is spread too thin you'll need to replenish it. Plant the seeds in the prepared gravel. Water the gravel well and keep it constantly moist, but not soggy, until the seedlings are established.

Weeding and Mulching

When preparing your beds for planting, it's important to pull or dig out the roots of perennial weeds, since even small fragments will resprout if left behind. Bindweed, couch grass, and goutweed are particularly difficult to remove when they invade a planting of creeping herbs like chamomile or thyme. Be vigilant and pluck out weed seedlings as soon as you spot them.

To suppress weeds around taller-growing herbs, spread a 2- to 4-inch layer of organic mulch around your plants. This will also help retain soil moisture and enrich the soil as it decays. Remember to keep the mulch an inch or two away from the crowns of the plants, however, to prevent rot. For plants that prefer a drier, leaner soil, use a mulch of sand, pea-sized gravel, or poultry grit.

In cold climates, an airy winter mulch of evergreen branches, straw, or salt hay will help plants

Pruning Lavender

To prevent lavender from becoming leggy and woody in the center, *prune back the previous year's growth by 1 to 2 inches in early spring, taking care to leave some green side shoots on the stems (below). This will stimulate new growth from the base of the plant as well as the production of healthy young side shoots on older stems.*

In summer, as soon as the flowers have bloomed, *cut off all the dried flower stalks, then prune the plant lightly to give it a neat, slightly mounded shape. Tie the fragrant flower stalks into bundles and lay them among clothing or linens, or scatter the clippings on a wood fire to release their scent.*

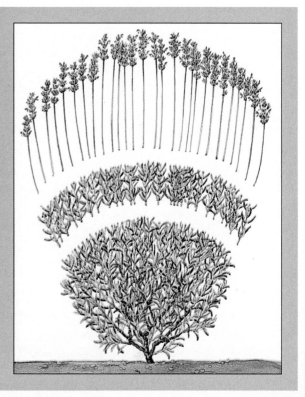

survive dipping temperatures and drying winds. Remove the mulch in the spring to allow the soil to warm up and the sun to reach new sprouts. If you are growing alkaline-loving herbs, it is especially important to remove evergreen branches before they shed their needles because they will acidify the soil as they decay.

The Fine Art of Watering

Knowing when to water your plants is a skill acquired by carefully attending to the requirements of the particular herbs in your garden. Species adapted to dry conditions are likely to perform poorly in soil that is constantly moist, while others require even moisture and must be checked frequently during dry weather *(list, right)*. Wilting is usually taken as a sign that a plant is short of water, but looks can be deceiving. On hot days, some thin-leaved herbs such as basil and hot peppers *(Capsicum* spp.) will wilt dramatically by early afternoon, even if the soil around their roots is moist. In the cool of the evening, the plants will perk up again. Always check the soil before watering herbs that wilt easily.

Although watering is largely a summertime chore, it may also be necessary in the winter. If there is no precipitation in your area for 3 or 4 weeks, give your beds a deep soaking to keep dormant herbs healthy. The following tips for when and how to water will help keep established herbs in good condition:

• For most herbs, allow the top inch or so of soil to become somewhat dry between waterings. To check whether it's time to water, dig down 3 to 4 inches with a trowel to see if the soil is still moist. If not, watering is in order.

• Drought-resistant herbs need no more than a half-inch of water per week. Other herbs should receive approximately 1 inch per week. Use a rain gauge to determine how much supplemental watering is needed.

• Give plants slow, deep soakings. Frequent light sprinklings encourage plants to produce shallow root systems, making them more vulnerable to drought.

Pointers for Pruning

Being quick to prune, pinch, or deadhead your herbs at the right time will repay you with more attractive and productive plants. For example, periodically pruning away deadwood from shrubby herbs like sage, southernwood, germander, and lavender encourages stronger, bushier growth. Remember, however, to stop pruning woody herbs approximately 4 weeks before the first expected frost in your area. Otherwise, the plants may waste their energy putting out new growth that could be damaged or killed by the cold.

Pinching back some herbs not only helps maintain a rounded, compact shape, it can also preserve flavor. Many culinary herbs valued for their foliage, such as basil, costmary, chervil, lemon balm, and oregano, will diminish in flavor if allowed to produce flowers. But if you promptly pinch off any new flower buds, the herbs will maintain their full flavor and aroma and continue to produce new foliage.

Unless you want to harvest seeds for cooking or to enjoy the ornamental seedpods of such plants as milkweed, boneset *(Eupatorium)*, or opium poppy *(Papaver somniferum)*, you should remove their spent flowers promptly. Deadheading prevents seeds from forming, so that the plants have more energy to spend on producing new flowers and foliage. French marigolds *(Tagetes patula)*, dyer's chamomile *(Anthemis tinctoria)*, yarrow, and other herbs that gardeners grow for their attractive flowers will bloom more profusely and over a longer period if deadheaded.

Angelica archangelica (angelica)

Herbs for Moist Soil

Acorus calamus
(sweet flag)
Angelica archangelica
(angelica)
Anthriscus cerefolium
(chervil)
Eupatorium purpureum
(Joe-Pye weed)
Filipendula ulmaria
(meadowsweet)
Gaultheria procumbens
(wintergreen)
Hydrastis canadensis
(goldenseal)
Laurus nobilis
(sweet bay)
Levisticum officinale
(lovage)
Lindera benzoin
(spicebush)
Melissa officinalis
(lemon balm)
Mentha aquatica
(water mint)
Mentha x piperita
(peppermint)
Mentha pulegium
(pennyroyal)
Mentha requienii
(Corsican mint)
Monarda didyma
(bee balm)
Myrrhis odorata
(sweet cicely)
Nepeta spp.
(catmint)
Ocimum basilicum
(sweet basil)
Panax quinquefolius
(American ginseng)
Polygonum odoratum
(Vietnamese coriander)
Saponaria officinalis
(soapwort)
Viola odorata
(sweet violet)

Note: The abbreviation "spp." stands for the plural of "species"; where used in lists it means that many, but not all, of the species in a genus meet the criterion of the list.

65

Propagating Your Herbs

The fastest way to get a garden going is with nursery-grown herbs, but don't overlook using your own mature plants to increase your stock. Dividing overcrowded clumps is simple, and growing new plants from cuttings is only a little more involved. If you need large numbers of plants for an expanse of ground cover or for a knot garden, seeding is a low-cost alternative. Most annual herbs are easy to grow from seed, and starting the cold-sensitive types indoors will give you a head start on the growing season.

Good light is vital for growing healthy seedlings indoors. A very sunny window sill may suffice for winter sowings, but if the intensity of the sunlight is too low the seedlings will be weak and leggy. If you plan to raise seedlings every year, it's smart to establish a propagation area in your basement or in a spare room. The setup can be as simple as a light fixture with two standard 4-foot-long fluorescent tubes suspended over a table or a sheet of plywood on sawhorse supports. Position the tubes so they will be about 4 inches above the seedlings. A timer set to 16 hours of light followed by 8 hours of darkness is a convenient way to ensure that the plants will get the light they need every day.

Double Potting for Easy Watering

For an effective way to keep your herb cuttings constantly moist, first fill a 6-inch clay pot halfway with moistened soilless growing medium. Plug the drainage holes of a 3-inch clay pot and set it on top of the medium. Fill the space between the pots with more of the growing medium and tamp it lightly. Plant the cuttings in the larger pot, then fill the small pot with water. It will seep through the pot and water your herbs.

Planting the Seed

A soilless growing medium, which you can buy or mix yourself *(opposite, below),* is the best choice for starting seeds. For containers, you can purchase inexpensive seed-starting trays with domed plastic lids that let in light and retain warmth and moisture. Individual plastic pots or cell packs with a covering of clear plastic wrap work just as well and are a good choice when you will be sowing only a few seeds of a variety. To minimize the chances of transmitting a disease to your seedlings, sterilize previously used containers with a solution of a half-cup of bleach to a gallon of water.

When you are ready to plant, moisten the growing medium and fill the containers no more than 2½ inches deep. Plant the seeds according to the instructions on the packets. Herbs that have a low rate of germination, such as lavender and parsley, should be sowed so thickly that the seeds touch one another. Make a label for each container with the name of the variety and the date of planting. Water thoroughly with a fine spray, then cover the container to keep the seedbed moist and warm. When using plastic wrap, choose the thinnest you can find and drape it loosely over a support of sticks, pencils, or arched hoops so that it is several inches above the seedbed.

Care of Seedlings

Place the containers in a warm (70° to 80°F), bright room out of direct sunlight. After a week, begin checking for signs of germination. As soon as a few seeds have sprouted, place the containers in a sunny window or under fluorescent lights and remove the covering. Seedlings left under cover in moist, warm conditions may be stricken with damping-off, a fungal disease that can quickly destroy an entire flat of young seedlings. To help prevent damping-off, try misting seedlings with an infusion of German chamomile: Add a handful of fresh chamomile or 2 tablespoons of the dried herb to 4 cups of boiling water. Steep the mixture for 10 minutes, strain it through cheesecloth, and let it cool before using.

Be careful not to overwater seedlings; soggy roots make them susceptible to root rot and foliage diseases. Water once each day in the morning, allowing the growing medium to dry out until the following morning. Once a week, feed the seedlings with a water-soluble organic fertilizer diluted as directed on the package.

Seedlings are ready for transplanting when they have two sets of leaves. Lift them carefully by their leaves, not by their fragile stems, and place them in 2- to 2½-inch plastic pots filled with dampened growing mix. After 3 to 6 weeks, the seedlings are ready to be hardened off. Set them outdoors in a sheltered, sunny spot for the day and bring them back inside at night. In a week they will be ready to be planted out in the garden.

New Plants from Cuttings and Division

If you have plants with long taproots that are hard to divide, you'll need to propagate them from stem cuttings. This method is also best for cultivars that don't come true from seed; the cuttings will yield offspring identical to the parent.

Spring is generally the best time to take cuttings, since fresh green growth roots quickly. First, prepare flats, trays, or shallow pots with dampened soilless growing medium. Using scissors or a sharp knife, make a clean cut just below a node or leaf 3 to 5 inches from the tip of the stem. If you will be taking cuttings for more than a few minutes, wrap each one as you go in dampened newspaper and place in a plastic bag to keep it moist and cool.

When you have enough cuttings, move to a shaded area to prepare them for potting. Strip all leaves from the lower half of the stem and pinch off all flowers or flower buds. To stimulate root formation, dip the base of the cuttings in rooting hormone, then plant the cuttings about an inch deep. Space them several inches apart to allow for air circulation. Water deeply and cover the container loosely with plastic wrap or a plastic bag held several inches above the cuttings by sticks or other supports. Keep the cuttings in a cool spot that gets plenty of bright, indirect light. Frequent misting—several times daily, if possible—will help maintain the high humidity needed to prevent wilting. Cuttings root most quickly when the air temperature is in the 60s and the root-zone temperature is around 75°F. For a steady source of bottom heat, set the container on an electric mat purchased at a garden center or through a garden supply catalog.

The appearance of new growth on a cutting signals that it has taken root and is ready to be transplanted to its own container and placed in a sunny window or under fluorescent lights. The new plant can be set out in the garden when a net-

PROPAGATION METHODS FOR 23 POPULAR HERBS	
Herb	**Propagation Method**
Allium schoenoprasum (chives)	seed, division
Anethum graveolens (dill)	seed
Angelica archangelica (angelica)	seed
Anthriscus cerefolium (chervil)	seed
Artemisia abrotanum (southernwood)	cuttings, layering
Artemisia dracunculus var. *sativa* (French tarragon)	cuttings, division
Calendula officinalis (calendula)	seed
Chamaemelum nobile (Roman chamomile)	seed, cuttings, division, layering
Galium odoratum (sweet woodruff)	cuttings, division
Laurus nobilis (bay laurel)	cuttings
Lavandula spp. (lavender)	seed, cuttings, layering
Melissa officinalis (lemon balm)	seed, cuttings, division
Mentha spp. (mint)	cuttings, division
Monarda didyma (bee balm)	cuttings, division
Myrrhis odorata (sweet cicely)	seed
Ocimum basilicum (sweet basil)	seed, cuttings
Pelargonium spp. (scented geranium)	seed, cuttings
Petroselinum crispum (parsley)	seed
Rosmarinus officinalis (rosemary)	cuttings, layering
Salvia spp. (sage)	seed, cuttings, layering
Santolina chamaecyparissus (lavender cotton)	cuttings, layering
Satureja montana (winter savory)	seed, cuttings, layering
Thymus spp. (thyme)	seed, cuttings, division, layering

Note: The abbreviation "spp." stands for the plural of "species"; where used in lists it means that many, but not all, of the species in a genus meet the criterion of the list.

Making Your Own Soilless Growing Medium

A soilless growing medium gets seedlings and cuttings off to a healthy start. Air and water penetrate it easily to reach growing roots and, unlike garden loam or commercial potting soil, it is free of disease organisms and weed seeds. To make a good mix yourself, combine 3 parts each of vermiculite, composted pine bark, and sphagnum moss with 1 part leaf mold. To each gallon of the mix add a heaping tablespoon of ground limestone and a half-cup of a slow-release fertilizer such as 17-6-10. Store in dry, clean containers or plastic bags. Just before using, dampen the mix with warm water.

work of roots has developed on the surface of the rootball; this will take several weeks. To check its appearance, gently slip the plant from its pot.

If you wish to propagate such herbs as basil, lemon verbena, mint, patchouli, pineapple sage, and Vietnamese coriander, you can also root them in water. Fill a clear glass jar with enough water to submerge only the stripped portion of the cutting's stem. Place it in bright, indirect light and change the water daily to keep it free of the bacteria that cause rot. When a cutting has roots ¼ to ½ inch long, which generally takes about 2 weeks, pot it in a soilless growing medium and place it under fluorescent lights or in direct sunlight. In a few weeks, the cuttings can be planted in the garden.

Division is the easiest and quickest way to increase your stock of healthy established herbs many times over. In cold climates, spring is the best season to divide plants; in milder climates you can choose between spring or fall. Work on a cloudy day, if possible, and dig up the plant with a sharp spade. Using your hands, a trowel, or a knife, divide the plant, roots and all, into several clumps. As a rule, a large clump will be less stressed than a small one and will establish itself quickly after planting. If a division has an ample root system and the weather is cool, it can be planted directly in the garden. Otherwise, plant the division in a container so that it can develop a larger root system before transplanting it to a permanent place. Water well with a soluble organic fertilizer to reduce the stress of transplanting.

The Simplicity of Layering

Creeping herbs often put down roots on their own wherever stems or branches touch moist soil. This process, known as layering, can be helped along by a gardener who wants new plants. Choose a young, flexible stem and strip the growth from a 5- to 6-inch section growing close to the ground. With a sharp knife, nick the bared section, then bury it 2 to 3 inches deep; leave several inches of the stem's tip exposed above the soil. You may need to anchor the buried stem with a small stone or a U-shaped wire to keep it in place. Mulch the layered area and water deeply. In about a month, check for roots by gently tugging on the buried stem. If you meet with resistance, roots have probably formed. Sever the stem from the parent plant, lift it gently, and transplant it to a pot or directly to the garden.

A special version of layering is used to propagate herbs that have upright, woody stems. This process, which is called mound layering, is explained in the drawings and text at right.

Mound Layering Shrubby Herbs

The stems of a number of shrubby upright herbs with woody bases will take root when mounded with soil, yielding new plants for the garden. Lavender, santolina, and other plants that are slow to root need to be cut back, as shown below in Step 1, then mounded with soil. You can skip this step with thyme, sage, rosemary, and other herbs that root easily and proceed to Steps 2 and 3.

1. In early spring, cut the stems of the plant to be mound layered back to within 2 to 3 inches of the ground. Within several weeks after pruning, new shoots should appear.

2. When the new shoots are about 5 inches long, mound a mixture of equal amounts of sand, peat moss, and soil over the plant's center, until only the tips of the new growth are showing. Keep the mound slightly moist. As the shoots continue to grow, add soil to the mound until it is 6 to 8 inches high. Be sure not to cover the tips of the shoots.

3. On an overcast day in late summer, gently wash away the mounded soil. Using hand pruners, cut each rooted stem at its base to separate it from the parent plant. Plant the rooted stems immediately in a well-prepared bed. The following year, you can mound layer the parent plant again or leave it to grow back into a rejuvenated healthy shrub.

Herbs to Propagate by Mound Layering

Artemisia abrotanum
(southernwood)
Artemisia absinthium
(wormwood)
Hyssopus officinalis
(hyssop)
***Lavandula* spp.**
(lavender)
Origanum dictamnus
(dittany-of-Crete)
Rosmarinus officinalis
(rosemary)
Salvia officinalis
(common sage)
***Santolina* spp.**
(santolina)
Satureja montana
(winter savory)
***Thymus* spp.**
(thyme)

Note: The abbreviation "spp." stands for the plural of "species"; where used in lists it means that many, but not all, of the species in a genus meet the criterion of the list.

Plants in this garden that can be mound layered include gray-leaved santolina and a trio of Spanish lavender (center), dark green spiky rosemary, and tall 'Alan Chickering' sage (rear).

CHAPTER FOUR

Reaping Homegrown Herbs

Herbs are truly one of nature's gifts to a gardener. Not only are they easy to grow, they also make congenial residents in virtually any landscape. And harvesting them for culinary, aromatic, and ornamental use is one of the more rewarding aspects of herb gardening.

Herbs still warm from the sun, such as the basketful of spring-tender chives, cilantro, parsley, rosemary, sage, and thyme at left, possess a pungent flavor difficult to resist. Beside the basket are the bright yellow blooms of Aurinia saxatilis (basket-of-gold), which add fragrant color to a potpourri.

Freshly picked or preserved in a multitude of ways, the uses for herbs—to flavor food and drink, decorate winter bouquets, or add scent and color to dried mixtures—are limitless. Learning when and how to pick, process, and store herbs as described in the following pages will safeguard their pleasures for your enjoyment long after their growing season has passed.

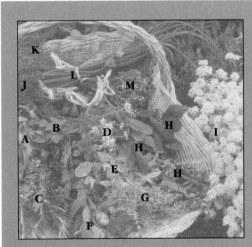

Please refer to the key at right to identify the plants in the garden shown.

A. *Artemisia dracunculus* (French tarragon) **B.** *Petroselinum crispum 'Italian'* (Italian parsley) **C.** *Rosmarinus officinalis 'Tuscan Blue'* (rosemary) **D.** *Matricaria recutita* (German chamomile) **E.** *Salvia officinalis 'Icterina'* (golden sage) **F.** *Salvia officinalis* (sage) **G.** *Thymus vulgaris 'Argenteus'* (silver thyme) **H.** *Salvia officinalis 'Purpurascens'* (sage) **I.** *Aurinia saxatilis* (basket-of-gold) **J.** *Petroselinum crispum* (curly parsley) **K.** *Foeniculum vulgare* (fennel) **L.** *Allium schoenoprasum* (chives) **M.** *Thymus vulgaris* (English thyme)

The Way to Harvest

When harvested and handled with care, home-grown fresh and dried herbs are far superior to any you can buy. Knowing when to harvest them ensures intense flavor, scent, and color. And storing herbs to retain their just-picked savoriness can be as simple as drying or freezing them.

Perhaps the easiest way to grow herbs is to start with a few pots or a small bed of herbs near your kitchen door. Several plants of parsley, chives, and mint—just waiting to be snipped into soup, salad, and teas—won't require much room or demand much care. Yet the wealth of flavor and sense of bounty you'll derive from them will soon spoil you for anything less.

Most herbs—including basil, borage, parsley, angelica, chives, and sage—may be picked at any time. Harvesting a few leaves for immediate use is an efficient way to keep your plants well groomed. Cut back a stray branch of rosemary or snip off the few roving sprigs of wild marjoram and use the trimmings in your kitchen. To shape a plant and also make it fuller, remove only the growing tip of a stem, a task called pinching back. You can induce dense, bushy growth on a sprawling mat of thyme, for example, by removing a few inches from the tips of scraggly branches.

How to Gather Leaves

Harvest leaves early in the morning as soon as the dew has evaporated but before the sun gets bright and hot, ideally on a dry day following a day of good weather. Choose healthy, vigorous growth with leaves unblemished by pests and disease. Using sharp pruners, scissors, or a knife, cut only as much as you'll need for the day's meals or for processing immediately for storage. Handle the leaves as little as possible to avoid bruising them.

Because herbs change in appearance as they dry, gather leaves from one type of herb at a time, keeping each kind separate and labeling the batches. Spread the cut leaves in a thin layer on a screen or in a basket; piling up herbs generates heat that makes them wilt.

Culinary Classics

Both weekend cooks and professional chefs know from experience how quickly the flavor of many herbs starts to wane once they're harvested. Widely available curly parsley, for example, is often relegated to use as a garnish because it has languished in your grocer's produce bin. But gardeners who grow it and its more assertive and longer-lasting cousin—flatleaf or Italian parsley—can enjoy them to the fullest extent: When minced with garlic and lemon peel, the herbs produce a tangy *gremolata,* adding a piquant finish to soups and stews. Fines herbes, a mixture of finely chopped chives, parsley or chervil, and more-pungent herbs such as tarragon, thyme, and savory, is basic to French cooking. The mixture can be bought dried, but the fresh version tastes far better.

Another indispensable component of French cooking is the bouquet garni, which is composed of three sprigs of parsley, a bay leaf, and a few sprigs of thyme tied into a bundle with string or wrapped in cheesecloth. After a bouquet has lent its blend of flavors to, say, a simmering pot of bean soup or a beef stew, it is removed before serving.

Unlike a bouquet garni, a chiffonade is made to be eaten. To make the delicate slivers that decorate and flavor a dish, gather clean, unblemished leaves of a large-leaved herb such as sorrel, washing them only if necessary and patting them dry. Roll the leaves into a cigar shape and slice the roll crosswise at one-quarter-inch intervals into fine strips. To make a visually striking salad or pep up a vegetable dish, use a mix of herbs with different leaf colors and compatible flavors such as basil, perilla, and mint.

Adventurous cooks can make use of *Cymbopogon citratus* (lemon grass), an herb traditional to the cuisines of Southeast Asia, whose unique flavor blends the bite of lemon with the scent of roses. The young, tender shoots of lemon grass are delectable stir-fried with chicken, stuffed into the middle of a whole fish before baking, and added to soup. Put them into the water in which you steam broccoli or other vegetables for a delicate hint of lemon. Where winters are cold—USDA Zone 7 and colder—pot up lemon grass and bring it inside to a sunny window. Its slender pale green leaves make it an attractive houseplant.

Herbs for Storage

Fresh herbs generally have more flavor than dried or frozen ones. One exception is bay leaves, which gain flavor when dried. In climates where even tender herbs grow year round they can always be enjoyed fresh. But in colder areas, bay leaves must be preserved for winter use.

Preserving herbs need not be mystifying or labor-intensive, especially if you begin on a small scale. Simply pluck a few leafy stems of basil, tarragon, marjoram, or any culinary herb and place them in a single layer in a colander. Set the colander in a dry, airy place out of direct sunlight. When the leaves are dry enough to crumble, break them into pieces, discarding the stems. Store the pieces in a tightly sealed jar and crush them just before using.

Gathering Herbs to Retain Quality

To preserve large quantities of herbs, you must know when to harvest them to capture their optimum flavor, fragrance, or color and how to retain those qualities through careful processing. The right time to harvest depends on which part of the plant is to be used. The maximum flow of essential oils, which furnish flavor and fragrance, generally occurs in leaves just before the plant's flowers open. But wait slightly longer to harvest blossoms—until they are newly opened. That's usually when a flower is richest in essential oils.

Because plants flower at different times, the precise moment to harvest leaves differs from plant to plant and, of course, with a growing season's particular climate and weather conditions. In most areas, many herbs flower in midsummer. Keep an eye on your plants so you'll know when each one is ready to bloom.

When harvesting, consider wearing gloves. Many people are allergic to the potent chemical compounds found in herbs. Rue, for instance, can cause severe dermatitis, and the hairy leaves of comfrey and borage can irritate sensitive skin. Reactions are generally worse if contact occurs during the heat of the day.

Use a sharp knife or pruning shears to cut the herbs. Remove a branch or cut back part of one, cutting directly above a node—the place where the leaf grows from the stem. This will stimulate the plants to produce new growth. For herbs that send up clumps of unbranched stems directly from the ground—parsley, chervil, and lemon grass, for example—cut the outer leaves at the base of the plant (box, below). If you like, you can cut back all the stems of stalwart perennial herbs such as lovage, comfrey, and chives; they will promptly grow back.

Slow and Moderate Growers

How much you can safely cut from an herb at any one time depends upon its vigor and growth habit. Some shrubby herbs—particularly bay, rosemary, and winter savory—grow slowly. Although you can pick a few leaves during their first year in the garden, wait until these plants are fully established and in lush growth before cutting them back. A few weeks before the first frost, take off one-quarter of the plants' growth. Pruning back to an outward-pointing bud encourages graceful branching (box, page 74).

Herbs that grow slightly faster—lavender, marjoram, pineapple sage, culinary sage, and thyme,

Culling Herbs from a Clump

Harvest the leafy growth of herbs that send up stems directly from the ground, such as the Italian parsley shown here, by cutting off individual stems at soil level from the outside edges of the plant. This will stimulate new growth at the center of the plant, keeping it compact and laden with leaves.

Clump-Forming Herbs

Angelica archangelica (angelica)
Anthriscus cerefolium (chervil)
Allium schoenoprasum (chives)
Allium tuberosum (garlic chives)
Cymbopogon citratus (lemon grass)
Petroselinum crispum var. *crispum* (curly parsley)
Petroselinum crispum var. *neopolitanum* (Italian parsley)

for instance—tolerate a somewhat sizable harvest once they are established. You can cut one-third off the top once, and sometimes twice, each year. Be sure to time your last pruning early enough in late summer or early fall so that new growth has a chance to harden off before winter.

Rambunctious growers like mint and lemon balm can withstand an extensive shearing. Cut as much as one-half of the new growth off the top twice—or even three times—during the growing season. Tarragon and sweet woodruff, while not as robust as mint and lemon balm, also tolerate severe pruning. Vigorous annuals like basil and summer savory can be cut back to 5 or 6 inches; be sure to save the lower foliage, however, which is needed for further growth.

Picking Flowers

The right time to harvest flowers depends on your use for them. Whole rosebuds, for example, are a lovely ingredient in a potpourri—an aromatic mixture of plant parts—providing a cushiony shape that contrasts with crumbled flowers and flakes of petals. Pick them when they are in tight bud. Flowers of lavender chosen for potpourri should be picked when the blossoms are fully formed and promising to open. At this stage, the top of the bud will show faint color and be intensely fragrant.

Rose petals to add scent to a potpourri are picked when the flower is freshly opened and at its most fragrant. Similarly, the color and flavor of golden yellow and orange calendula florets and showy red or pink-lavender bee balm petals, which are used to perk up salads and blend into soft cheese and butter for flavor and bright color, peak when they have just bloomed.

Slow-Growing Herbs

Woody herbs, including the potted bay laurel pictured here, *grow less rapidly than their herbaceous counterparts. Pick only a few leaves their first season. Wait until the plant is fully established in the fall of its second year before cutting one-quarter off the top. Cut back to a leaf node, preferably an outward-pointing one, to stimulate growth.*

Moderately Fast Growers

Herbs that grow at a moderate pace, *such as the thyme at left, tolerate two light shearings per season. Cut off one-third of the new growth in early summer and another third in early fall. Time the last harvest to allow any new growth to harden off before heavy frost.*

Harvesting Seeds

An herb grown for its edible seeds must be watched carefully—once the plant flowers, its seedpods and seed heads will soon follow. Gather seeds when they start losing their green color and begin turning light brown and the plant's stems and pods—if it has any—begin to wither and look dry. After the seed heads are cut from the plant, the seeds will continue to ripen. The seeds of many herbs such as caraway, coriander, and sweet fennel don't all ripen at the same time. With these herbs, harvest the seed heads when there are still immature seeds present. Both immature and ripe seeds can be spread out on paper towels and left to cure in a warm, dry place. Above all, don't wait too long to gather seeds. Leaving seeds exposed to the vagaries of weather will turn them black, an indication that they have deteriorated. If you were planning to save some for spring planting, they will probably not germinate.

After a day of drying, seed heads should be checked carefully for insects. Unwelcome pests such as tiny aphids will make their presence known by crawling away from seeds that have begun to lose moisture. If you see or suspect that there are insect eggs or larvae hidden in the seeds, pop them into the freezer for 48 hours. Store the seeds in an airtight container such as a screw-top glass jar in a cool, dark place.

Seeds for Sowing

Seeds destined to start next year's herb garden should be allowed to ripen on the plant until no trace of green remains. This helps to ensure a higher rate of germination next spring. Some herbs—dill, German chamomile, and angelica, among others—will self-sow. Simply allow their ripe seeds to drop to the ground.

Make sure seeds to be held until spring are completely dry, then place them in an airtight

Robust Herbs

Some perennial herbs— such as the lemon verbena shown at left—as well as most annual herbs grow so vigorously that they tolerate two or more harvests a year. One-half of their lush new growth can be cut off once in late spring, a second time in summer, and again in early fall, when their volatile oils are at their peak.

The Growth Rate of Different Herbs

SLOW GROWERS

Laurus nobilis
(bay)
Rosmarinus officinalis
(rosemary)
Satureja montana
(winter savory)

MODERATE GROWERS

Lavandula spp.
(lavender)
Origanum x majoricum
(hardy marjoram)
Salvia elegans
(pineapple sage)
Salvia officinalis
(common sage)
Thymus spp.
(thyme)

VIGOROUS GROWERS

Artemisia absinthium
(wormwood)
Artemisia dracunculus
var. *sativa*
(French tarragon)
Galium odoratum
(sweet woodruff)
Melissa officinalis
(lemon balm)
Mentha spp.
(mint)
Ocimum spp.
(basil)
Origanum vulgare
(oregano)
Satureja hortensis
(summer savory)
Symphytum spp.
(comfrey)
Tanacetum vulgare
var. *crispum*
(fern-leaved tansy)

Note: The abbreviation "spp." stands for the plural of "species"; where used in lists it means that many, but not all, of the species in a genus meet the criterion of the list.

Herbs with Tasty Flowers

Allium schoenoprasum
(chives)
Calendula officinalis
(calendula—petals only)
Chamaemelum nobile
(Roman chamomile)
Hyssopus officinalis
(hyssop)
Lavandula spp.
(lavender)
Monarda spp.
(wild bergamot)
Ocimum spp.
(basil)
Pelargonium spp.
(geranium)
Plectranthus

amboinicus
(Indian borage)
Rosa spp.
(rose—buds or petals)
Tropaeolum majus
(nasturtium)
Viola spp.
(violet)

Note: The abbreviation
"spp." stands for the
plural of "species"; where
used in lists it means
that many, but not all,
of the species in a genus
meet the criterion of
the list.

*The bright yellow and orange daisies
of calendula mingle with the soft blue
of borage in an edible planting.*

glass jar with a package of commercial desiccant or an inch of powdered milk to keep the humidity low. Store the sealed jar in your refrigerator.

Saving Other Plant Parts

In addition to leaves, seeds, and flowers, the aromatic roots of herbs such as *Zingiber officinale* (ginger) and *Vetiveria zizanioides* (vetiver) and the fragrant and colorful stigmas of *Crocus sativus* (saffron crocus) are highly prized. To dry ginger-root, harvest the roots in fall, when their moisture content is low and the length of time it takes them to dry will be minimal.

Vetiver's slender, spongy roots possess a rich, spicy scent used in potpourri and sachets. Grow this tall, slender-bladed grass in a 3-gallon container; its tough root system is difficult to dig out of open ground. Turn the rootball out of the container every 2 or 3 years at the end of summer and cut the roots back by one-half to two-thirds. Cut the foliage back to 14 inches in height and repot with fresh soil. To prepare the pieces of root

you've cut away, thoroughly scrub and dry them. Slice them into 3-inch lengths, then split each piece in half lengthwise. Wrap several pieces together in cheesecloth and put the bundles in dresser drawers and linen closets, which will become suffused with a fresh, woodsy fragrance. Vetiver is a tender perennial and, except in areas that are frost free, needs to be overwintered in a basement or garage where the temperature doesn't fall much below freezing. Set the plant out in a sunny place when daytime temperatures reach 60° F.

Saffron, the world's most expensive spice, is the dried stigmas of the autumn-blooming saffron crocus. Labor alone accounts for its costliness, for it takes many thousands of its threadlike stigmas—which must be gathered by hand—to produce a single ounce. Fortunately, you'll need only a pinch to flavor cookies or rice. A few dozen bulbs grown in your garden will supply you with enough for a handful of uses. Pluck the bright orange stigmas when the flowers open over several weeks in the fall. Saffron threads will quickly dry spread out on a kitchen towel; store them in a tightly sealed glass container away from heat and light.

The Art of Preserving Herbs

Air-drying, the time-honored method of preserving herbs, remains one of the best ways today. Speed is of the essence, because the faster an herb dries, the more flavor and color it will retain and the less likely it is to become contaminated or moldy. Conventional ovens, however, even at low temperatures, are too hot for drying herbs. Use them only in an emergency, when herbs are so wet that they are in danger of becoming moldy.

Two conditions important for drying herbs are good air circulation and a temperature that stays constant between 80° and 85° F. Higher temperatures and sunlight dissipate an herb's essential oils. Another crucial factor in speedy drying is low humidity. For this reason, don't wash herbs unless it's absolutely necessary. Give mud-spattered or dusty herbs a shower with a garden hose a day or two before harvesting them.

The place you choose to dry your herbs will influence the finished product. In some climates, dry, breezy days in late summer render almost any

room in the house ideal. In hot, muggy climates, however, you'll have to keep your herbs in an air-conditioned room or one equipped with a dehumidifier for them to dry properly. Avoid a basement that, while dry and cool, harbors stagnant air. And an attic, though airy and dry, may get too hot.

Hanging herbs in bunches tied with decorative knots of raffia and ribbon may be picturesque, but this method works well only for thyme and other tiny-leaved herbs that dry quickly. If you choose to hang-dry herbs, keep the bunches relatively small and tie them loosely; otherwise, the innermost leaves may mildew.

Most herbs, and especially those with thick, fleshy leaves, should be dried in a single layer on a flat surface that allows for adequate air flow, like the shallow basket shown below. A large window screen that has been scrubbed and dried also makes an ideal drying tray. For smaller quantities, try cookie or oven racks covered with kitchen towels, or hanging wicker baskets.

SAVING SAGE
Freshly picked sage leaves line this flat-bottomed wicker basket, where they will dry. Their arrangement in a single layer and the coarse weave of the basket permit air to circulate around each leaf, promoting quick drying. The faster an herb dries, the more color and flavor it retains in storage.

Helpful Appliances

Dehydrators, which force warm air through a series of screens, are excellent for drying herbs quickly. The fastest method, however, is drying with a microwave oven. Microwaves differ in power wattage, so you'll have to experiment if you chose this drying method, which works best for herbs with resinous leaves such as rosemary, bay, and sage. Place the leaves between two sheets of paper towels and microwave on low for 20 seconds. Check the leaves for crispness. If they are still pliable, microwave them for several seconds more, then check them again. Avoid overdrying the leaves; they will be brittle and turn to powder when crumbled. You can also dry herbs between between paper towels in a frost-free refrigerator. They should be dry and crisp in about 24 hours.

When your herbs are dry, remove the remaining stems, but take care to keep the leaves as intact as possible. The larger the pieces, the longer they retain their flavor in storage. Crumble them into smaller pieces right before you use them.

Herbal Teas

You need not be so careful when you prepare a harvest for making herbal tea, a beverage made from dried herbs steeped in hot water. Because the tea is strained before serving, whole leaves, stems, and flowers can go into it. You can make a tea of just one herb or several. A particularly refreshing tea combines the dried leaves of lemon grass with other citrusy herbs such as lemon verbena and lemon balm.

Packaging and Storing Herbs

Because dried herbs can reabsorb moisture from the air, it's important to package them as soon as they are dry. Further exposure to air will cause them to lose volatile oils, collect dust, and quite possibly become infested with insects. Use airtight glass or plastic containers for storage. Although clear containers let you see what's inside, opaque

PUTTING HERBS BY
The leaves of feathery chervil, broad-leaved sorrel, and sage, with blue-violet flower spikes, all taste best fresh. To keep chervil, freeze leafy stems in plastic bags or make an herb butter. Freeze shredded sorrel leaves in oil or layer them in salt. Sage can be dried or frozen and makes a delicious flavored vinegar.

Fleshy Leaves and Tender Tissues

Fleshy leaves such as those of scented geraniums contain a lot of moisture. To dry their thick tissues successfully, strip them from their stems to shorten the drying time and place them in a shallow basket or on a screen in one layer, with plenty of room surrounding each leaf.

Thin, tender leaves such as those of basil require great care in handling; they are easily bruised and crushed, which compromises their quality. Their fragility also makes them difficult to store without sacrificing flavor. Freezing is a good method of storage for the leaves of herbs with delicate tissues, such as basil, chervil, tarragon, lovage, and cilantro.

Aloysia triphylla
(lemon verbena)
***Artemisia* spp.**
(wormwood)
Borago officinalis
(borage—flowers)
***Calendula
officinalis***
(calendula—flowers)
***Citrus* spp.**
(orange and
lemon—peel)
***Cymbopogon
citratus***
(lemon grass)
Galium odoratum
(sweet woodruff)
Laurus nobilis
(bay)
Lavandula
(lavender)
Melissa officinalis
(lemon balm)
***Mentha* spp.**
(mint)
***Origanum
majorana***
(sweet marjoram)
Origanum vulgare
(oregano)
***Rosmarinus
officinalis***
(rosemary)
***Salvia* spp.**
(sage)
***Vetiveria
zizanioides***
(vetiver—root)
***Viola* spp.**
(violet—flower)
Zingiber officinale
(ginger—root)

*Note: The abbrevia-
tion "spp." stands for
the plural of "species";
where used in lists it
means that many, but
not all, of the species
in a genus meet the
criterion of the list.*

*Sage, Lavender,
and Orange Peel*

or colored ones are better because they keep out damaging light. Find a cool, dark place to store your herbs. Heat from any source such as an oven or cooktop will sap their potency.

Freezing is a quick way to preserve herbs, especially hard-to-dry herbs such as chives, chervil, parsley, and fresh coriander, or cilantro *(Coriandrum sativum).* The easiest way to freeze these herbs is simply to enclose them in a plastic bag labeled to show its contents and the date. Wait to chop a frozen herb until you are ready to use it.

You can also try freezing herbs in oil. Start with clean, dry leaves that have been stripped from their stems. Chop them and mix with just enough oil to form a paste. Then pack into containers, label, date, and store them in the freezer. You'll be able to scrape out what you need with a spoon without thawing the whole containerful first because oil doesn't freeze as hard as water.

Culinary Treats

Herbs can also be preserved in oil, butter, salt, vinegar, or wine. Each of these preparations has a specific shelf life. Herb butter, a mixture of one-half pound of softened butter and 3 tablespoons of finely chopped herbs such as parsley or tarragon or a combination of herbs, must be refrigerated. It is best used within a week unless it is frozen, in which case it should be good for as long as 2 months.

Herbal oils must be used within 2 weeks. To infuse oil with herbal essence, combine one-half cup of oil and sprigs of an herb such as rosemary, thyme, or marjoram in a metal measuring cup or small metal bowl. Simmer in the lower third of a preheated 300° oven for 1 hour to flavor the oil and destroy any bacteria that cause botulism. Strain the oil, bottle it, and keep it refrigerated at all times. Herbal vinegars, made by steeping fresh herbs in vinegar or wine, last up to a year and don't require refrigeration.

You can also use salt to dry herbs. In an airtight canning jar that will keep the salt from caking, layer leaves of, say, basil or lovage, over salt—the large crystals of kosher salt are best—covering each layer with more salt. In a week the herbs will be ready to use.

Sweetly scented geranium leaves and rose petals can be steeped in sugar, which will absorb their aromatic oils. Discard the leaves and petals after they are dry and use the flavored sugar to make cake icings, cookies, and candy.

Potpourri

An aromatic potpourri—a blend of dried flowers, spices, and leaves—lends the delectable scent of a summer garden to a room. Although there are many recipes for potpourri, there are basically two methods: the moist and the dry. The moist method is time-consuming and results in a highly fragrant but unattractive product. The dry method is far simpler and looks as pretty as it smells.

Favorite potpourri ingredients are listed opposite. If you haven't made potpourri before, a good place to begin is with this classic recipe: Prepare a quart of bone-dry rose petals or a combination of petals and rosebuds from fragrant varieties such as the fruit-scented bourbon rose 'Madame Isaac Pereire'. Intoxicatingly fragrant gallica and dam-

ask roses such as 'Camaieux' and 'Madame Hardy' also are perfect for potpourri.

Gently stir into the roses 1 pint of completely dry scented geranium leaves, a pint of dried lavender flowers, and 2 tablespoons each of cloves, cinnamon, and allspice. Blend in a fixative—an ingredient that extends the life of potpourri by absorbing aromatic oils and releasing them slowly. You can use 1 level tablespoon of orrisroot or gum benzoin for every cup of the potpourri mixture. Another excellent fixative is vetiver root, which also adds its own woodsy fragrance to the final product. Chop the dried root and crush it slightly, but do not pulverize it; using it powdered may make the potpourri look dusty. Mix the fixative with the flowers and spices and store the potpourri in a tightly sealed container for at least a month to allow the fragrances to meld.

A QUINTET OF
SEASONED VINEGARS
Decorative glass bottles hold sparkling, unclouded vinegars infused with, from left, purple basil, salad burnet, rosemary, sage, and garlic chives. Make sure herbs are free of surface moisture before steeping them in vinegar or the infusion may become murky. To retain their full flavor, store the vinegars in a cool, dark place.

Answers to Common Questions

I live in a contemporary house. Is there an herb garden design particularly appropriate for this style of architecture?

You have tremendous freedom in the way you design your herb garden. Look closely at the lines of your house and consider repeating these shapes in your garden. For example, if your house has curved walls and rounded angles, mimic them with swirls and loose drifts of herbs. Or you can draw from historic herb garden designs and plant herbs in beds flanking a central path or in quadrants formed by two intersecting paths. If you choose a traditional design, remember that formal herb gardens are enhanced by a sense of enclosure.

A cottage garden would fit in perfectly outside my kitchen door. How can I achieve the look of lush informality using herbs?

Herbs are particularly well suited to a cottage garden design. But don't let the seemingly random nature of a cottage garden fool you; it takes careful planning to achieve the casual effect. Begin by listing the plants and combinations you want to include. When you plant, place herbs, annuals, and perennials close together so that bare soil is covered quickly. If some plants die or simply don't look good together, remove them and experiment until the planting pleases you. Try arranging foliage and flowers in specific color combinations such as gray and red or blue and gold. Or plant freely and see what pairings of foliage, plant shape, and flower form and color arise.

I've always wanted a knot garden, but I don't have a big yard. Any suggestions?

Create a miniature knot garden in a container. Select herbs that take well to container culture such as basil, thyme, chamomile, and rosemary and keep them neatly pruned. Devise a knot pattern that looks good when viewed from above—star shapes and figure eights are only two of the possibilities. If you can't overwinter the miniature knot garden, harvest the herbs at the end of the growing season and start over in the spring.

I love to grow roses and wonder if I can plant my herbs with them.

Absolutely. Roses and herbs make ideal companions. Plant sun-loving herbs such as lavender, rosemary, thyme, rue, and sage near roses to highlight their blooms. But be sure to space the plants generously to give roses good air circulation. In shady spaces at the base of a rose, try violets, lady's-mantle, and sweet woodruff.

Which herbs are best grown from seed and which ones should I start from plants?

Sow fast-growing, short-lived annuals such as dill, coriander, arugula, and nasturtium directly in your garden. Many biennials, including angelica, clary sage, and mullein, also take best to direct-sowing. Perennial herbs can be grown from seed, division, cuttings, or layering. The method will vary depending on the plant. For example, thyme, lavender, rosemary, and mint hybridize freely and are best grown from cuttings. Other perennials such as lovage and comfrey are best propagated by division.

I would like to harvest seeds from my herbs, but I don't know when or how to harvest them.	Seeds are ripe when they have just turned brown. Cut the seed heads on a dry day and place them in a brown bag. Let the seeds dry for 1 to 2 weeks, and when they are completely dry store them in airtight jars. For more information on harvesting seeds to start next year's herb garden and a list of herbs with aromatic seeds see pages 75-77.
When I order new herb plants, how do I know if they are correctly labeled?	First check the plants against the encyclopedia descriptions and photographs starting on page 100. If you believe a plant is labeled incorrectly but can't identify it yourself, cut a stem of the plant when it is in bloom and take both leaves and flowers to a nursery or garden center for identification. You can also press the specimen and have it identified at a later date. If the herb in question may be poisonous, be sure not to ingest it.
Are there any culinary herbs that will grow in a shady container?	Sweet cicely *(Myrrhis odorata),* sweet woodruff *(Galium odoratum),* and chervil *(Anthriscus cerefolium)* prefer shade; and mint, angelica, and lovage grow well in light shade. Although you can grow sun-loving herbs in light shade, their flavor will be less intense and often they will not flower. In hot climates, some gardeners plant herbs in a location that gets midday shade to prevent them from being scorched by the summer sun.
Can I have a productive herb garden indoors?	Herbs generally grow best in the garden, where they can enjoy full sun, fresh air, and plenty of soil. If you want to cultivate herbs indoors, they will perform better under commercial plant lights. During warm seasons, the herbs will need more water, but take care not to overwater them in winter.

CARE AND MAINTENANCE

Is it true that herbs have better flavor if they are grown in poor soil?	No. Herbs have the fullest flavor when planted in moderately fertile soil that encourages healthy, strong growth. Soil that is too rich or too poor will result in herbs with compromised flavor and a greater susceptibility to disease.
Will the flavor of an herb decrease if I fertilize it? Should I limit the amount of compost applied to the soil?	Using moderate amounts of fertilizer will not diminish an herb's flavor. However, heavy fertilization will encourage weak and unhealthy growth, particularly in culinary herbs. Compost is a great soil amendment for herbs, but again, don't overdo it.
What is poultry grit? Why should I add it to the soil in which I grow herbs?	Poultry grit is finely crushed rock—usually granite—given to chickens and other poultry to aid their digestion. It is available in three sizes and can be purchased at a farm-supply store. Medium-sized poultry grit added to soil improves drainage best and increases aeration around plant roots. In heavy clay soils it works better than sand because its particles are larger than grains of sand. Since poultry grit is inorganic and does not break down over time, add it to the soil only once. Herb gardeners can also use poultry grit as a mulch, spreading a 3-inch layer over the soil surface.

Should I mulch my herbs? Which mulches do you recommend?

Like all plants, herbs should be mulched for weed control and in soils where moisture retention is a problem. But be sure to use a mulch that does not hold in too much moisture, and keep the mulch away from the crown of the plant to prevent rot. Mediterranean herbs are especially prone to rotting if a heavy mulch is used. Gravel, sand, and poultry grit are good choices for herbs that like good drainage. Other options include cocoa hulls, fine pine chips, and pine needles, all of which add a handsome finish of color and texture to the garden.

When should I pinch back my herbs to make them bushier?

It varies with the life cycle of each herb. Rosemary, for example, benefits from an early, low pinch to encourage side branching. Most perennial herbs take well to a midspring pinching back to stimulate dense growth. Annual herbs with a short life cycle, such as dill and coriander, do not require any pinching. When harvesting them, take the entire plant. Annual herbs whose leaves you plan to harvest throughout the growing season, such as basil and chervil, should be pinched back in early summer to encourage bushiness. Removing their flower buds whenever they appear will hasten the growth of new foliage.

I want to rejuvenate an established lavender plant that has grown leggy and produces few blooms. Will pruning it do the job?

Yes. Prune your lavender in early spring just as new growth emerges. To rejuvenate an old plant, cut it back close to the base instead of pruning it lightly. Although you may lose the plant completely if it has grown weak and feeble, more likely it will return stronger and healthier than before.

PESTS AND DISEASES

The branches of my bay tree (Laurus nobilis) are often covered with a brown crust. What is the problem and what is the best way for me to get rid of it?

Piercing-sucking scale insects—shiny brown and shell-like in appearance—are a common problem on bay trees. To control a small infestation, try scrubbing them off with a cotton-tipped swab or soft toothbrush dipped in soapy water or a solution of 1 part each of rubbing alcohol and water. For a larger infestation spray on a horticultural oil; once this is done, however, you must refrain from using the leaves for culinary purposes. Left untreated, scale will spread to the foliage of a bay tree and eventually kill it.

Some of my herbs die out in summer when the weather gets hot and humid. What is the problem and what can I do about it?

In regions of the country with extended periods of hot, humid weather, the branches of herbs may turn brown and die as a result of diseases caused by soil fungi. These disease organisms are activated when plants are stressed and the weather is humid. Removing all the diseased portions of the plant will help it to revive, but if the herb is severely infected, dispose of it entirely. Then try a new plant in a different location in soil that has been amended with poultry grit, which enhances air circulation at the root zone.

I've heard a lot about companion planting. What exactly is it?

Proponents of companion planting believe that neighboring plants influence each other in predictable and specific ways. They can enhance or interfere with a nearby plant's growth, repel or trap pests, or attract beneficial insects. Chamomile, for example, is sometimes referred to as a "physician plant" because it is said to revive nearby ailing plants. Herbs planted with some vegetables are said to amplify their flavor, such as basil with tomatoes, and summer savory with beans. French marigolds are said to repel nematodes, and catnip and nasturtiums are possibly effective against green peach aphids. Other herbs used to keep insects away include rue, southernwood, tansy, pennyroyal, and garlic.

What are beneficial insects and what herbs attract them?

Beneficial insects include predators that kill other insects, parasites that lay their eggs on other insects, and pollinators that carry pollen from male to female flowers. Creeping predators such as ground beetles like dense, low-growing herbs such as thyme and rosemary; flying predators such as hover flies prefer chamomile and mint. Parasitic wasps like dill, anise, and flowering members of the carrot family such as Queen Anne's lace. Most predators and parasites are excellent pollinators, too. ·

What is biological pest control?

Biological pest control does not eradicate populations of insects but reduces them to acceptable levels. Predators, parasites, and diseases are introduced into the garden to target a particular pest. For example, there are biological predators to reduce populations of aphids, whiteflies, spider mites, mealybugs, thrips, and caterpillars. Naturally derived botanical sprays include neem, whose active ingredient is azadirachtin—an extract from the seeds of the neem tree, which is native to India. Neem controls common herb pests including Japanese beetles, leaf miners, vine borers, thrips, and leafhoppers. It is not harmful to honeybees, butterflies, ladybugs, earthworms, or pets. Insecticidal soap is another excellent nontoxic biological control effective against soft-bodied insects such as aphids, spittlebugs, earwigs, and spider mites. It is not harmful to humans, pets, or the environment.

CHILDREN AND HERBS

I want to create an herb garden for my children. What's the best way to get started?

Giving children their own container to plant is a surefire way for them to take ownership of a garden and can be a tremendous source of pride for them. Take your children to a nursery or garden center and help them pick out the plants they like. Appearance, fragrance, and texture—the smiling face of a pansy, the fluffy texture of lavender cotton, the intense citrus scent of lemon verbena, the tart taste of mint, or the woolly texture of lamb's ears—often draw children to certain plants. Along with the herbs, grow fun plants such as four-o'clocks, which open their blooms in late afternoon; busy Lizzy impatiens, with bursting seedpods that catapult seeds as far as 20 feet; sensitive plant, which folds up its leaves when touched; and snapdragons, with jaws that snap shut.

What are some other kinds of gardens with herbs that children will enjoy?

Kids love to take part in harvesting plants, so concentrate on culinary herbs and decorative herbs that can be used for crafts. A pizza garden with tomatoes, oregano, basil, and onions will delight a child. A cutting garden filled with plants whose stems and flowers can be dried and used for wreaths and bouquets is another option. Good choices for drying include amaranth, cockscomb, safflower, artemisia, lavender, and sage.

Is there a fun way to teach children about the life cycle of plants from seed to harvest using herbs?

Try making a salad farm using edible herbs that grow easily from seed. In tending a miniature farm, children will learn about seed germination, a seedling's growth cycle, plant care, and when and how to harvest. If you have seeds that were collected from the garden, show children how to separate the ripe seeds from the rest of the plant. Sow the seed in rows and label each row. Watch the plants grow and harvest them for salads. Some of the best plants to grow from seed are coriander, corn salad, dill, lettuce, nasturtium, purple hyacinth bean, arugula, and sweet fennel.

CULINARY TREATS

How do you make an herb tea?

Herb teas can be made with either fresh or dried herbs, but fresh herbs result in a more pungent brew. Place the shredded leaves, seeds, or chopped root or bark in a teapot, using about 3 teaspoons of fresh or 1 heaping teaspoon of dried ingredients per cup. Add boiling water, let the tea steep for 3 to 5 minutes, strain, and serve. If you like strong tea, use a larger quantity of herbs; brewing the tea more than 5 minutes may result in an off taste.

What herbs should I grow for herb tea?

Delicious herb teas are made from pungent herbs such as lemon verbena, which has a tart, lemon flavor; chamomile, which is fragrant and relaxing; sage, which tastes best in the cold months because it has a warming quality; and anise seed, which possesses a warm and wonderful licorice flavor. Create blends—peppermint and spearmint combined make a soothing tea—to suit your own taste.

Is there any trick to preparing herbal vinegars?

No, they are easy to make. To quickly extract herbal essences, warm up any type of vinegar—wine vinegar is a good choice—and pour it into a sterile bottle filled with your favorite culinary herbs. Avoid using metal utensils, which may react with the vinegar, producing an unpleasant taste. You can also make flavored vinegar by adding herbs to a bottle of vinegar and setting it in the sun for 2 weeks. Strain the vinegar and replace the herbs with attractive fresh ones if you plan to display the vinegar or give it as a gift. Choice herbs to flavor vinegars include tarragon, lemon verbena, basil, garlic, and chili peppers.

How do I make herb-flavored liqueurs?

Steep the herbs in vodka with sugar to taste; put the brew aside for 6 months so the vodka can absorb the herbal flavors. Herbs and fruit together make terrific liqueurs; try combining blackberries and rosemary, or apricots and lemon balm, and use the liqueur as a sauce over ice cream and fruit.

FUN WITH HERBS

What herbs are used in cosmetics? Are there any cosmetics I can easily make with homegrown herbs?

Aloe soothes sun-damaged skin; pot marigold moisturizes dry and sensitive skin; chamomile helps heal superficial cuts and wounds and also conditions hair; peppermint is an antibacterial agent widely used in mouthwashes and oral hygiene products; rose petals are used in skin creams; and rosemary improves scalp and hair health. Most herbal cosmetics are made with an herb's essential oil, which is added to an emollient such as glycerin or paraffin. It takes a huge volume of a fresh herb to make a small amount of essential oil, which is extracted by distillation, a process that requires laboratory equipment and expertise. However, you can still make skin cream, for example, by buying essential oils and combining them with lanolin. But make sure the oils are fresh and not adulterated with less desirable synthetic oils.

I am interested in aromatherapy. How can I use herbs in this way?

Although aromatherapy also relies on the essential oils that are extracted from herbs by steam distillation, you can use harvests from your own garden to enjoy aromatic benefits. To make a wonderfully refreshing and relaxing herbal bath, wrap lavender flowers, rosemary leaves, and rose petals in cheesecloth and steep the bundle in hot bathwater.

What is a tussie-mussie?

A tussie-mussie is a small, artfully arranged hand-held bouquet whose flowers and herbs convey a message from the giver to the recipient. Sentiments such as true love, devotion, and admiration symbolized by flowers and herbs appeared in flower-language dictionaries during the Victorian era.

I'd like to make a tussie-mussie for a wedding. What herbs and flowers do you recommend?

A romantic tussie-mussie for a bride might consist of a rose symbolizing unity and love surrounded by herbs such as lavender for devotion, sweet marjoram for joy and happiness, myrtle for married bliss, and rue for virtue and virginity, as well as flowers of honeysuckle for bonds of love and orange blossoms for fecundity. Sprigs of rosemary, an ancient symbol of loving remembrance and fidelity, are traditionally worn by the groom.

Is it possible to dry the tussie-mussie or somehow preserve it?

Hang the bouquet upside down in a place that is dry and dark to avoid bleaching the colors. In 2 to 3 weeks it should be dry enough to put in a vase or container as a memento. Hair spray also helps preserve the herbs and flowers.

Troubleshooting Guide

Although herbs are remarkably resistant to serious damage from pests and diseases, problems can arise in even the best-tended garden. It's always better to catch an infestation or infection at an early stage, so make it a habit to inspect your plants regularly for warning signs. Keep in mind that a lack of nutrients, improper pH levels, and other environmental conditions can cause symptoms resembling those typical of some diseases. As a rule, if wilting or yellowing appears on neighboring plants, the source is probably environmental; pest and disease damage is usually more random.

This guide is intended to help you identify and solve the oc-casional pest or disease problem you may encounter. In general, good drainage and air circulation will help prevent infection, and the many insects, such as ladybugs and lacewings, that prey on pests should be encouraged. *For pest problems on culinary herbs, apply only natural solutions such as handpicking.* Any diseased culinary herb is best removed and destroyed. For other plants, natural solutions are preferable, but if you must use chemicals, treat only the affected plant. Try to use insecticidal soap or the botanical insecticide neem; these products are the least disruptive to beneficial insects and will not destroy the soil balance that is at the foundation of a healthy garden.

PESTS

PROBLEM: Leaves curl, are distorted in shape, and may be sticky and have a black, sooty appearance. Buds and flowers are deformed, new growth is stunted, and leaves and flowers may drop off.

CAUSE: Aphids are pear-shaped, semitransparent, wingless sucking insects, about ⅛ inch long and ranging in color from green to red, pink, black, or gray. Aphids suck plant sap and may spread viral disease. Infestations are worst in spring and early summer, when pests cluster on tender new shoots, on the undersides of leaves, and around flower buds. Aphids secrete a sticky substance known as honeydew onto leaves, which fosters the growth of a black fungus called sooty mold.

SOLUTION: Spray plants frequently with a steady stream of water from a garden hose to knock aphids off plants and discourage them from returning. In severe cases, prune off infested areas and use a diluted insecticidal soap solution. Ladybugs, green lacewings, gall midges, and syrphid flies prey on aphids and may be introduced into the garden.
SUSCEPTIBLE PLANTS: MANY HERBS.

PROBLEM: Holes appear in leaves, buds, and flowers; stems may also be eaten.

CAUSE: Caterpillars, including the larvae of the violet sawfly, verbena bud moth, sunflower moth, and painted lady butterfly, come in varied shapes, sizes, and colors. They can be smooth, hairy, or spiny. These voracious pests are found in gardens in spring and summer.

SOLUTION: Handpick to control small populations. The bacterial pesticide *Bacillus thuringiensis* (Bt) kills many types without harming plants. Identify the caterpillar species to determine the control options and timing of spray applications. Several species are susceptible to sprays of insecticidal soap. Introduce beneficials that prey on caterpillars, such as parasitic braconid wasps, tachinid flies, and beneficial nematodes. Destroy all visible cocoons and nests.
SUSCEPTIBLE PLANTS: MANY HERBS, INCLUDING BEE BALM, CARAWAY, GERANIUM, HOT PEPPER, MARIGOLD, MINT, NASTURTIUM, PARSLEY, AND PINKS.

PROBLEM: Leaves become stippled or flecked, then discolor, curl, and wither. Webbing may appear, particularly on undersides of leaves.

CAUSE: Mites are pinhead-sized, spider-like sucking pests that can be reddish, pale green, yellow, or brown. They are worst in hot, dry weather, and several generations of mites may appear in a single season. Eggs and the adults of some species hibernate over the winter in sod and bark and on weeds and plants that retain foliage.

SOLUTION: Keep plants watered and mulched, especially during hot, dry periods. To control nymphs and adults, spray the undersides of leaves regularly, since this is where mites feed and lay eggs, using a strong stream of water or a diluted insecticidal soap solution. Introduce predators such as ladybugs and green lacewing larvae. In severe cases, apply neem or pyrethrins. *SUSCEPTIBLE PLANTS: MANY HERBS, PARTICULARLY THOSE RAISED IN GREENHOUSES OR BROUGHT INDOORS OVER THE WINTER.*

PROBLEM: Ragged holes are eaten in leaves, especially those near the ground. New shoots and seedlings may disappear entirely. Telltale silver streaks appear on leaves and garden paths.

CAUSE: Slugs or snails hide during the day and feed on low-hanging leaves at night or on overcast or rainy days. They prefer damp soil in a shady location and are most damaging in summer, especially in wet regions or during rainy years.

SOLUTION: Keep garden clean to minimize hiding places. Handpick slugs or trap them by placing saucers of beer, sunk into the soil with rims at soil level, near plants. Slugs will also collect under a board laid on the ground or under inverted grapefruit halves or melon rinds. Salt kills slugs and snails but may damage plants. Barrier strips of coarse sand or cinders, or copper garden edging also act as deterrents. Encourage rove beetles, which prey on slugs. Turning the soil in spring helps destroy dormant slugs and eggs. *SUSCEPTIBLE PLANTS: MANY HERBS WITH TENDER FOLIAGE, PARTICULARLY BASIL, FLEUR-DE-LIS, GERANIUM, HOLLYHOCK, JOB'S-TEARS, MARIGOLD, OREGANO, SAGE, SAVORY, AND VIOLET.*

PROBLEM: Buds do not open, or flowers are tattered and deformed. Petals may be darkened or have brownish yellow or white streaks and small dark spots or bumps. Leaves and stems may be twisted, and plants may be stunted.

CAUSE: Thrips are quick-moving sucking insects barely visible to the naked eye; they look like tiny slivers of yellow, black, or brown wood. They emerge in early spring and are especially active in hot, dry weather. The larvae are wingless and feed on stems, leaves, and flower buds. Adults are weak fliers but are easily dispersed by wind and can, therefore, travel great distances.

SOLUTION: Controlling thrips is difficult, especially when they are migrating in early summer. Lacewings, minute pirate bugs, and several predaceous mites feed on them; late in the growing season such predators often check thrips populations. Remove and destroy damaged buds and foliage, and for severe cases, spray plants with an insecticidal soap or, *for nonedible plants only,* with a systemic insecticide. *SUSCEPTIBLE PLANTS: ARTEMISIA, EUCALYPTUS, FLEUR-DE-LIS, HOLLYHOCK, MARIGOLD, MYRTLE, NASTURTIUM, ONION, POT MARIGOLD, ROSE, AND YARROW.*

PROBLEM: Leaves turn yellow and plants are stunted. When plants are shaken, a white cloud appears.

CAUSE: Whiteflies, sucking insects ⅟₁₆ inch long that look like tiny white moths, generally collect on the undersides of young leaves. Found year round in warmer climates but only in summer in colder climates, they like warm, still air. Both adults and nymphs suck sap from stems and leaves, causing an infested plant to wilt. Whiteflies are often brought home with greenhouse-raised plants and can carry a virus and secrete honeydew, which promotes sooty mold.

SOLUTION: Keep the garden well weeded. Spray affected plants with a diluted soap solution or, in extreme cases, *and for nonedible plants only,* an insecticide. Because whiteflies are attracted to the color yellow, sticky traps hung in the garden will help control the population.
SUSCEPTIBLE PLANTS: BASIL, FLEUR-DE-LIS, GERANIUM, HIBISCUS, HOLLYHOCK, HOT PEPPER, NASTURTIUM, POT MARIGOLD, ROSE, ROSEMARY, AND SAGE.

DISEASES

PROBLEM: Overnight, young seedlings suddenly topple over and die. Stems are rotted through at the soil line.

CAUSE: Damping-off is a disease caused by several soil fungi that infect seeds and the roots of seedlings. The problem often occurs in wet, poorly drained soil with a high nitrogen content.

SOLUTION: Use fresh or treated seeds. Plant in a sterile medium topped with a thin layer of sand or perlite to keep seedlings dry at the stem line. Plants in containers are more susceptible than those growing outdoors. Give them well-drained soil with plenty of light and avoid overcrowding. Do not overwater seed flats or seedbeds.
SUSCEPTIBLE PLANTS: VIRTUALLY ALL.

PROBLEM: Leaves develop small yellow spots that gradually turn brown. Spots are frequently surrounded by a ring of yellow or brownish black tissue. Spots often join to produce large, irregular blotches. The entire leaf may turn yellow, wilt, and drop. Extensive defoliation can occur, weakening the plant. The problem usually starts on lower leaves and moves upward.

CAUSE: Leaf-spot diseases, caused by various fungi and bacteria, are spread by wind and splashing water. They are most prevalent from summer into fall, and thrive when humidity and rainfall are high.

SOLUTION: Destroy infected leaves as they appear; do not leave infected material in the garden over the winter. Water only in the mornings. Space and thin plants to encourage air circulation. A baking-soda solution can protect healthy foliage but will not destroy fungi on infected leaves.
SUSCEPTIBLE PLANTS: BEE BALM, CELERY, GERANIUM, HOLLYHOCK, HORSERADISH, PARSLEY, POT MARIGOLD, AND PRIMROSE.

PROBLEM: Leaves are covered with spots or a thin layer of grayish white powdery material. Infected parts may distort and curl, then turn yellow or purplish, and leaves may finally drop off. Badly infected buds will not open properly.

CAUSE: Powdery mildew, a fungal disease, is especially noticeable in late summer and early fall when cool, humid nights follow warm days. More unsightly than harmful, it rarely kills the plant.

SOLUTION: Grow mildew-resistant varieties. Place susceptible plants in areas with good air circulation, mist frequently, and spray with a baking-soda solution. *In the case of nonedible plants only,* spraying infected plants with compost tea in the evening can limit the disease's spread. *SUSCEPTIBLE PLANTS: ARTEMISIA, BEE BALM, CATNIP, GOLDENROD, HOLLYHOCK, HOT PEPPER, LEMON BALM, PINKS, POT MARIGOLD, SAGE, AND YARROW.*

PROBLEM: Leaves turn yellow or brown or are stunted and wilted; the entire plant may wilt and die. Roots are dark brown or black, feel soft and wet to the touch, and emit a slightly foul odor.

CAUSE: Root rot, a common soil-borne disease, is caused by a variety of fungi found in moist soils.

SOLUTION: Remove and destroy affected plants and surrounding soil. Plant in well-drained soil; do not overwater; keep mulch away from base of plants. Avoid damaging roots when digging. *SUSCEPTIBLE PLANTS: VIRTUALLY ALL, PARTICULARLY FOXGLOVE, GERANIUM, LAVENDER, MARIGOLD, PINKS, POT MARIGOLD, AND ROSEMARY.*

PROBLEM: Leaves and stems rapidly turn yellow, wilt, and die. Plants with fleshy roots quickly rot and die as well. A white cottony growth may be visible on stems and surrounding soil, and tiny tan globules about the size of mustard seeds may also be visible on or near the plant and in the surrounding soil or mulch.

CAUSE: Southern blight is a soil-borne fungal disease that occurs mainly in the eastern United States from New York south. It is most serious in the Southeast because of its rapid spread in areas of hot, humid weather.

SOLUTION: Remove and destroy diseased plants and any white cottony growth around them. Solarize the soil of new beds, thin plants to improve air circulation, and mulch them with a thin layer of solarized or sterile sharp sand. *SUSCEPTIBLE PLANTS: BASIL, BEE BALM, CATMINT, FLEUR-DE-LIS, HOT PEPPER, LEMON VERBENA, MYRTLE, ONION, POT MARIGOLD, ROSE, AND VIOLET.*

PROBLEM: A side or a branch of the plant wilts. Leaves turn yellow, then brown, and finally wilt and die. Wilt progresses upward and outward. A cut made across the stem near the base may reveal dark, discolored tissue inside.

CAUSE: Vascular wilt caused by either fusarium or verticillium fungi in the soil displays similar symptoms. Fusarium wilt is more prevalent in hot weather, verticillium wilt in cooler weather. In both diseases, the fungus responsible forms strands that penetrate the roots and stems and eventually clog the water-conducting vessels. Both fungi are long-lived, remaining in the soil for years after the host plant has died.

SOLUTION: Destroy infected plants; substitute resistant varieties. Wash hands thoroughly and disinfect tools. Don't site susceptible plants in an area that has been infected previously. Solarize the soil to kill fungi. *SUSCEPTIBLE PLANTS: BASIL, GERANIUM, HOT PEPPER, MARIGOLD, MINT, NASTURTIUM, POPPY, AND SAGE.*

Plant Selection Guide

Organized by plant type, this chart provides information needed to select species and varieties that will thrive in the particular conditions of your garden. For additional information on each plant, refer to the encyclopedia that begins on page 100.

	HARDINESS			HEIGHT				LIGHT			SOIL			BLOOM SEASON				PARTS USED				
ANNUALS AND BIENNIALS	HARDY	HALF-HARDY	TENDER	UNDER 1 FOOT	1 TO 3 FEET	3 TO 5 FEET	OVER 5 FEET	FULL SUN	LIGHT SHADE	SHADE	DRY	WELL-DRAINED	MOIST	SPRING	SUMMER	FALL	WINTER	LEAVES	FLOWERS	ROOT/BULB	SEEDS/FRUIT	STEMS/BARK
ALOE VERA			✓	✓				✓	✓			✓			✓			✓				
AMARANTHUS HYPOCHONDRIACUS		✓				✓	✓	✓			✓	✓			✓						✓	
ANETHUM GRAVEOLENS 'MAMMOTH'		✓			✓		✓	✓				✓			✓						✓	
ANGELICA ARCHANGELICA*	✓					✓	✓	✓	✓				✓		✓			✓			✓	
ANGELICA GIGAS*	✓					✓	✓	✓	✓				✓		✓			✓			✓	
ANTHRISCUS CEREFOLIUM		✓		✓					✓	✓		✓			✓	✓		✓				
APIUM GRAVEOLENS*	✓				✓			✓	✓			✓	✓		✓			✓			✓	
ARTEMISIA ANNUA	✓					✓		✓			✓	✓			✓			✓	✓			
ATRIPLEX HORTENSIS	✓					✓	✓	✓				✓	✓		✓			✓				
BORAGO OFFICINALIS 'ALBA'	✓				✓			✓			✓	✓			✓			✓	✓			
BRASSICA JUNCEA	✓				✓			✓				✓			✓			✓			✓	
CALENDULA OFFICINALIS	✓				✓			✓				✓		✓	✓	✓			✓			
CAPSICUM ANNUUM VAR. ANNUUM		✓		✓				✓			✓	✓	✓								✓	
CAPSICUM CHINENSE 'HABANERO'		✓		✓				✓			✓	✓	✓								✓	
CARTHAMUS TINCTORIUS		✓		✓				✓			✓	✓			✓				✓		✓	
CARUM CARVI*	✓				✓			✓	✓			✓	✓	✓	✓			✓		✓	✓	
CATHARANTHUS ROSEUS		✓		✓				✓	✓		✓	✓	✓	✓	✓	✓		✓				
CENTAUREA CYANUS		✓		✓				✓				✓		✓	✓			✓	✓			
CHENOPODIUM AMBROSIOIDES	✓				✓			✓				✓			✓	✓		✓			✓	
CHENOPODIUM BOTRYS	✓			✓				✓				✓			✓	✓		✓				
COIX LACRYMA-JOBI		✓				✓	✓	✓				✓			✓			✓			✓	
CORIANDRUM SATIVUM		✓		✓				✓	✓			✓			✓			✓		✓	✓	
DIGITALIS LANATA*	✓				✓			✓	✓			✓			✓				✓			
DIGITALIS PURPUREA*	✓					✓		✓	✓			✓			✓				✓			
ERUCA VESICARIA SSP. SATIVA	✓				✓			✓	✓				✓	✓	✓			✓	✓			
FOENICULUM VULGARE 'PURPURASCENS'		✓				✓	✓	✓				✓			✓	✓		✓		✓	✓	✓
HEDEOMA PULEGIOIDES	✓		✓					✓	✓			✓			✓	✓		✓				
HIBISCUS SABDARIFFA			✓			✓		✓	✓			✓			✓	✓		✓			✓	

*BIENNIAL

ANNUALS AND BIENNIALS

	HARDINESS			HEIGHT				LIGHT			SOIL			BLOOM SEASON				PARTS USED				
	HARDY	HALF-HARDY	TENDER	UNDER 1 FOOT	1 TO 3 FEET	3 TO 5 FEET	OVER 5 FEET	FULL SUN	LIGHT SHADE	SHADE	DRY	WELL-DRAINED	MOIST	SPRING	SUMMER	FALL	WINTER	LEAVES	FLOWERS	ROOT/BULB	SEEDS/FRUIT	STEMS/BARK
ISATIS TINCTORIA*	✓				✓			✓				✓	✓	✓					✓			
MATRICARIA RECUTITA		✓		✓				✓				✓		✓	✓			✓	✓			
NICOTIANA RUSTICA		✓			✓			✓				✓			✓	✓		✓	✓			
NIGELLA SATIVA		✓		✓				✓				✓			✓						✓	
OCIMUM 'AFRICAN BLUE'		✓			✓			✓				✓			✓	✓		✓	✓			
OCIMUM BASILICUM 'CINNAMON'		✓		✓				✓				✓			✓	✓		✓	✓			
OCIMUM BASILICUM 'DARK OPAL'		✓		✓				✓				✓			✓	✓		✓	✓			
OCIMUM BASILICUM 'MIMIMUM'		✓	✓					✓				✓			✓	✓		✓	✓			
OCIMUM SANCTUM		✓		✓				✓				✓			✓	✓		✓	✓			
ORIGANUM DICTAMNUS		✓		✓					✓			✓			✓	✓		✓	✓			
ORIGANUM MAJORANA		✓		✓					✓			✓			✓	✓		✓	✓			
ORIGANUM X MAJORICUM		✓		✓					✓			✓			✓	✓		✓	✓			
ORIGANUM ONITES		✓		✓					✓			✓			✓	✓		✓	✓			
PAPAVER RHOEAS		✓		✓				✓				✓		✓	✓				✓		✓	
PELARGONIUM CAPITATUM		✓		✓				✓				✓			✓			✓	✓			
PELARGONIUM X FRAGRANS 'VARIEGATUM'		✓	✓					✓				✓			✓			✓	✓			
PELARGONIUM ODORATISSIMUM		✓	✓					✓	✓			✓		✓	✓			✓	✓			
PELARGONIUM QUERCIFOLIUM		✓			✓			✓				✓		✓	✓			✓	✓			
PELARGONIUM TOMENTOSUM		✓		✓				✓	✓			✓		✓	✓			✓	✓			
PERILLA FRUTESCENS 'ATROPURPUREA'		✓		✓				✓	✓			✓				✓	✓	✓		✓		
PETROSELINUM CRISPUM VAR. CRISPUM*	✓			✓				✓				✓			✓			✓				
PETROSELINUM CRISPUM VAR. NEAPOLITANUM*	✓			✓				✓				✓			✓			✓				
PLECTRANTHUS AMBOINICUS		✓		✓				✓	✓			✓			✓			✓				
RICINUS COMMUNIS 'CARMENCITA'		✓					✓	✓				✓			✓			✓				
SALVIA COCCINEA	✓			✓				✓			✓	✓			✓			✓	✓			
SALVIA VIRIDIS*	✓			✓				✓			✓	✓			✓			✓	✓			
SATUREJA HORTENSIS	✓			✓				✓				✓			✓	✓		✓				
TAGETES LUCIDA		✓		✓				✓				✓			✓	✓		✓	✓			
TAGETES MINUTA		✓		✓				✓				✓			✓	✓		✓	✓			
TAGETES PATULA		✓	✓					✓				✓			✓	✓			✓			
TROPAEOLUM MAJUS		✓		✓	✓	✓	✓	✓	✓			✓			✓	✓		✓	✓		✓	
VERBASCUM THAPSUS*	✓					✓	✓	✓				✓			✓	✓		✓	✓			

*BIENNIAL

PERENNIALS, FERNS, AND BULBS

	ZONES								HEIGHT				LIGHT			SOIL			BLOOM SEASON				PARTS USED				
	Zone 3	Zone 4	Zone 5	Zone 6	Zone 7	Zone 8	Zone 9	Zone 10	Under 1 foot	1 to 3 feet	3 to 5 feet	Over 5 feet	Full sun	Light shade	Shade	Dry	Well-drained	Moist	Spring	Summer	Fall	Winter	Leaves	Flowers	Root/bulb	Seeds/fruit	Stems/bark
ACHILLEA MILLEFOLIUM	✓	✓	✓	✓	✓	✓				✓			✓				✓			✓	✓		✓	✓			
ACORUS CALAMUS	✓	✓	✓	✓	✓	✓	✓	✓			✓		✓	✓				✓		✓			✓		✓		
ADIANTUM CAPILLUS-VENERIS				✓	✓	✓	✓		✓					✓	✓		✓	✓					✓				
AGASTACHE FOENICULUM		✓	✓	✓	✓	✓				✓			✓	✓			✓	✓		✓			✓	✓			
ALCEA ROSEA	✓	✓	✓	✓	✓						✓	✓	✓				✓			✓				✓			
ALCHEMILLA ALPINA	✓	✓	✓	✓	✓				✓				✓	✓			✓			✓			✓				
ALLIUM AMPELOPRASUM VAR. AMPELOPRASUM		✓	✓	✓	✓	✓			✓				✓				✓			✓	✓				✓		
ALLIUM SATIVUM		✓	✓	✓	✓	✓			✓				✓				✓			✓	✓		✓	✓	✓	✓	
ALLIUM SCHOENOPRASUM	✓	✓	✓	✓	✓	✓	✓		✓				✓	✓			✓			✓	✓		✓	✓			
ALLIUM TUBEROSUM	✓	✓	✓	✓	✓	✓	✓		✓				✓	✓			✓			✓	✓		✓	✓			
ALTHAEA OFFICINALIS	✓	✓	✓	✓	✓	✓					✓		✓					✓		✓				✓	✓		
ANTHEMIS TINCTORIA	✓	✓	✓	✓	✓	✓	✓		✓				✓				✓	✓		✓	✓		✓	✓			
ARCTOSTAPHYLOS UVA-URSI	✓	✓	✓	✓	✓	✓			✓				✓				✓		✓							✓	
ARMORACIA RUSTICANA	✓	✓	✓	✓	✓	✓	✓			✓			✓					✓		✓			✓		✓		
ARNICA MONTANA			✓	✓	✓	✓			✓				✓				✓			✓				✓			
ARTEMISIA ABSINTHIUM 'LAMBROOK SILVER'	✓	✓	✓	✓	✓	✓			✓				✓	✓		✓	✓						✓				
ARTEMISIA ARBORESCENS				✓	✓				✓				✓	✓		✓	✓			✓	✓		✓				
ARTEMISIA DRACUNCULUS VAR. SATIVA		✓	✓	✓					✓				✓	✓		✓	✓						✓				
ARTEMISIA LUDOVICIANA 'SILVER KING'		✓	✓	✓	✓	✓				✓			✓			✓	✓						✓				
ASARUM CANADENSE	✓	✓	✓	✓	✓				✓					✓	✓		✓	✓	✓				✓		✓		
ASCLEPIAS TUBEROSA	✓	✓	✓	✓	✓	✓				✓			✓			✓				✓				✓	✓		
CALAMINTHA GRANDIFLORA		✓	✓	✓	✓	✓	✓			✓			✓	✓			✓			✓			✓				
CENTELLA ASIATICA				✓	✓	✓			✓				✓	✓				✓		✓			✓	✓			
CHAMAEMELUM NOBILE		✓	✓	✓	✓	✓			✓				✓				✓		✓	✓	✓			✓			
CICHORIUM INTYBUS	✓	✓	✓	✓	✓	✓	✓			✓			✓					✓		✓	✓		✓	✓	✓		
CIMICIFUGA RACEMOSA	✓	✓	✓	✓	✓	✓					✓	✓	✓	✓			✓			✓				✓			
COLCHICUM AUTUMNALE		✓	✓	✓	✓				✓				✓	✓			✓				✓				✓		
CONVALLARIA MAJALIS	✓	✓	✓	✓	✓	✓				✓				✓	✓		✓	✓	✓					✓			
CROCUS SATIVUS		✓	✓	✓					✓				✓	✓			✓				✓			✓			
CYMBOPOGON CITRATUS					✓	✓	✓			✓			✓	✓			✓			✓			✓				
DIANTHUS X ALLWOODII		✓	✓	✓	✓	✓			✓				✓	✓			✓		✓	✓	✓			✓			
DIANTHUS CARYOPHLLUS			✓	✓	✓	✓			✓				✓	✓			✓		✓	✓	✓			✓			

PERENNIALS, FERNS, AND BULBS

	ZONES								HEIGHT				LIGHT			SOIL			BLOOM SEASON				PARTS USED				
	ZONE 3	ZONE 4	ZONE 5	ZONE 6	ZONE 7	ZONE 8	ZONE 9	ZONE 10	UNDER 1 FOOT	1 TO 3 FEET	3 TO 5 FEET	OVER 5 FEET	FULL SUN	LIGHT SHADE	SHADE	DRY	WELL-DRAINED	MOIST	SPRING	SUMMER	FALL	WINTER	LEAVES	FLOWERS	ROOT/BULB	SEEDS/FRUIT	STEMS/BARK
DICTAMNUS ALBUS	✓	✓	✓	✓	✓	✓	✓			✓			✓	✓			✓	✓	✓	✓				✓	✓		
EUPATORIUM PURPUREUM	✓	✓	✓	✓	✓	✓	✓	✓			✓		✓	✓				✓		✓	✓			✓			
FILIPENDULA ULMARIA	✓	✓	✓	✓	✓	✓					✓	✓	✓	✓				✓		✓	✓			✓			
GALIUM ODORATUM	✓	✓	✓	✓	✓	✓			✓				✓	✓	✓	✓	✓	✓					✓	✓			
GERANIUM MACULATUM	✓	✓	✓	✓	✓				✓				✓	✓		✓		✓	✓					✓			
GERANIUM ROBERTIANUM	✓	✓	✓	✓	✓				✓					✓	✓	✓		✓	✓	✓			✓				
GLYCYRRHIZA GLABRA				✓	✓	✓					✓		✓	✓			✓		✓						✓		
HELICHRYSUM ANGUSTIFOLIUM					✓	✓	✓		✓				✓			✓	✓			✓			✓	✓			
HEUCHERA AMERICANA		✓	✓	✓	✓	✓			✓					✓	✓	✓	✓		✓	✓				✓			
HIEROCHLOE ODORATA	✓	✓	✓	✓	✓	✓			✓				✓	✓			✓	✓	✓				✓				
HUMULUS LUPULUS	✓	✓	✓	✓	✓						✓	✓	✓				✓	✓		✓			✓				✓
HYDRASTIS CANADENSIS		✓	✓	✓	✓	✓						✓		✓	✓	✓	✓	✓	✓				✓				
HYPERICUM PERFORATUM		✓	✓	✓	✓	✓			✓				✓					✓		✓				✓			
HYSSOPUS OFFICINALIS	✓	✓	✓	✓	✓	✓			✓				✓	✓		✓	✓		✓	✓	✓		✓	✓			
INULA HELENIUM	✓	✓	✓	✓	✓	✓					✓	✓	✓	✓			✓	✓		✓	✓			✓	✓		
IRIS VERSICOLOR	✓	✓	✓	✓	✓	✓				✓								✓		✓				✓			
LAVANDULA ANGUSTIFOLIA			✓	✓	✓	✓				✓			✓				✓			✓				✓			
LAVANDULA LANATA				✓	✓	✓					✓		✓				✓			✓			✓	✓			
LAVANDULA STOECHAS				✓	✓	✓	✓		✓				✓				✓		✓					✓			
LEVISTICUM OFFICINALE	✓	✓	✓	✓	✓	✓					✓	✓	✓	✓			✓	✓	✓	✓			✓				✓
MARRUBIUM VULGARE		✓	✓	✓	✓					✓			✓			✓	✓		✓	✓			✓				
MELISSA OFFICINALIS		✓	✓	✓	✓	✓				✓			✓				✓		✓	✓	✓		✓				
MENTHA X PIPERITA		✓	✓	✓	✓	✓				✓			✓	✓			✓	✓		✓			✓				
MENTHA REQUIENII				✓	✓	✓		✓						✓				✓		✓			✓				
MENTHA SPICATA	✓	✓	✓	✓	✓	✓				✓			✓	✓		✓	✓		✓				✓				
MONARDA DIDYMA		✓	✓	✓	✓	✓	✓			✓			✓	✓				✓		✓	✓		✓	✓			
MONARDA FISTULOSA	✓	✓	✓	✓	✓	✓				✓			✓			✓				✓	✓		✓	✓			
MYRRHIS ODORATA	✓	✓	✓	✓	✓	✓				✓				✓			✓	✓	✓				✓	✓	✓		
NEPETA CATARIA	✓	✓	✓	✓	✓	✓				✓			✓	✓			✓		✓	✓	✓		✓	✓			
ORIGANUM ONITES					✓	✓	✓		✓				✓			✓	✓			✓	✓		✓	✓			
ORIGANUM VULGARE			✓	✓	✓	✓			✓				✓			✓	✓			✓	✓		✓	✓			
PANAX PSEUDOGINSENG		✓	✓	✓	✓	✓			✓					✓	✓		✓	✓	✓	✓				✓			

PERENNIALS, FERNS, AND BULBS

	ZONES								HEIGHT				LIGHT			SOIL			BLOOM SEASON				PARTS USED				
	ZONE 3	ZONE 4	ZONE 5	ZONE 6	ZONE 7	ZONE 8	ZONE 9	ZONE 10	UNDER 1 FOOT	1 TO 3 FEET	3 TO 5 FEET	OVER 5 FEET	FULL SUN	LIGHT SHADE	SHADE	DRY	WELL-DRAINED	MOIST	SPRING	SUMMER	FALL	WINTER	LEAVES	FLOWERS	ROOT/BULB	SEEDS/FRUIT	STEMS/BARK
POGOSTEMON CABLIN								✓		✓			✓					✓		✓			✓				
POLYGONUM ODORATUM				✓	✓				✓				✓					✓		✓			✓				
POTERIUM SANGUISORBA	✓	✓	✓	✓	✓	✓			✓				✓				✓		✓				✓	✓			
PRIMULA VERIS	✓	✓	✓	✓	✓				✓				✓				✓	✓	✓				✓	✓			
PRIMULA VULGARIS		✓	✓	✓	✓				✓				✓				✓	✓	✓				✓	✓			
PRUNELLA VULGARIS		✓	✓	✓	✓	✓				✓			✓	✓			✓			✓			✓	✓			
PULMONARIA SACCHARATA	✓	✓	✓	✓	✓					✓				✓	✓		✓	✓	✓				✓	✓			
PYCNANTHEMUM VIRGINIANUM		✓	✓	✓	✓	✓				✓			✓	✓			✓	✓		✓			✓	✓			
ROSMARINUS OFFICINALIS				✓	✓	✓					✓		✓	✓			✓					✓	✓		✓		
RUBIA TINCTORUM			✓	✓	✓	✓	✓			✓			✓				✓			✓					✓		
RUMEX ACETOSA		✓	✓	✓	✓					✓			✓					✓		✓			✓				
RUMEX SCUTATUS			✓	✓	✓				✓				✓	✓			✓			✓			✓				
RUTA GRAVEOLENS			✓	✓	✓	✓		✓		✓			✓				✓	✓		✓			✓	✓			
SALVIA CLEVELANDII							✓	✓		✓			✓			✓	✓			✓			✓				
SALVIA DORISIANA											✓		✓				✓				✓	✓	✓	✓			
SALVIA LAVANDULIFOLIA				✓	✓	✓			✓				✓				✓	✓		✓			✓	✓			
SALVIA OFFICINALIS		✓	✓	✓	✓	✓				✓			✓				✓	✓		✓			✓	✓			
SANGUINARIA CANADENSIS	✓	✓	✓	✓	✓	✓			✓					✓	✓		✓	✓	✓				✓		✓		
SANTOLINA CHAMAECYPARISSUS				✓	✓	✓				✓			✓			✓	✓			✓			✓	✓			
SAPONARIA OFFICINALIS	✓	✓	✓	✓	✓					✓			✓	✓			✓			✓			✓	✓	✓		✓
SATUREJA MONTANA 'NANA'			✓	✓	✓				✓				✓				✓			✓	✓		✓				
SATUREJA THYMBRA					✓	✓				✓			✓				✓			✓			✓				
SESAMUM INDICUM								✓		✓			✓				✓			✓						✓	
SOLIDAGO ODORA	✓	✓	✓	✓	✓	✓	✓			✓			✓			✓				✓	✓		✓	✓			
STACHYS OFFICINALIS		✓	✓	✓	✓	✓	✓			✓			✓	✓			✓	✓		✓	✓		✓				
SYMPHYTUM OFFICINALE	✓	✓	✓	✓	✓	✓				✓			✓	✓	✓			✓	✓	✓	✓		✓	✓			
TANACETUM BALSAMITA			✓	✓	✓	✓					✓		✓	✓		✓	✓			✓			✓	✓			
TANACETUM CINERARIIFOLIUM			✓	✓	✓	✓				✓			✓				✓			✓			✓	✓			
TANACETUM PARTHENIUM			✓	✓	✓	✓				✓			✓	✓			✓			✓			✓	✓			
THYMUS CAPITATUS							✓	✓	✓				✓				✓	✓		✓			✓	✓			
THYMUS X CITRIODORUS			✓	✓	✓	✓			✓				✓				✓	✓		✓			✓				
THYMUS PRAECOX SSP. ARCTICUS		✓	✓	✓	✓	✓	✓		✓				✓				✓	✓		✓			✓	✓			

PERENNIALS, FERNS, AND BULBS

	ZONES								HEIGHT				LIGHT			SOIL			BLOOM SEASON				PARTS USED				
	Zone 3	Zone 4	Zone 5	Zone 6	Zone 7	Zone 8	Zone 9	Zone 10	Under 1 foot	1 to 3 feet	3 to 5 feet	Over 5 feet	Full sun	Light shade	Shade	Dry	Well-drained	Moist	Spring	Summer	Fall	Winter	Leaves	Flowers	Root/Bulb	Seeds/Fruit	Stems/Bark
THYMUS SERPYLLUM		✓	✓	✓	✓	✓			✓				✓			✓	✓			✓			✓	✓			
THYMUS VULGARIS		✓	✓	✓	✓	✓			✓				✓			✓	✓			✓			✓	✓			
TULBAGHIA VIOLACEA						✓	✓		✓				✓	✓			✓	✓		✓			✓	✓			
VALERIANA OFFICINALIS		✓	✓	✓	✓	✓	✓				✓		✓	✓			✓	✓		✓				✓	✓		
VETIVERIA ZIZANIOIDES						✓	✓					✓	✓	✓			✓	✓		✓					✓		
VIOLA ODORATA	✓	✓	✓	✓	✓	✓	✓	✓	✓				✓	✓			✓	✓	✓	✓		✓	✓	✓			
VIOLA TRICOLOR	✓	✓	✓	✓	✓	✓	✓						✓	✓			✓	✓	✓	✓			✓	✓			
ZINGIBER OFFICINALE						✓	✓			✓				✓				✓		✓					✓		

SHRUBS AND TREES

	ZONES								HEIGHT				LIGHT			SOIL			BLOOM SEASON				PARTS USED				
	Zone 3	Zone 4	Zone 5	Zone 6	Zone 7	Zone 8	Zone 9	Zone 10	Under 1 foot	1 to 3 feet	3 to 5 feet	Over 5 feet	Full sun	Light shade	Shade	Dry	Well-drained	Moist	Spring	Summer	Fall	Winter	Leaves	Flowers	Root/Bulb	Seeds/Fruit	Stems/Bark
ALOYSIA TRIPHYLLA						✓	✓				✓		✓	✓			✓			✓			✓	✓			
ARTEMISIA ABROTANUM			✓	✓	✓	✓					✓		✓			✓	✓			✓							
CEDRONELLA CANARIENSIS							✓				✓		✓				✓			✓	✓		✓	✓			
CINNAMOMUM CAMPHORA						✓	✓	✓				✓	✓	✓			✓	✓	✓	✓			✓				
CINNAMOMUM ZEYLANICUM						✓	✓					✓	✓	✓			✓	✓	✓								✓
CITRUS AURANTIUM						✓	✓					✓	✓	✓			✓	✓	✓					✓		✓	
CITRUS LIMON						✓	✓					✓	✓	✓			✓	✓	✓	✓				✓		✓	
COMPTONIA PEREGRINA	✓	✓	✓	✓	✓						✓		✓	✓		✓	✓			✓			✓				
EUCALYPTUS CITRIODORA						✓	✓					✓	✓	✓			✓				✓	✓	✓			✓	✓
GAULTHERIA PROCUMBENS	✓	✓	✓	✓	✓	✓	✓	✓	✓					✓	✓		✓	✓		✓			✓			✓	
LAURUS NOBILIS 'AUREA'					✓	✓	✓					✓	✓	✓	✓		✓			✓			✓				
LINDERA BENZOIN		✓	✓	✓	✓	✓					✓			✓			✓	✓	✓							✓	✓
LIPPIA GRAVEOLENS						✓	✓				✓		✓	✓			✓			✓			✓				
MYRICA CERIFERA					✓	✓	✓					✓	✓			✓	✓	✓	✓							✓	
MYRICA GALE	✓	✓	✓	✓	✓	✓	✓			✓							✓	✓	✓							✓	
MYRTUS COMMUNIS 'FLORE PLENO'						✓	✓					✓	✓	✓			✓		✓	✓			✓	✓			
PUNICA GRANATUM VAR. NANA				✓	✓	✓	✓			✓			✓				✓			✓				✓		✓	
ROSA CANINA	✓	✓	✓	✓	✓	✓	✓					✓	✓				✓		✓	✓				✓		✓	
ROSA DAMASCENA			✓	✓	✓	✓	✓					✓	✓				✓			✓	✓			✓		✓	
ROSA GALLICA 'OFFICINALIS'		✓	✓	✓	✓	✓					✓		✓				✓			✓	✓			✓		✓	
ROSA GALLICA 'VERSICOLOR'		✓	✓	✓	✓	✓					✓		✓				✓			✓	✓			✓		✓	
ROSA RUGOSA	✓	✓	✓	✓	✓	✓	✓					✓	✓				✓		✓	✓				✓		✓	
TEUCRIUM CHAMAEDRYS			✓	✓	✓	✓				✓			✓	✓			✓			✓			✓				
VITEX AGNUS-CASTUS					✓	✓	✓	✓				✓	✓	✓		✓		✓		✓	✓					✓	

A Zone Map of the U.S. and Canada

A plant's winter hardiness is critical in deciding whether it is suitable for your garden. The map below divides the United States and Canada into 11 climatic zones based on average minimum temperatures, as compiled by the U.S. Department of Agriculture. Find your zone and check the zone information in the plant selection guide *(pages 92-97)* or the encyclopedia *(pages 100-149)* to help you choose the plants most likely to flourish in your climate.

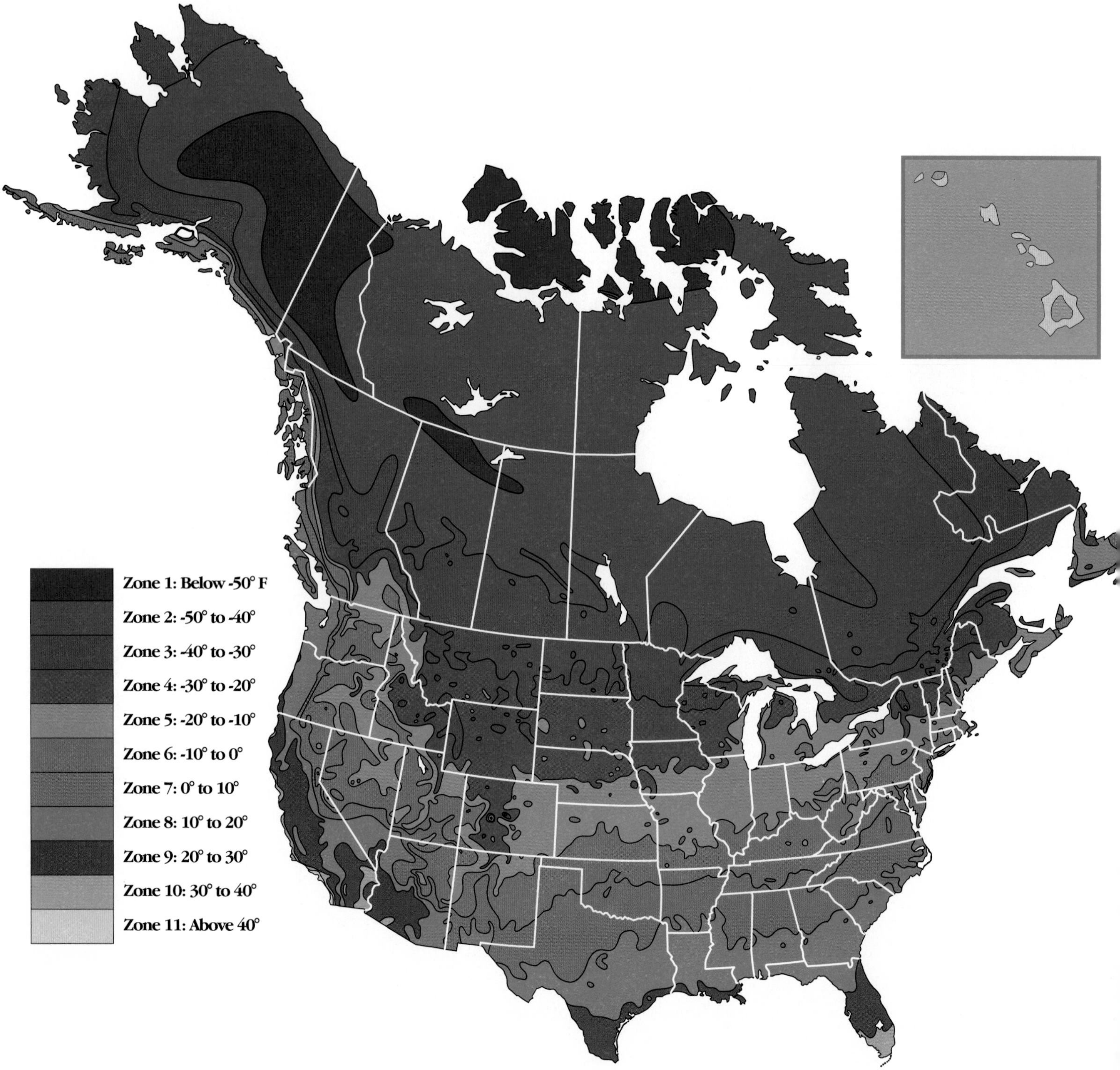

Zone 1: Below -50° F
Zone 2: -50° to -40°
Zone 3: -40° to -30°
Zone 4: -30° to -20°
Zone 5: -20° to -10°
Zone 6: -10° to 0°
Zone 7: 0° to 10°
Zone 8: 10° to 20°
Zone 9: 20° to 30°
Zone 10: 30° to 40°
Zone 11: Above 40°

Cross-Reference Guide to Plant Names

Absinthe—*Artemisia absinthium*
Alumroot—*Heuchera*
Ambrosia—*Chenopodium botrys*
Arugula—*Eruca*
Autumn crocus—*Colchicum*
Bachelor's-button—*Centaurea*
Balm—*Calamintha*
Balm—*Melissa*
Balm—*Monarda*
Balm-of-Gilead—*Cedronella*
Basil—*Ocimum*
Basil—*Pycnanthemum*
Bay—*Laurus*
Bayberry—*Myrica*
Bedstraw—*Galium*
Bee balm—*Melissa*
Bee balm—*Monarda*
Bergamot—*Monarda*
Betony—*Stachys*
Black cohosh—*Cimicifuga*
Black cumin—*Nigella sativa*
Black snakeroot—*Cimicifuga*
Bloodroot—*Sanguinaria*
Boneset—*Eupatorium*
Bouncing Bet—*Saponaria*
Burnet—*Poterium*
Butterfly weed—*Asclepias*
Candleberry—*Myrica cerifera*
Caraway—*Carum*
Castor bean—*Ricinus*
Catnip—*Nepeta cataria*
Chamomile—*Anthemis*
Chamomile—*Chamaemelum*
Chamomile—*Matricaria*
Chaste tree—*Vitex*
Chervil—*Anthriscus*
Chicory—*Cichorium*
Chives—*Allium*
Cilantro—*Coriandrum*
Cinnamon—*Cinnamomum zeylanicum*
Comfrey—*Symphytum*
Coriander—*Coriandrum*
Coriander—*Nigella sativa*

Cornflower—*Centaurea cyanus*
Costmary—*Tanacetum balsamita*
Cowslip—*Primula veris*
Cranesbill—*Geranium*
Curry plant—*Helichrysum*
Dill—*Anethum*
Dittany-of-Crete—*Origanum dictamnus*
Dock—*Rumex*
Elecampane—*Inula helenium*
Everlasting—*Helichrysum*
False saffron—*Carthamus*
Fennel—*Foeniculum*
Feverfew—*Tanacetum parthenium*
Flag—*Iris*
Foxglove—*Digitalis*
Garden heliotrope—*Valeriana*
Garlic—*Allium*
Gas plant—*Dictamnus*
Geranium—*Pelargonium*
Germander—*Teucrium*
Ginger—*Asarum*
Ginger—*Zingiber*
Ginseng—*Panax*
Goldenrod—*Solidago*
Goldenseal—*Hydrastis*
Heal-all—*Prunella vulgaris*
Herb Robert—*Geranium robertianum*
Hollyhock—*Alcea*
Horehound—*Marrubium*
Horsemint—*Mentha*
Horsemint—*Monarda*
Horseradish—*Armoracia*
Hyssop—*Agastache*
Hyssop—*Hyssopus*
Hyssop—*Pycnanthemum*
Indian paintbrush—*Asclepias*
Job's-tears—*Coix*
Joe-Pye weed—*Eupatorium*
Johnny-jump-up—*Viola tricolor*
Lady's-mantle—*Alchemilla*
Lamb's ears—*Stachys*
Laurel—*Laurus*

Lavender cotton—*Santolina*
Leek—*Allium*
Lemon—*Citrus limon*
Lemon balm—*Melissa*
Lemon grass—*Cymbopogon*
Lemon verbena—*Aloysia*
Licorice—*Glycyrrhiza*
Lily of the valley—*Convallaria*
Lovage—*Levisticum*
Lungwort—*Pulmonaria*
Madder—*Rubia*
Maidenhair—*Adiantum*
Mallow—*Althaea*
Mallow—*Hibiscus*
Marguerite—*Anthemis*
Marigold—*Calendula*
Marigold—*Tagetes*
Marjoram—Origanum
Meadow saffron—*Colchicum*
Mint—*Agastache foeniculum*
Mint—*Mentha*
Mint—*Monarda*
Mint—*Plectranthus*
Mint—*Polygonum*
Mint—*Pycnanthemum*
Mugwort—*Artemisia vulgaris*
Mullein—*Verbascum*
Mustard—*Brassica*
Myrtle—*Myrica cerifera*
Myrtle—*Myrtus*
Nasturtium—*Tropaeolum*
Navelwort—*Centella*
Nutmeg flower—*Nigella sativa*
Onion—*Allium*
Orange—*Citrus aurantium*
Oregano—*Lippia*
Oregano—*Origanum*
Orris—*Iris germanica*
Oswego tea—*Monarda*
Pansy—*Viola tricolor*
Parsley—*Coriandrum*
Parsley—*Petroselinum*
Patchouli—*Pogostemon*
Pennyroyal—*Hedeoma*
Pennyroyal—*Mentha pulegium*

Pepper—*Capsicum*
Periwinkle—*Catharanthus*
Pink—*Dianthus*
Pomegranate—*Punica*
Poppy—*Papaver*
Primrose—*Primula*
Prince's-feather—*Amaranthus*
Pyrethrum—*Tanacetum cinerariifolium*
Queen-of-the-meadow—*Filipendula*
Ramp—*Allium tricoccum*
Rocket—*Eruca*
Rue—*Ruta*
Safflower—*Carthamus*
Saffron—*Crocus sativus*
Sage—*Artemisia ludoviciana*
Sage—*Pulmonaria*
Sage—*Salvia*
Savory—*Calamintha*
Savory—*Satureja*
Self-heal—*Prunella*
Society garlic—*Tulbaghia*
Sorrel—*Hibiscus*
Sorrel—*Rumex*
Southernwood—*Artemisia abrotanum*
Spicebush—*Lindera*
St.-John's-wort—*Hypericum*
Storksbill—*Pelargonium*
Sweet anise—*Foeniculum*
Sweet Annie—*Artemisia annua*
Sweet cicely—*Myrrhis*
Sweet flag—*Acorus*
Sweet grass—*Hierochloë*
Sweet woodruff—*Galium*
Tansy—*Tanacetum*
Tarragon—*Artemisia dracunculus*
Thyme—*Plectranthus*
Thyme—*Satureja*
Thyme—*Thymus*
Tobacco—*Nicotiana*
Turmeric—*Hydrastis*
Wild celery—*Apium*
Wintergreen—*Gaultheria*
Wormwood—*Artemisia*
Yarrow—*Achillea*

Encyclopedia of Herbs

Presented here is an array of herbs suitable for borders, kitchen gardens, and containers. Each plant genus is listed alphabetically by its Latin botanical name, with the pronunciation given in parentheses. The common name of the genus follows in bold type. If you know only a plant's common name, see the cross-reference chart on page 99 or the index.

A botanical name consists of the genus and, usually, a species, both commonly written in italics. After its first mention in the entry, the Latin genus is abbreviated to an initial letter followed by a period. Species often have common names of their own, which appear in parentheses here, and many species have cultivars, whose names appear in single quotation marks. An "x" indicates plants that are hybrid offspring of two different species.

Hardiness zones for biennials, perennials, trees, and shrubs are keyed to the USDA Plant Hardiness Zone Map on page 98. For biennials, hardiness refers to their ability to survive winter after their first growing season. Hardiness for annuals refers to their ability to withstand frost after being set out in the ground in spring: Tender annuals should not be placed outdoors until all danger of frost is past; half-hardy annuals can survive a light frost; hardy annuals tolerate all but extreme cold. Distinctions between annuals and perennials are not always clear-cut; some hardy annuals self-sow so readily that they perform almost like perennials, while some perennials that are hardy only in the warmest zones should be considered annuals or grown as houseplants in cooler regions.

Each entry outlines the herb's specific uses and cites the plant parts appropriate for each use. The medicinal uses of the herbs, often based on folklore or centuries-old tradition, are noted only where modern scientific support exists for them or, contrariwise, where following them is no longer advised. Note that many herbs once considered therapeutic are now known to be toxic.

Achillea
(ak-il-EE-a)
YARROW

Achillea millefolium 'Paprika'

Hardiness: *Zones 3-8*
Height: *1 to 3 feet*
Light: *full sun*
Soil: *average, well-drained*
Plant type: *perennial*
Uses: *landscaping, arrangements*

Yarrow's broad, flat clusters of tiny summer-to-fall flowers on stems lined with soft, aromatic, ferny leaves are long-lasting in both fresh and dried arrangements. Yarrow spreads into dense, weed-suppressing mats good for covering difficult garden sites. Reminiscent of sage and somewhat bitter, the leaves are sometimes chopped into salads. Yarrow yields yellow and olive green dyes and has a long tradition in herbal medicine.

Selected species and varieties: *A. millefolium* (common yarrow, sanguinary, milfoil, thousand-seal, nosebleed)—gray-white to faded pink flowers on 2- to 3-foot stems; 'Cerise Queen' has deep pink flowers on stems 18 to 24 inches tall and is less invasive than the species; 'Paprika', long-lasting orange-red flowers on 12- to 18-inch plants.

Growing conditions and maintenance: Sow yarrow seeds or plant divisions in spring, setting them 12 inches apart. Gather leaves and flowers in late summer to dry; cut low to the ground to promote a second bloom. Hang in bunches to dry. Divide yarrow every 2 years in spring or fall to propagate or to control its spread.

Acorus
(AK-o-rus)
SWEET FLAG

Acorus gramineus 'Variegatus'

Hardiness: *Zones 3-10*

Height: *1 to 5 feet*

Light: *full sun to partial shade*

Soil: *moist*

Plant type: *perennial*

Uses: *landscaping, potpourri*

The creeping rhizomes of sweet flag thrive in wet soils along stream banks or in aquatic gardens. The grasslike leaves smell of tangerine; the rhizomes have a spicy cinnamon aroma prized in potpourri. Once used in herbal medicine, sweet flag is now considered hazardous. It is being researched as an insecticide.

Selected species and varieties: *A. calamus* (sweet flag)—sword-shaped ¾-inch-wide leaves up to 5 feet tall and tiny yellow-green summer flowers; Zones 3-10. *A. gramineus* (Japanese sweet flag)—narrow leaves up to 20 inches long and a 2- to 3-inch spadix in summer; 'Ogon' has 12-inch leaves striped golden green and cream; 'Variegatus', white-edged 1½-foot leaves only ¼ inch wide; Zones 7-10.

Growing conditions and maintenance: Plant sweet flag in a constantly moist site, even under as much as 2 inches of water. It can be propagated from seed, but the seed must not be allowed to dry out. Otherwise, divide rhizomes in spring or fall. Collect rhizomes that are at least 2 to 3 years old in spring, wash well, slice, and dry; do not peel them, as much of their aromatic oil is in the outer layers.

Adiantum
(ad-ee-AN-tum)
MAIDENHAIR

Adiantum capillus-veneris

Hardiness: *Zones 7-10*

Height: *12 to 24 inches*

Light: *partial to full shade*

Soil: *moist, well-drained, acid*

Plant type: *perennial*

Uses: *landscaping, pot culture*

Delicate maidenhair ferns provide a fine-textured embellishment to shade gardens when massed as ground covers, used as fillers among larger plants, or allowed to cascade over the edges of banks and walls. They also do well as container specimens for patio use. Native Americans and traditional herbalists use maidenhair fronds for medicinal purposes.

Selected species and varieties: *A. capillus-veneris* (southern maidenhair, Venus's-hair, common maidenhair, dudder grass) —deep green arching, branching deciduous fronds up to 2 feet long with glossy purple-black stems and several broad, triangular leaflets composed of tiny fan-shaped ¾-inch segments; Zones 7-10.

Growing conditions and maintenance: Sow maidenhair spores or set out divisions of the fern's slender rhizome in spring; spores take 6 weeks to germinate. For pot culture, set whole plants or divisions in a mixture of equal parts garden loam, leaf mold, peat moss, and sand. Keep ferns moist; plants that dry out completely may shed their fronds, although these will regrow when moisture reaches normal levels.

Agastache
(a-GAH-sta-kee)
GIANT HYSSOP

Agastache barberi 'Tutti-Frutti'

Hardiness: *Zones 4-9*

Height: *2 to 5 feet*

Light: *full sun to light shade*

Soil: *moist, well-drained*

Plant type: *perennial*

Uses: *landscaping, culinary, dried arrangements*

Clumps of erect stems lined with fragrant leaves and tipped with spikes of colorful flowers make giant hyssop a bold border accent. The nectar-filled summer flowers are edible, attract bees, and dry well for everlasting arrangements. Scatter the leaves in salad or infuse them for teas.

Selected species and varieties: *A. barberi* —red-purple flowers with a long season of bloom on stems to 2 feet tall; 'Firebird' has copper orange blooms; 'Tutti-Frutti', raspberry pink to purple flavorful flowers; Zones 6-9. *A. foeniculum* (anise hyssop, blue giant hyssop, anise mint, licorice mint)—licorice-scented leaves and purple-blue flowers on 3-foot stems; 'Alba' has white blossoms; Zones 4-9. *A. rugosa* (Korean anise hyssop)—wrinkly, mint-scented leaves and small purple flower spikes on 5-foot stems; Zones 5-9.

Growing conditions and maintenance: Start giant hyssop seeds indoors 10 to 12 weeks before the last frost, and set seedlings out 18 inches apart to bloom the first year. Established plantings self-sow; or propagate by division in spring or fall every 3 to 5 years. Hang flowers upside down in bunches to dry.

Alcea
(al-SEE-a)
HOLLYHOCK

Alcea rosea

Hardiness: *Zones 2-9*

Height: *4 to 9 feet*

Light: *full sun*

Soil: *well-drained*

Plant type: *biennial (perennial to Zone 5)*

Uses: *landscaping*

Hibiscus-like, 3- to 4-inch-wide flowers blooming in spires at the tips of hollyhock's erect stems make a bold statement in a summer border. The heart-shaped, rough-textured leaves lining the stems create an effective temporary screen or backdrop when the 2-foot-wide clumps are closely spaced. The cup-shaped blossoms yield a yellow dye and figure in herbal medicine.

Selected species and varieties: *A. rosea* (garden hollyhock)—single- or double-petaled flowers in shades of white, yellow, pink, or purple; 'Chater's Double' has double-petaled flowers like small peonies in yellow, pink, or deep purple; 'Nigra', deep maroon-black single-petaled blooms.

Growing conditions and maintenance: Although hollyhocks are a short-lived perennial, they are most commonly grown as biennials. Sow seed in spring or late summer for bloom the second season. To coax a second bloom in fall from mature plantings, cut stems to the ground after plants bloom in summer and feed with any good garden fertilizer.

Alchemilla
(al-kem-ILL-a)
LADY'S-MANTLE

Alchemilla mollis

Hardiness: *Zones 3-8*

Height: *4 to 18 inches*

Light: *partial shade*

Soil: *moist, well-drained*

Plant type: *perennial*

Uses: *landscaping, arrangements*

Lady's-mantle carpets the ground with large cupped leaves that reveal silvery undersides when tipped by a breeze. Use the frothy clusters of tiny greenish flowers that rise above the semievergreen foliage in summer as fillers in fresh or dried arrangements. Young leaves are sometimes tossed with salads or added to tea; they also yield a green dye. Lady's-mantle was traditionally used in herbal remedies.

Selected species and varieties: *A. alpina* (Alpine lady's-mantle)—broad leaves composed of pointed, lobed leaflets arranged like fingers on a hand and clusters of green flowers on creeping plants 4 to 8 inches tall, ideal for informal edgings. *A. mollis*—scalloped, fan-shaped leaves up to 6 inches across and yellow-green flowers on plants to 18 inches tall.

Growing conditions and maintenance: Sow seeds of lady's-mantle in spring; transplant divisions or the freely self-sown seedlings in spring or fall. Cut plants back hard to keep them compact; they recover readily. Plants can tolerate full sun in cool, moist northern areas. To dry, cut flowers just as they open and hang in bunches in a well-ventilated area.

Allium
(AL-lee-um)
ONION

Allium ampeloprasum var. ampeloprasum

Hardiness: *Zones 3-9*

Height: *8 to 36 inches*

Light: *full sun to partial shade*

Soil: *rich, moist, well-drained*

Plant type: *bulb*

Uses: *culinary, landscaping, arrangements*

This large genus produces round or domed umbels of white to blue, pink, or purple flowers amid grassy leaves from summer through fall. Depending on the species, edible underground bulbs, aerial bulbils, the flat or cylindrical leaves, or young flowers provide texture, color, and a range of flavors for culinary use. Some species are suited to the flower border, others add interest to winter bouquets, and still others figure in herbal medicine.

Selected species and varieties: *A. ampeloprasum* var. *ampeloprasum* (elephant garlic)—plants to 3 feet tall with several large, mildly sweet cloves forming bulbs 4 inches or more across that can be sliced for flavoring or prepared alone as a side dish. *A. cepa* var. *proliferum* (tree onion, Egyptian onion)—stiff stalks to 3 feet tall, tipped with small aerial bulbs or bulbils from late summer through fall, grown ornamentally or for the bulbils that are used whole for cooking or pickling. *A. fistulosum* (Welsh onion, Spanish onion, ciboule, two-bladed onion)—small, cylindrical bulbs elongating into pencil-thick blanched stems topped with pungent 12- to 36-inch leaves, all parts of which can be sliced fresh for flavoring or garnish. *A. sativum* (garlic)—up to 15 pungently flavored small cloves in bulbs 2 to 3 inches across with edible pale violet flowers tipping stems up to 36 inches tall from late summer through fall; softneck artichoke varieties have three to five layers of cloves in lumpy bulbs; softneck silverskin

Allium sativum

varieties, uniform bulbs that are sometimes braided into decorative ropes for storage; hardneck varieties, coiled stalks and decorative seedpods that are prized in dried arrangements; all varieties are used for flavoring. *A. schoenoprasum* (chive)—clumps of slender foot-long leaves with mild onion flavor and stalks tipped with edible pale purple flowers from summer through fall, all varieties of which are used fresh, frozen, or dried as garnishes or flavoring or planted as border accents; 'Forescate' is a particularly vigorous variety with rose pink flowers on stalks to 18 inches. *A. scorodoprasum* (rocambole, Spanish garlic)—inch-wide bulbs with mild garlicky flavor and 3-foot stalks tipped with edible bulbils; both leaves and bulbils are used for flavoring. *A. tricoccum* (ramp, wild leek)—2-inch-wide arrow-shaped leaves that wither before white summer-to-fall flowers bloom on 12- to 18-inch stalks; the extremely pungent bulbs and leaves are used for flavoring, the flowers as ornamentals. *A. tuberosum* (garlic chive, Oriental garlic, Chinese leek)—scented white summer flowers on 1- to 1½-foot stalks grown ornamentally for fresh or dried bouquets; the summer flowers and mildly flavored flat leaves are used in cooking or salads.

Growing conditions and maintenance: Sow allium seeds indoors 10 to 12 weeks before the last frost or outdoors in fall 8 to 12 weeks before the first frost; alliums require two growing seasons to produce eating-size bulbs from seed. For earlier harvest, plant sets of *A. fistulosum* or *A. schoenoprasum* in spring or plant the small aerial bulbils or cloves of other allium species in fall for harvest the following year; left unharvested, bulbils self-sow. Most alliums do best in moist but very well-drained organic soils; ramp prefers constantly moist soils and tolerates shade; rocambole tolerates drier soils. Set bulbs or cloves 1 to 3 inches deep. Space sets or cloves of smaller

Allium tuberosum

species such as *A. fistulosum* or *A. schoenoprasum* 4 to 6 inches apart, those of larger species such as *A. cepa* var. *proliferum, A. sativum,* or *A. ampeloprasum* var. *ampeloprasum* 8 to 10 inches apart. Wider spacing produces larger bulbs. Grow chives in containers and move indoors for harvest through the winter. Divide clumps of chives and garlic chives every 3 to 4 years to maintain vigor. Harvest allium leaves any time during the growing season; chives do best sheared close to the ground and allowed to regrow. Harvest flowers of garlic, chives, and garlic chives for salads and garnishes just after opening. Cut seed heads of garlic chives to prevent proliferation of seedlings. Pick aerial bulbils of tree onion and rocambole in fall. Dig allium bulbs for fresh use in fall as leaves begin to wither. To dry elephant garlic or garlic for long-term storage, allow skins to dry for several days, then either braid stems or cut them off 2 inches from bulb; store with good air circulation and use within 6 to 10 months.

Aloe
(AL-oh)
ALOE

Aloe vera

Hardiness: *tender or Zone 10*

Height: *2 to 3 feet*

Light: *full sun to light shade*

Soil: *well-drained, sandy*

Plant type: *annual*

Uses: *landscaping, houseplant*

Aloes produce rosettes of fleshy, pointed leaves that twist and arch to create architectural border specimens. Where aloe can be grown outdoors, plants produce a flower stalk in summer, but potted plants maintained indoors seldom bloom. Science has proved the truth of folklore and demonstrated that the sap inside aloe leaves soothes burns and skin irritations.

Selected species and varieties: *A. vera* [also classified as *A. barbadensis*] (medicinal aloe, Barbados aloe, unguentine cactus)—mottled gray-green leaves up to 3 feet long and 3- to 4-foot-tall flower stalks with dense clusters of 1-inch yellow to orange or red flowers.

Growing conditions and maintenance: Grow aloes from the small offsets produced by mature plants, removing 1-inch offsets for potted plants or 6- to 8-inch offsets for outdoor specimens. Allow offsets to harden 2 days before replanting outdoors or potting in a 50:50 mixture of compost and sand. Water aloes infrequently. To use the gel-like sap, split leaves lengthwise and rub the cut surface on the skin; fresh sap is best, as stored sap loses its healing properties.

Aloysia
(a-LOYZ-ee-a)
LEMON VERBENA

Aloysia triphylla

Hardiness: *Zones 9-10*

Height: *2 to 8 feet*

Light: *full sun*

Soil: *average, well-drained*

Plant type: *deciduous shrub*

Uses: *potpourri, culinary, houseplant*

The lemon-lime aroma of *Aloysia*'s narrow leaves perfumes the garden from spring through fall. Its fragrance is this shrub's primary attraction; where it can be grown outdoors, it is often pinched and pruned as an espalier or standard to give it shape. Use fresh leaves in cold drinks, salads, and fish or poultry dishes or infused in liquids to flavor baked goods and puddings. Steep fresh or dried leaves for tea. Dried leaves retain their fragrance for several years in potpourri.

Selected species and varieties: *A. triphylla* (lemon verbena, cidron, limonetto)— whorls of lemon-scented leaves along open, sprawling branches growing 6 to 8 feet outdoors, 2 to 4 feet as a potted plant, and loose clusters of tiny white to lilac late-summer flowers.

Growing conditions and maintenance: Sow lemon verbena seeds 3 feet apart in spring. Where frost is a possibility, cut stems to 6 to 12 inches in fall and provide protective winter mulch. Potted plants drop their leaves in winter and do best if moved outdoors during warmer months. Propagate lemon verbena from seed or from cuttings taken in summer.

Althaea
(al-THEE-a)
MARSH MALLOW

Althaea officinalis

Hardiness: *Zones 3-9*

Height: *4 to 5 feet*

Light: *full sun*

Soil: *moist*

Plant type: *perennial*

Uses: *landscaping, culinary*

Marsh mallows create colorful border backdrops and temporary screens in marshy, wet garden sites. Tender young leaves at the tips of stems and the cup-shaped flowers growing where leaves and stems join can be tossed in salads, as can the nutlike seeds contained in the plant's ring-shaped fruits, called cheeses. Steam leaves or fry roots after softening by boiling and serve as a side dish. Roots release a thick mucilage after long soaking, which was once an essential ingredient in the original marshmallow confection and is sometimes used in herbal medicine.

Selected species and varieties: *A. officinalis* (marsh mallow, white mallow)— clumps of stiffly erect 4- to 5-foot-tall stems lined with velvety triangular leaves and pink or white summer flowers.

Growing conditions and maintenance: Sow seeds of marsh mallow in spring or divisions in spring or fall, setting plants 2 feet apart. Keep marsh mallow's woody taproot constantly moist. Pick leaves and flowers just as the flowers reach their peak. Dig roots of plants at least 2 years old in fall, remove rootlets, peel bark, and dry whole or in slices.

Amaranthus
(am-a-RAN-thus)
AMARANTH

Amaranthus hypochondriacus

Hardiness: *tender*

Height: *4 to 6 feet*

Light: *full sun*

Soil: *dry, well-drained*

Plant type: *annual*

Uses: *culinary, landscaping*

Flowering spikes rise from amaranth's clumps of spinachlike leaves in late summer. While amaranth can be used in the border, its primary value is as a food crop. Young leaves are steamed or boiled as a side dish. The high-protein seeds are cooked as a cereal, popped like popcorn, or ground into flour. Seed heads can also be saved as a winter treat for birds.

Selected species and varieties: *A. hypochondriacus* [also listed as *A. hybridus* var. *erythrostachys*] (golden amaranth, prince's-feather)—purple-green or golden green 6-inch leaves and tiny long-lasting deep burgundy flowers on 4- to 6-foot-tall stalks followed by red-brown or golden bronze seeds.

Growing conditions and maintenance: Sow amaranth seeds ¼-inch deep in rows 2 to 3 feet apart and thin seedlings to stand 4 to 10 inches apart. Keep soil moist until seed germinates; plants tolerate dry conditions thereafter. Harvest seeds after frost. Thresh by walking on seed heads or pushing them through ½-inch hardware cloth, then through window screening. Winnow in front of an electric fan to remove chaff.

Anethum
(a-NEE-thum)
DILL

Anethum graveolens

Hardiness: *tender*

Height: *3 to 4 feet*

Light: *full sun*

Soil: *average to rich, well-drained*

Plant type: *annual*

Uses: *culinary, dried arrangements*

Dill's aromatic feathery leaves and flat, open clusters of yellow summer flowers add delicate texture to garden beds. Dill also thrives in window-sill gardens. Snippets of tangy, fresh leaves are a culinary staple in fish, egg, meat, and vegetable dishes; immature flower heads flavor cucumber pickles; and the flat, ribbed seeds season breads and sauces.

Selected species and varieties: *A. graveolens* (dill)—soft 3- to 4-foot stems lined with fine, threadlike foliage; 'Bouquet' is a compact cultivar producing more leaves than flowers; 'Mammoth' is fast-growing with blue-green foliage.

Growing conditions and maintenance: Sow dill seed in the garden and thin seedlings to stand 8 to 10 inches apart. Plants may need staking. Dill self-sows readily; remove flower heads to prevent self-sowing and to encourage leaf production. Snip leaves and immature flower heads as needed. Harvest seed heads just before they turn brown and place in paper bags until seeds loosen and fall. Preserve leaves by freezing whole stems or drying in a microwave oven; dried conventionally, dill loses flavor.

Angelica
(an-JEL-i-ka)
ANGELICA

Angelica gigas

Hardiness: *Zones 3-9*

Height: *3 to 8 feet*

Light: *partial shade to full sun*

Soil: *rich, moist*

Plant type: *biennial or short-lived perennial*

Uses: *landscaping, culinary, potpourri*

Tall columns of coarse-textured, licorice-scented leaves make angelica a bold border specimen or backdrop. In their second year, plants produce broad, flat clusters of tiny summer flowers, then die. Fresh angelica leaves are used to flavor acidic fruits such as rhubarb, stems are steamed as a vegetable or candied for a garnish, and seeds add sweet zest to pastries. Dried leaves can be used to scent potpourri. Angelica can cause dermatitis. It should be eaten sparingly, as some herbalists believe it may be carcinogenic. Do not attempt to collect angelica in the wild, as it closely resembles poisonous water hemlock.

Selected species and varieties: *A. archangelica* (archangel, wild parsnip)—plants to 8 feet tall with 6-inch-wide clusters of greenish white flowers. *A. gigas*—specimens to 6 feet tall, with 8-inch clusters of burgundy flowers.

Growing conditions and maintenance: Sow very fresh angelica seed in the garden in spring or fall. Remove flower stalks to prolong the life of the plants. Angelica self-sows readily; transplant seedlings before taproots become established.

Anthemis
(AN-them-is)
CHAMOMILE

Anthemis tinctoria

Hardiness: *Zones 3-7*

Height: *2 to 3 feet*

Light: *full sun*

Soil: *rich, moist, well-drained*

Plant type: *short-lived perennial*

Uses: *landscaping, arrangements*

Chamomile forms mounds of lacy, pungent foliage ideal as a border filler. Masses of daisylike flowers on thin stalks that bloom from summer through late fall are long-lasting as cut flowers. The blossoms yield a range of dye colors from yellow through khaki; the finely cut foliage yields a pale green shade.

Selected species and varieties: *A. tinctoria* (dyer's chamomile, yellow chamomile, dyer's marguerite, golden marguerite)—pale cream to deep gold petals rimming golden brown centers on 2-inch-wide blossoms.

Growing conditions and maintenance: Sow chamomile seeds in spring, and thin seedlings to stand 1 to 2 feet apart. Mulch to suppress weeds, and fertilize to prolong blooming period. Deadhead to shape plants and extend blooming. Stake plants if flowering stems become floppy. Divide yearly or every other year, discarding the dead center of each clump. To ensure flowers of a particular hue, propagate by rooting stem cuttings taken in summer. Dyer's chamomile self-sows freely and can be treated as a self-sown annual.

Anthriscus
(an-THRIS-kus)
CHERVIL

Anthriscus cerefolium

Hardiness: *tender*

Height: *1 to 2 feet*

Light: *light to full shade*

Soil: *average, well-drained*

Plant type: *annual*

Uses: *culinary, containers, arrangements*

One of the fines herbes of French cuisine, chervil's finely divided leaves resemble parsley with a hint of warm anise flavor. Chervil is an ideal outdoor container plant. Chop fresh chervil into fish, vegetable, egg, and meat dishes. Use flower stalks in fresh or dried arrangements, and add dried leaves to herbal potpourri.

Selected species and varieties: *A. cerefolium* (chervil, salad chervil)—mounds 1 to 2 feet tall of lacy bright green leaves topped by small, open clusters of tiny white flowers in summer.

Growing conditions and maintenance: Sow chervil seeds in the garden for harvestable leaves in 6 to 8 weeks. Make successive sowings for a continuous supply of fresh leaves; seeds sown in fall produce a spring crop. Remove flowers to encourage greater leaf production; alternatively, allow plants to go to seed and self-sow, producing both early- and late-summer crops. Pick leaves before flowers appear, starting when plants reach 4 inches in height, and preserve by freezing alone or mixed with butter. Flavor fades when leaves are dried. Hang flower stalks to dry for use in winter bouquets.

Apium
(A-pee-um)
WILD CELERY

Apium graveolens

Hardiness: *hardy*

Height: *1 to 3 feet*

Light: *full sun to light shade*

Soil: *rich, moist, well-drained*

Plant type: *biennial*

Uses: *culinary*

The ridged stems, parsleylike leaves, and tiny seeds of wild celery all share the scent of the cultivated vegetable beloved as an aromatic culinary staple. While their bitterness limits their use raw to a sprinkling in salads, fresh stems and fresh or dried leaves substitute for celery in soups, stews, and stuffings. Use wild celery sparingly, as it is toxic in large amounts. Proponents of herbal medicine include wild celery in various remedies.

Selected species and varieties: *A. graveolens* (wild celery, smallage)—rosettes of flat, fan-shaped leaflets with toothed edges the first year, followed by elongated, ridged, branching stems tipped with small clusters of greenish cream summer flowers the second year.

Growing conditions and maintenance: Sow wild celery seeds in sites sheltered from drying winds. Thin out the seedlings to stand 12 to 16 inches apart. Dry the leaves flat in a single layer in a shady, well-ventilated area. To obtain seed, pick flower heads as they begin to brown and store in paper bags until they dry and release seeds.

Arctostaphylos
(ark-toh-STAF-i-los)
BEARBERRY

Arctostaphylos uva-ursi

Hardiness: *Zones 2-6*

Height: *6 to 12 inches*

Light: *full sun to light shade*

Soil: *well-drained, acid, sandy or organic*

Plant type: *ground cover*

Uses: *landscaping*

Bearberry's long trailing stems lined with tiny dark green oval leaves root wherever they touch the soil. Spreading into low mats of evergreen foliage, bearberry makes an ideal ground cover to control erosion on difficult rocky or sandy banks. Dangling flower clusters lining the stems in spring are followed by bright red oval berries in fall. Native Americans used the berries for necklaces, in rattles, and as a survival food. Bearberry figures in herbal medicine, and its leaves, stems, and berries yield yellow, gray, and green dyes.

Selected species and varieties: *A. uva-ursi* (common bearberry, hog cranberry, bear's grape, mealberry, kinnikinnick, sandberry, mountain box, creashak, trailing manzanita)—slender arching stems to 5 feet long, producing ¼-inch urn-shaped red-tinged white flowers.

Growing conditions and maintenance: Sow bearberry seeds or set out rooted cuttings in spring, spacing plants 1 to 2 feet apart. Bearberry will tolerate dry conditions as long as it receives periodic deep watering. Propagate bearberry from seed, from stem cuttings, or by layering stems and moving rooted runners.

Armoracia
(ar-mo-RAH-kee-a)
HORSERADISH

Armoracia rusticana

Hardiness: *Zones 3-10*

Height: *2 to 4 feet*

Light: *full sun to light shade*

Soil: *moist, well-drained*

Plant type: *perennial*

Uses: *culinary*

Spring clumps of oblong leaves with ruffled, wrinkled edges grow from horseradish's fleshy taproot, followed by clusters of tiny white summer flowers. The pungent bite of fresh horseradish root grated into vinegar, cream, or mayonnaise for sauces and dressings is enjoyed in German cuisine. Chop fresh young leaves and toss in salad. Horseradish was used as a medicinal plant before it became popular as a condiment, and its dried leaves yield a yellow dye.

Selected species and varieties: *A. rusticana* (horseradish, red cole)—thick, branching white-fleshed roots a foot long or longer with leaves to 2 feet and flower stalks to 4 feet; 'Variegata' has leaves streaked white.

Growing conditions and maintenance: Plant pieces of mature root at least 6 inches long in spring or fall. Set root pieces 3 to 4 inches deep and 1 to 2 feet apart. Dig roots in fall and store in dry sand; slice and dry for later grinding, or grate into white vinegar to preserve. Horseradish can be invasive, as new plants grow from any root pieces left in the garden.

Arnica
(AR-ni-ka)
ARNICA

Arnica montana

Hardiness: *Zones 6-9*

Height: *6 to 24 inches*

Light: *full sun*

Soil: *well-drained, sandy, acid*

Plant type: *perennial*

Uses: *rock gardens, wildflower gardens*

Slender flower stalks rise from arnica's rosettes of narrow aromatic leaves in summer, each with up to three daisylike flowers. Arnica once figured in herbal medicine but is now regarded as toxic when taken internally and is legally restricted in some countries. Arnica preparations for external use, however, are important homeopathic remedies, and ointments made from its flowers are used in Europe for sprains and bruises, though they may cause dermatitis in some.

Selected species and varieties: *A. montana* (leopard's-bane)—tufts of 2- to 5-inch-long blunt-tipped, finely toothed leaves and golden yellow 3-inch flowers composed of narrow petals surrounding a buttonlike center.

Growing conditions and maintenance: Sow arnica seeds in fall or divide mature plants in spring, setting divisions 6 to 8 inches apart. Arnica does not do well in hot, humid sites or where winters are wet. Flower stems become leggy and floppy in rich soils. For an aromatic muscle liniment, pick flowers when fully open, heat equal parts of flowers and oil or lard, then strain and cool.

Artemisia
(ar-tem-IS-ee-a)
WORMWOOD

Artemisia absinthium 'Lambrook Silver'

Hardiness: *hardy annual or Zones 3-10*

Height: *1 to 8 feet*

Light: *full sun to partial shade*

Soil: *average, dry to moist*

Plant type: *annual, perennial, or shrub*

Uses: *landscaping, culinary, dried arrangements*

Artemisia's aromatic filigreed foliage in shades of green through gray-green to silver and almost white is prized as a border filler or background. The foliage dries well for use in arrangements and sachets. While most species bear inconspicuous flowers or none at all, a few produce airy sprays of tiny, fragrant, early- to late-summer blossoms useful as fillers in fresh bouquets. One variety is used as an ingredient in fines herbes, but some bitterer species contain a poisonous narcotic legally restricted in several countries, including the United States—especially *A. absinthium,* the source of absinthe, a liquor alleged to induce bizarre behavior and cause mental deterioration. Herbal tradition ascribes medicinal and insect repellent properties to wormwoods, and boiled stems yield a yellow dye.

Selected species and varieties: *A. abrotanum* (southernwood)—a deciduous subshrub or perennial 3 to 6 feet tall with gray-green camphor- or citrus-scented foliage; Zones 5-9. *A. absinthium* 'Lambrook Silver' (absinthe, common wormwood)—an evergreen shrub or perennial with filigreed silver gray foliage in neat

Artemisia arborescens

18- to 36-inch-high mounds; Zones 3-9. *A. annua* (sweet Annie)—an annual growing quickly into a pyramid of feathery foliage up to 8 feet tall accented by frothy clusters of tiny light green to yellow flowers in summer. *A. arborescens* (tree wormwood)—an evergreen or semi-evergreen shrub or perennial forming mounds 3 feet high and almost as wide of threadlike silver gray leaves, with loose sprays of tiny yellow flowers from summer through fall; Zones 8-9. *A. dracunculus* var. *sativa* (French tarragon, estragon)—a sprawling perennial to 2 feet high with glossy green leaves whose peppery anise flavor is prized in cooking and seasoning; Zones 4-7. *A. lactiflora* (white mugwort)—a perennial producing upright columns of narrow dark green leaves with pale gray undersides and branched clusters of tiny creamy white flowers on purple stems up to a foot long from summer through fall; Zones 4-8. *A. ludoviciana* 'Silver King' (western mugwort, white sage)—a bushy perennial with silvery white leaves in mounds up to 4 feet high and as wide; 'Silver Queen' grows to only 2 feet with silvery white leaves; Zones 5-9. *A. pontica* (Roman wormwood)—an upright perennial 1 to 4 feet tall with feathery silver gray leaves used to flavor vermouth; Zones 5-9. *A.* x *'Powis Castle'*—a perennial to 30 inches with mounds of woolly white stems and silvery fernlike foliage; Zones 6-9. *A. vulgaris* (mugwort)—an upright perennial to 5½ feet high and half as wide with lacy green white-speckled leaves having downy silver undersides; Zones 4-10.

Growing conditions and maintenance: Sow seeds of sweet Annie in spring; plant rooted stem cuttings or divisions

of other wormwoods 1 to 2 feet apart for low hedges, 3 to 4 feet apart as specimens or backdrop plantings, in spring or fall. Most wormwoods prefer dry, average to poor, well-drained soil, becoming leggy in fertile soils and rotting under hot, humid conditions. White mugwort, however, grows best in moist, rich soil. *A. absinthium* makes a poor companion plant, as the substance absinthin flushed from its leaves by rain or watering acts as a growth inhibitor to nearby plants. All wormwoods grow in full sun; French tarragon, *A. absinthium* 'Lambrook Silver',

Artemisia x 'Powis Castle'

white mugwort, and *A. vulgaris* 'Variegata' tolerate partial shade. Prune southernwood to control its size and shape, Roman wormwood to train as a hedge or curb its invasiveness. Propagate sweet Annie from seed or by replanting its self-sown seedlings; propagate shrubby 'Lambrook Silver', Roman wormwood, southernwood, and tree wormwood from rooted stem cuttings taken in spring or fall. Propagate all perennial wormwood species by division every 3 to 4 years in spring or fall. Grow French tarragon in patio containers, or pot divisions in fall, leaving them outdoors for 2 to 3 months of exposure to colder temperatures, then bringing indoors to pick fresh leaves for culinary use. Gather flowers of sweet Annie or white mugwort for filler; use the foliage of all wormwoods as an aromatic addition to fresh bouquets. Weave fresh foliage into wreaths or swags for drying, or hang foliage in bunches in a shady, warm location with good ventilation to dry. Use dried branches in arrangements or crumble leaves into herbal mixes for potpourri and sachets.

Asarum
(AS-a-rum)
WILD GINGER

Asarum canadense

Hardiness:	*Zones 3-8*
Height:	*6 to 12 inches*
Light:	*full to light shade*
Soil:	*moist, well-drained, acid*
Plant type:	*perennial*
Uses:	*ground cover, rock gardens*

Pairs of deciduous heart-shaped leaves on thin, arching stems hide wild ginger's bell-shaped spring flowers growing at ground level. The attractive foliage, resembling that of cyclamen, grows along creeping rhizomes that develop into ground-covering carpets. While the edible roots are seldom used, they can substitute for fresh or dried ground ginger. Young leaves add flavor to salads, though they may cause dermatitis. Wild ginger figures in traditional herbal medicine.

Selected species and varieties: *A. canadense* (Canadian wild ginger, snakeroot)—broad, hairy dark green leaves up to 7 inches across on 12-inch-tall stems with inch-wide brown to purple flowers.

Growing conditions and maintenance: Sow wild ginger seeds in spring, or plant divisions in spring or fall, cutting sections of rhizome with at least one pair of leaves. Set sections 1 inch deep in beds prepared with ample leaf mold or other organic amendments, and space plants 12 inches apart. Keep new beds evenly moist; once established, wild ginger becomes a low-maintenance, weed-suppressing ground cover.

Asclepias
(as-KLEE-pee-as)
MILKWEED, SILKWEED

Asclepias tuberosa

Hardiness: *Zones 3-9*

Height: *1 to 2 feet*

Light: *full sun*

Soil: *dry, sandy*

Plant type: *perennial*

Uses: *landscaping, arrangements*

In summer, milkweed's thick, stiff stems lined with willowy deep green leaves are tipped with broad domed clusters of tiny nectar-rich flowers attractive to bees and butterflies. The flowers are long-lasting in arrangements. Those left on plants are followed by boat-shaped pods, prized in dried arrangements, that burst to release tiny seeds with tufts of silky, downy hair. Milkweed's stems and leaves are thought to be poisonous to animals. The roots have figured in herbal medicine.

Selected species and varieties: *A. tuberosa* (butterfly weed, tuberroot, Indian paintbrush, chigger flower)—deep orange flower clusters throughout summer on thick stems filled with milky sap and lined with narrow 4-inch-long leaves.

Growing conditions and maintenance: Propagate milkweeds from seed or root cuttings in spring or fall, spacing plants 12 inches apart. Because of their long taproots, milkweeds resent division or transplanting. Once established, they often self-sow. For long-lasting arrangements of milkweed cut for fresh use, sear the stems. To dry pods, cut before the seeds are released and hang.

Atriplex
(AT-ri-plex)
ORACH, SALTBUSH

Atriplex hortensis 'Rubra'

Hardiness: *hardy*

Height: *2 to 6 feet*

Light: *full sun*

Soil: *rich, moist, organic*

Plant type: *annual*

Uses: *culinary, landscaping, arrangements*

Garden orach sends up stiff stems lined with arrowhead-shaped leaves that can be massed together as an effective seasonal screen. The leaves add color and a slightly salty tang to salads. Leaves and young shoots can be boiled like spinach. Use the colorful foliage as a filler in fresh arrangements. Orach once figured in herbal medicine.

Selected species and varieties: *A. hortensis* (mountain spinach)—smooth deep green leaves and branching clusters of tiny yellow-green flowers tinged red in summer on stems to 6 feet; 'Rubra' (purple orach) has deep red leaves and stems.

Growing conditions and maintenance: Sow orach seeds in spring and thin plants to stand 8 to 12 inches apart. Orach will tolerate both saline soils and dry conditions but produces the most succulent leaves when kept constantly moist. Successive sowings every 2 weeks ensure a continuous supply of young salad leaves. Pinch out flower heads to encourage greater leaf production. Allowed to form seed, orach self-sows freely. Dip stem ends in boiling water to seal them before using in arrangements.

Borago
(bor-RAY-go)
BORAGE

Borago officinalis

Hardiness: *hardy*

Height: *1 to 3 feet*

Light: *full sun*

Soil: *rich, moist, well-drained*

Plant type: *annual*

Uses: *culinary, houseplant, arrangements*

Borage forms sprawling mounds of hairy, cucumber-scented oval leaves. Bees find the nodding clusters of star-shaped summer flowers with black stamens extremely attractive. Chop borage leaves into salads, soups, and dips for a cucumber flavor without gastric distress; brew leaves as tea, or sauté for a side dish. Toss flowers with salads for color, freeze them into ice cubes to garnish cool drinks, or candy them to decorate cakes and other sweets. Borage can be grown as a houseplant, and its flowers used in fresh arrangements.

Selected species and varieties: *B. officinalis* (talewort, cool-tankard)—leaves 6 to 8 inches long and deep blue flowers; 'Alba' has white blossoms.

Growing conditions and maintenance: Sow borage in the garden in spring and thin seedlings to stand 12 inches apart. Borage will tolerate dry soils but grows best with constant moisture. Plants will self-sow. Indoors, plant borage in large pots to accommodate its spreading roots. Pick rosettes of young leaves for fresh use; borage does not dry or freeze well but can be preserved in vinegar.

Brassica
(BRASS-ik-a)
MUSTARD, COLE

Brassica juncea

Hardiness: *hardy*

Height: *3 to 4 feet*

Light: *full sun*

Soil: *average, well-drained*

Plant type: *annual*

Uses: *culinary*

Mustard's pungent oval leaves add zest to salads and can be boiled or sautéed as a side dish. The four-petaled summer flowers are followed by pods filled with tiny round seeds used whole to flavor pickles and curries or ground to create mustard spread. Mustard can be grown in pots indoors for a continuous supply of young salad greens in winter.

Selected species and varieties: *B. juncea* (brown mustard, Chinese mustard, Indian mustard, mustard cabbage, mustard greens)—leaves 6 to 12 inches long, with open, branching clusters of pale yellow flowers followed by 1½-inch beaked pods filled with dark reddish brown seeds.

Growing conditions and maintenance: Sow mustard seeds ¼ inch deep in spring in rows 18 inches apart and thin plants to stand 8 inches apart. Use the thinnings in salads; young leaves are ready for salad picking in 8 to 10 days. Mustard self-sows freely for future crops. Harvest pods as they begin to brown, and finish drying them in paper bags to collect the ripening seed. Brown mustard develops its hottest flavor when ground and mixed with cold liquids.

Calamintha
(kal-a-MIN-tha)
CALAMINT

Calamintha grandiflora 'Variegata'

Hardiness: *Zones 5-10*

Height: *12 to 24 inches*

Light: *full sun to light shade*

Soil: *average, well-drained, neutral to alkaline*

Plant type: *perennial*

Uses: *landscaping, culinary, potpourri*

Calamint forms neat spreading clumps of erect stems lined with mint-scented oval leaves and tipped with spikes of tiny tubular flowers in summer. Ideal as a border edging, where a passing touch releases its aroma, calamint also grows well in patio containers. Use fresh leaves to garnish summer drinks; steep fresh or dried leaves in boiling water for tea. Mix dried leaves into herbal potpourri.

Selected species and varieties: *C. grandiflora* (mountain balm, ornamental savory)—brown-fringed, slightly hairy deep green leaves on 12- to 18-inch-tall stems and pink flowers; 'Variegata' has a bushy habit and leaves flecked off-white. *C. nepeta* ssp. *nepeta* [also classified as *Satureja calamintha*] (lesser calamint)—shiny green leaves on 18- to 24-inch stems and pale lilac to white flowers.

Growing conditions and maintenance: Sow calamint seed in spring or fall or set out divisions in spring, spacing plants 12 inches apart. Cut stems back in fall and provide winter mulch in cooler climates. Calamint spreads by creeping rhizomes and also self-sows. Dry the leaves on screens in a shady, well-ventilated area.

Calendula
(kal-EN-dew-la)
MARIGOLD

Calendula officinalis

Hardiness: *hardy*

Height: *18 to 24 inches*

Light: *full sun*

Soil: *average, well-drained*

Plant type: *annual*

Uses: *landscaping, culinary, potpourri*

Pot marigold's thick stems lined with hairy oval leaves each bear one or two blossoms resembling zinnias from spring through frost. Their long season of bloom makes them valuable in borders, and they also grow well in patio containers or as houseplants. Pot marigolds are long-lasting as cut flowers. Young leaves were once used like spinach in salads and stews. Use the fresh, slightly salty flower petals to add color to salads, soups, sandwiches, and pâtés. Dried and ground, the petals can substitute for saffron in rice dishes and baked goods. Mix dried petals into potpourri for color.

Selected species and varieties: *C. officinalis* (pot marigold, common marigold, Scotch marigold, ruddles)—coarse 2- to 3-inch leaves and 1½- to 4-inch-wide pale yellow to deep orange flowers.

Growing conditions and maintenance: Sow pot marigold seeds in early spring and thin plants to 10 inches apart. Deadhead to encourage flower production. To dry, pull petals and lay in a single layer on paper (the petals will stick to screens). Dry in a shady, well-ventilated area, and store in moisture-proof containers.

Capsicum
(KAP-si-kum)
PEPPER

Capsicum frutescens 'Tabasco'

Hardiness: *tender or Zone 10*

Height: *1 to 3 feet*

Light: *full sun*

Soil: *rich, moist, well-drained*

Plant type: *annual or short-lived perennial*

Uses: *culinary, landscaping, containers*

Peppers produce hundreds of small, colorful fruits from summer through fall, held above low clumps of narrow oval leaves. Use them as border edgings, massed in beds, or in patio containers. Chop the fiery fruits into salsa, chutneys, marinades, vinegar, salad dressings, and baked goods. The tiny peppers are even spicier when dried.

Selected species and varieties: *C. annuum* var. *annuum* 'Jalapeno' (chili pepper)—narrow, conical 2½- to 4-inch-long fruits ripening from green to red. *C. chinense* 'Habañero' (papaya chili)—extremely hot, bell-shaped 1- to 2-inch fruits ripening from green to yellow-orange. *C. frutescens* 'Tabasco' (tabasco pepper)—small, upright green fruits with a slightly smoky flavor ripening to red.

Growing conditions and maintenance: Start peppers indoors 8 to 10 weeks before the last frost and transplant to the garden when soil temperature reaches 65° F or more. Set plants 18 inches apart and mulch from midsummer on to prevent drying out. Harvest by cutting stems when green or ripe. To dry, string on a line or pull entire plants and hang.

Carthamus
(KAR-tha-mus)
SAFFLOWER

Carthamus tinctorius

Hardiness: *tender*

Height: *1 to 3 feet*

Light: *full sun*

Soil: *well-drained to dry*

Plant type: *annual*

Uses: *landscaping, culinary, arrangements*

Both safflower's stiff stems lined with spiny leaves and its thistlelike summer flowers add texture and color to seasonal borders. Surrounded by a cuff of spiny bracts, the blossoms make excellent cut flowers. Dried flower petals are ground and used as a substitute for saffron in sauces, soups, and other dishes. They also yield dyes for textiles and cosmetics in shades from yellow through red. The seeds are pressed for oil.

Selected species and varieties: *C. tinctorius* (safflower, saffron thistle, false saffron, bastard saffron)—yellow to yellow-orange tousled flowers up to 1 inch across followed by white seeds yielding polyunsaturated oil for cooking.

Growing conditions and maintenance: Sow safflower seeds in spring and thin seedlings to stand 6 inches apart. Safflowers grow best under dry conditions and are subject to disease in rainy or humid areas. Cut and dry the mature flowers, storing in airtight containers for up to a year to grind as food coloring. Alternately, carefully pluck petals from mature blossoms and allow the oily seeds to develop so that plants can self-sow.

Carum
(KAY-rum)
CARAWAY

Carum carvi

Hardiness: *Zones 3-8*

Height: *2 feet*

Light: *full sun to light shade*

Soil: *rich, well-drained*

Plant type: *biennial*

Uses: *culinary*

Carum's feathery, aromatic carrotlike leaves grow in loose clumps from thick branching roots. In late spring or early summer of their second year, plants send up branching flower stalks tipped with flat clusters of tiny flowers followed by flavorful seeds. Chop the leaves, which have a parsley-dill flavor, into salads, and cook the roots like carrots or parsnips. Use the anise-flavored seeds in breads and cakes; add them to meat, cabbage, and apple dishes; or crystallize them in sugar for an after-dinner candy to sweeten the breath and settle the stomach.

Selected species and varieties: *C. carvi* (caraway)—ferny leaves up to 10 inches long and white flowers followed by ¼-inch dark brown seeds.

Growing conditions and maintenance: Sow caraway in the garden in spring or fall and thin seedlings to stand 8 inches apart; once established, it self-sows. Snip leaves at any time. Harvest seeds as flower clusters turn brown but before the seed capsules shatter. Hang to dry over a tray or cloth, and store the seeds in airtight containers. Dig 2-year-old roots to serve as a side dish.

Catharanthus
(kath-ah-RAN-thus)
PERIWINKLE

Catharanthus roseus

Hardiness: *tender or Zone 10*

Height: *1 to 2 feet*

Light: *full sun to light shade*

Soil: *moist, well-drained*

Plant type: *annual*

Uses: *landscaping, containers*

Periwinkle's main stems divide into multiple erect branches lined with shiny, fleshy leaves and tipped with small clusters of flat-faced flowers. Perennial in tropical climates, it is often grown as an annual bedding plant elsewhere for its long season of bloom—which runs from spring through fall—and neat, compact habit. Madagascar periwinkle also makes a showy greenhouse specimen and is useful as a cut flower. It yields alkaloids used in cancer chemotherapy; the plants are highly toxic if eaten.

Selected species and varieties: *C. roseus* (Madagascar periwinkle, rose periwinkle, cayenne jasmine)—2-inch smooth, oval leaves with spiny tips and 1½-inch five-petaled pink flowers with darker pink centers in clusters of twos and threes.

Growing conditions and maintenance: In warm climates, sow Madagascar periwinkle outdoors in spring. Elsewhere, start seed indoors 3 to 4 months before the last frost or take fall cuttings of nonflowering stems and grow them through the winter for transplanting in spring. Space plants 10 to 12 inches apart. Pinch early growth to promote bushiness.

Cedronella
(see-dro-NEL-la)
BALM-OF-GILEAD

Cedronella canariensis

Hardiness: *Zone 10*

Height: *5 feet*

Light: *full sun*

Soil: *organic, well-drained*

Plant type: *perennial subshrub*

Uses: *landscaping, houseplant, potpourri*

Balm-of-Gilead's aromatic leaves scent the garden with a musky blend of cedar, camphor, and lemon. The pointed, oval leaves line square stems tipped with tufts of small tubular flowers from summer through fall. In frost-free gardens, train it against trellises or walls or grow it in patio containers where its fragrance can be enjoyed. Elsewhere, it grows as a houseplant. Brew the fresh leaves as tea alone or blended with other herbs. Dried leaves and flower buds add aroma to potpourri.

Selected species and varieties: *C. canariensis* (balm-of-Gilead, canary balm)—toothed leaves up to 4 inches long and dense spikes of pink to lilac flowers.

Growing conditions and maintenance: Sow balm-of-Gilead seeds or plant divisions of mature plants in spring, spacing transplants or thinning seedlings to stand 18 inches apart. Prune in early spring and again in fall after flowering to encourage branching and bushiness. Pick leaves just before flowers open, or use leaves from pruned branches. Dry the leaves and buds in a single layer in a shady, well-ventilated area.

Centaurea
(sen-TOR-ee-a)
KNAPWEED

Centaurea cyanus

Hardiness: *tender*

Height: *8 to 36 inches*

Light: *full sun*

Soil: *well-drained*

Plant type: *annual*

Uses: *landscaping, potpourri, arrangements*

Cornflowers form colorful clumps of slender, branching stems with clinging gray-green foliage ideal for massing in a summer border. From summer through fall plants are crowned with buttonlike tufted flowers in bright hues. Both flowers and foliage are attractive in fresh arrangements. Toss flower petals into summer salads for color or dry them to add color to potpourri.

Selected species and varieties: *C. cyanus* (cornflower, bachelor's-button, blue bottle)—narrow leaves up to 6 inches long and single or double blue, sometimes purple, pink, or white flowers up to 1½ inches across.

Growing conditions and maintenance: Sow cornflower seeds in fall in mild winter areas, in spring elsewhere, and thin seedlings to stand 1 foot apart. Soil that is too rich or has too much fertilizer encourages foliage growth at the expense of flowers. Cornflower often self-sows. To dry for potpourri, cut flowers and dry whole blossoms or pull florets apart to dry. Cornflowers retain their bright colors when dried.

Centella
(KEN-tel-a)
NAVELWORT

Centella asiatica

Chamaemelum
(ka-mee-MAY-lum)
ROMAN CHAMOMILE

Chamaemelum nobile

Chenopodium
(ken-o-PO-dee-um)
GOOSEFOOT, PIGWEED

Chenopodium ambrosioides

Hardiness: *Zones 8-10*

Height: *6 to 20 inches*

Light: *light shade to full sun*

Soil: *moist*

Plant type: *perennial*

Uses: *ground cover, containers, houseplant*

Hardiness: *Zones 4-8*

Height: *1 to 6 inches*

Light: *full sun to light shade*

Soil: *dry, well-drained*

Plant type: *perennial*

Uses: *ground cover, lawn, potpourri, culinary*

Hardiness: *hardy*

Height: *2 to 5 feet*

Light: *full sun*

Soil: *rich, well-drained*

Plant type: *annual*

Uses: *culinary, arrangements, potpourri*

Dainty cupped leaves with scalloped edges line centella's slender, trailing reddish green stems. Centella, designated by many authorities as *Hydrocotyle,* spreads to form mats of soft-textured ground cover as leaf nodes root wherever they touch the ground to develop new plants. Tiny flowers hide beneath the leaves. Allow gotu kola *(C. asiatica)* to ramble, or confine it in patio containers or as a houseplant. Its colorful trailing stems make it an ideal basket plant. Gotu kola figures in Eastern herbal medicine, but its safety has recently been called into question.

Selected species and varieties: *C. asiatica* [also classified as *Hydrocotyle asiatica*] (gotu kola, tiger grass)—kidney-shaped 1- to 2-inch bright green leaves and white to pink flowers in summer.

Growing conditions and maintenance: Sow gotu kola seeds in spring or fall in moist, or even wet, sites. Plants grow best in light shade but will tolerate full sun if there is ample moisture. Alternately, cut rooted daughter plants from main stems and replant, spacing them 1 to 2 feet apart. Gotu kola can be invasive where conditions are favorable for its growth.

Roman chamomile's feathery leaves release an apple scent when crushed. The roots spread quickly into dense mats ideal as informal ground covers or as fillers among paving stones. Dry the leaves for potpourri. The flowers that bloom from late spring through early fall can be dried and steeped for a tea. Chamomile figures in many herbal remedies.

Selected species and varieties: *C. nobile* [formerly classified as *Anthemis nobilis*] (Roman chamomile, garden chamomile) —lacy, ferny bright green leaves and 1-inch white flowers with golden centers; 'Flore Pleno' has double-petaled cream flowers on plants 6 inches high spreading 18 inches wide; 'Treneague' is a nonflowering cultivar that grows 1 to 2 inches tall and 18 inches wide.

Growing conditions and maintenance: Sow Roman chamomile seeds in spring or fall or plant divisions in spring; the species self-sows freely, but cultivars only come true from division. For lawns, space plants 4 to 6 inches apart and allow to spread before mowing. Harvest flowers as petals begin to fade, and dry on screens in a shady, well-ventilated area.

Epazote's leaves are prized for flavoring beans, corn, and fish in Central American cuisines. They should be used sparingly, however, as the plant's oils are a potent, sometimes toxic vermifuge and insecticide. Ambrosia's fragrant foliage and plumy flower spikes are valued in both fresh and dried arrangements; leaves and seeds can be used in potpourri.

Selected species and varieties: *C. ambrosioides* (epazote)—spreading clumps of woody stems to 5 feet tall, lined with both broad, toothed, oval leaves and finely lacy leaves. *C. botrys* (ambrosia)—lobed ½- to 4-inch leaves that are deep green above and red below, and airy sprays of tiny yellow-green summer flowers without petals along arching 2-foot stems.

Growing conditions and maintenance: Sow epazote and ambrosia seeds in spring or fall, and thin seedlings to stand 12 inches apart. Pinch plants to keep them bushy. Both species self-sow freely and can become invasive weeds. Use epazote leaves either fresh or dried for cooking. For dried arrangements, hang ambrosia in a shady, well-ventilated area or stand stems in vases without water.

Cichorium
(si-KOR-ee-um)
CHICORY

Cichorium intybus

Hardiness: *Zones 3-10*

Height: *1 to 5 feet*

Light: *full sun*

Soil: *poor to average, well-drained, slightly alkaline*

Plant type: *perennial*

Uses: *culinary, landscaping, potpourri*

Chicory forms loose mounds of coarsely toothed leaves with a branching central flower stalk. Common chicory forms conical heads of young leaves called chicons. While it can be grown for ornament in a wildflower garden, chicory is most useful in the kitchen. Steam or braise young seedlings and roots. Toss bitter young leaves into salads. Roast and grind the young caramel-flavored roots to blend with coffee. Cultivars can be forced to produce blanched chicons ideal for salads or braising. Dried flowers add color to potpourri.

Selected species and varieties: *C. intybus* (common chicory, witloof, barbe-de-capuchin, succory)—daisylike 1- to 1½-inch sky blue—in rare cases white or pink— flowers the second year from seed.

Growing conditions and maintenance: Sow chicory seeds in spring and thin to 18 inches. Chicory self-sows freely. To roast, lift year-old roots in spring, slice and dry at 350° F. For blanched chicons, lift roots their first fall, cut back all but 1 inch of foliage and shorten root 1 inch; bury in moist, sandy compost and keep in total darkness at 50° F for 4 weeks.

Cimicifuga
(si-mi-SIFF-yew-ga)
BUGBANE, RATTLETOP

Cimicifuga racemosa

Hardiness: *Zones 3-8*

Height: *3 to 8 feet*

Light: *partial shade to full sun*

Soil: *rich, moist, acid*

Plant type: *perennial*

Uses: *landscaping*

Black cohosh forms lacy mounds of large leaves composed of many coarsely toothed, pointed leaflets. In summer, tall, wiry stems bear wands of fuzzy flowers to provide a vertical accent in shady borders. The creeping rhizomes by which the plants spread were once used by Native Americans for remedies, including snakebite antidote. The strong odor of the flowers is said to repel garden insects.

Selected species and varieties: *C. racemosa* (black cohosh, black snakeroot)— leaves to 1½ feet long in mounds up to 24 inches wide and small, creamy white flowers in elongated bottle-brush spikes to 3 feet long on stems to 8 feet tall.

Growing conditions and maintenance: Sow black cohosh seeds in fall to flower in 3 years, or divide mature clumps anytime, spacing plants 2 to 3 feet apart. Black cohosh grows best in light shade, particularly in hot climates, but will grow in full sun if given ample moisture; if late-summer weather turns leaves brown, cut plants back. Plants seldom need staking despite their height. Top-dress annually with aged manure or compost, and provide protective winter mulch.

Cinnamomum
(sin-am-O-mum)
CINNAMON

Cinnamomum zeylanicum

Hardiness: *Zones 9-11*

Height: *to 100 feet*

Light: *full sun*

Soil: *rich, moist, well-drained*

Plant type: *tree*

Uses: *specimen, houseplant, potpourri*

Cinnamon and camphor tree have glossy evergreen leaves that are red, pink, or bronze when young. Use either species as a specimen tree, as their competitive roots crowd out other plants. Alternately, pot them for indoor enjoyment. Use camphor tree's foliage in potpourri or moth-repellent sachets. When cut and dried, the inner bark of cinnamon curls into sticks or quills, which can be used whole or powdered to flavor teas, baked goods, and fruit dishes and to scent potpourri.

Selected species and varieties: *C. camphora* (camphor tree)—trees to 100 feet and half as wide or wider with 3- to 6-inch oval leaves and yellow-green spring-to-summer flowers. *C. zeylanicum* (cinnamon, Ceylon cinnamon)—trees to 30 feet and half as wide with papery outer bark, leathery 7-inch leaves, and clusters of yellowish white summer flowers.

Growing conditions and maintenance: Sow camphor tree or cinnamon seeds in spring, or root cuttings of semiripe wood taken in spring or summer. Roots will rot if sites are not well drained. Pinch and prune potted specimens to a height of 6 to 8 feet.

Citrus
(SIT-rus)
LEMON, ORANGE

Citrus aurantium

Hardiness: *Zones 9-11*

Height: *8 to 30 feet*

Light: *full sun*

Soil: *rich, moist, well-drained*

Plant type: *tree*

Uses: *landscaping, containers, culinary*

Glossy evergreen foliage, fragrant white flowers, and juicy fruits with aromatic skins all recommend *Citrus* species as specimen trees. Space them closely for hedges or grow them in containers. Chop bitter (Seville) oranges for piquant marmalade or dry their peels for potpourri. Slice lemons for garnish, add slices to tea, squeeze the juice for cool drinks. Grate lemon peels for flavoring, candy them for garnishes, or dry them for potpourri.

Selected species and varieties: *C. aurantium* (bitter orange)—trees 30 feet tall and as wide with bright orange fruits. *C. limon* (lemon)—'Eureka' is a nearly thornless spreading tree to 20 feet tall; 'Meyer' is a cold-resistant 8- to 12-foot-tall dwarf with sweet yellow fruits; 'Ponderosa' has grapefruit-sized yellow fruits.

Growing conditions and maintenance: Sow lemon seeds in spring or propagate from cuttings of semiripe wood in summer. Choose sites protected from wind and frost. Keep plants constantly moist but ensure good drainage; mulch to conserve moisture. Grow potted citruses in containers 18 inches in diameter or larger, and prune both branches and roots.

Coix
(KO-ix)
JOB'S-TEARS

Coix lacryma-jobi

Hardiness: *tender*

Height: *3 to 4 feet*

Light: *full sun to light shade*

Soil: *average, moist*

Plant type: *annual grass*

Uses: *landscaping, containers*

Job's-tears produces long, narrow leaves clasping tall, jointed stems that create a lacy vertical accent as a border backdrop or temporary screen. It also does well as a container plant. In summer, arching flower spikes rise like froth above the foliage, and female flowers, enclosed in hard, oval husks, hang decoratively in strings like dripping tears. Children enjoy stringing the small beads into bracelets and necklaces. Dry the stems for everlasting arrangements.

Selected species and varieties: *C. lacryma-jobi* (Job's-tears)—leaves 2 feet long and 1½ inches wide on stems to 4 feet tipped with spiky flower clusters, male at the end, female at the base, encased in hard green husks that turn pearly white, gray, or iridescent violet as they ripen.

Growing conditions and maintenance: Sow Job's-tears in spring when soil warms to 68° F; in colder climates, start seed indoors 2 to 3 months in advance. Keep soil constantly moist. Potted specimens do best in light shade. To dry, pick stems before seeds dry and shatter.

Colchicum
(KOL-chi-kum)
AUTUMN CROCUS

Colchicum autumnale 'Plenum'

Hardiness: *Zones 5-7*

Height: *1 foot*

Light: *full sun to light shade*

Soil: *moist, well-drained*

Plant type: *bulb*

Uses: *landscaping*

Meadow saffron's broad, straplike spring leaves fade away by midsummer, but in early fall, clusters of stemless flowers in shades from white to pink-lavender or deep purple with prominent yellow anthers rise to brighten the landscape. Scatter meadow saffron under shrubs, in rock gardens, or in lawns for a splash of fall color or use them along the edges of perennial borders. Though it was used medicinally in ancient times, all parts of meadow saffron are now known to be extremely poisonous.

Selected species and varieties: *C. autumnale* (meadow saffron, mysteria, wonder bulb)—deep green 1- to 1½-inch-wide leaves up to 12 inches long and stemless flowers composed of petal-like pointed tepals 1¼ inch to 1¾ inch long; 'Plenum' has double lilac-pink blooms.

Growing conditions and maintenance: Propagate meadow saffron by lifting corms in summer and removing and replanting the tiny offsets, setting them 2 to 3 inches deep and 3 to 9 inches apart. Meadow saffron can be grown from seed, but corms take 3 to 6 years to reach blooming size.

Comptonia
(komp-TONE-ee-a)
SWEET FERN

Comptonia peregrina

Hardiness: *Zones 2-6*

Height: *3 to 5 feet*

Light: *full sun to light shade*

Soil: *well-drained, acid*

Plant type: *shrub*

Uses: *landscaping*

In the morning and evening, sweet fern perfumes the air in the wildflower garden or perennial border, where it makes an ideal specimen planting. Sweet fern's lacy deciduous leaves covered with rusty brown hairs form mounds of foliage almost as wide as they are tall. The leaves were used by Native Americans for both herbal remedies and as a poison.

Selected species and varieties: *C. peregrina*—fans of narrow, pointed 5-inch leaves with red-brown dangling male catkins and smaller, round female flowers in summer followed by shiny conical brown nutlets in fall.

Growing conditions and maintenance: Sow ripe sweet fern seeds in fall, and overwinter in cold frames to transplant in spring. Otherwise, remove and transplant rooted suckers in spring or layer branches to develop rooted cuttings. Sweet fern can be difficult to transplant; to disturb roots as little as possible, dig up a large rootball when moving suckers or layered cuttings. Sweet fern grows best in loose, open soils and tolerates dry conditions.

Convallaria
(kon-va-LAIR-ee-a)
LILY OF THE VALLEY

Convallaria majalis 'Albistriata'

Hardiness: *Zones 2-8*

Height: *9 to 12 inches*

Light: *light to full shade*

Soil: *rich, moist, organic*

Plant type: *perennial*

Uses: *ground cover, arrangements, pot culture*

Lily of the valley's fragrant white flower bells are a welcome sight in spring planted beneath deciduous trees in shade or wildflower gardens. The tiny blossoms lining arching, square stems clasped by a pair of broad green leaves add fragrance to nosegays or small bouquets. Lily of the valley can be forced for indoor enjoyment. The plant is poisonous.

Selected species and varieties: *C. majalis*—deeply veined 9- to 12-inch-long leaves up to 4 inches across and five to 13 small flower bells followed by orange to red fall berries; 'Albistriata' [also called 'Striata'] has leaves veined white.

Growing conditions and maintenance: Plant lily of the valley pips in late fall, setting them 1 inch deep and 6 to 12 inches apart. In subsequent years, mulch with compost or aged manure in fall. *C. majalis* 'Albistriata' tends to lose its color in deep shade. To force lily of the valley, buy prechilled pips or hold pips in the refrigerator in a plastic bag for 8 weeks or more; pot with tips just below the surface and bring into a warm room to grow and flower. Propagate lily of the valley by division in fall.

Coriandrum
(kor-ri-AND-rum)
CORIANDER

Coriandrum sativum

Hardiness: *tender*

Height: *1 to 3 feet*

Light: *full sun to light shade*

Soil: *rich, well-drained*

Plant type: *annual*

Uses: *culinary, potpourri*

Coriander's pungent young leaves, commonly known as cilantro or Chinese parsley, are a staple in East Asian, Mexican, and Indian cuisines. With a hint of citrus, the round, ribbed seeds are used whole or ground in baked goods, curries, chutneys, and vegetable dishes. Add them to potpourri for a lingering lemon fragrance. The unpleasant odor of immature fruits earned coriander the nickname stinkplant; the characteristic agreeable fruity aroma develops as they ripen. Chop coriander roots into curries or steam them as a nutty vegetable.

Selected species and varieties: *C. sativum*—young leaves grow in small, scalloped fans resembling parsley; older leaves look ferny and threadlike, with flat, loose clusters of tiny white to mauve summer flowers; 'Long Standing' is a slow-to-bolt cultivar.

Growing conditions and maintenance: Sow coriander seed in spring and thin seedlings to stand 8 inches apart. Use fresh, immature leaves for best flavor; cilantro loses flavor if dried. To collect seed, mature seeds heads and dry in a paper bag to catch seeds. Dig roots in fall.

Crocus
(KRO-kus)
CROCUS

Crocus sativus

Hardiness: *Zones 5-7*

Height: *6 to 12 inches*

Light: *light shade to full sun*

Soil: *well-drained*

Plant type: *bulb*

Uses: *landscaping, pot culture, culinary*

In fall, saffron crocus's bright cups open to reveal three prominent red branching stigmas. Picked and dried as saffron, they can be used to color food and textiles a delicate yellow. It takes 5,000 flowers to yield an ounce of saffron, but a dozen or so produce enough for a single recipe. *Caution:* Be careful not to confuse saffron crocus with the poisonous meadow saffron *(Colchicum autumnale),* which blooms at the same time. Mass saffron crocuses in rock gardens or scatter them in lawns. Force for indoor bloom.

Selected species and varieties: *C. sativus* (saffron crocus)—pale purple—though sometimes lavender, white, or reddish—1½- to 2-inch flowers and grassy leaves with a white midrib.

Growing conditions and maintenance: Remove cormels growing alongside mature saffron crocus corms in spring and replant 3 to 4 inches deep at 6-inch intervals. Divide corms every few years. Pick stigmas when flowers open, dry on paper, and store in airtight containers. To force, plant 12 to 18 corms in a 6-inch bulb pan. Refrigerate for at least 8 weeks, then put in a warm place to bloom.

Cymbopogon
(sim-bo-PO-gon)
OIL GRASS

Cymbopogon citratus

Hardiness: *Zones 10-11*

Height: *2 to 6 feet*

Light: *full sun to light shade*

Soil: *well-drained, sandy, slightly acid*

Plant type: *perennial grass*

Uses: *landscaping, culinary*

Lemon grass's fragrant leaves are a staple in Thai and Vietnamese cuisine. The tough stems are sliced and simmered to release their citrus flavor, then discarded before serving. Steep fresh or dried leaves for tea. Use clumps of lemon grass with its gracefully arching leaf blades in the middle of a border in warm-climate gardens. Elsewhere, grow as an annual and pot it to overwinter indoors.

Selected species and varieties: *C. citratus* (lemon grass, fever grass)—inch-wide aromatic evergreen leaves with sharp edges growing from bulbous stems in clumps to 6 feet tall and 3 feet wide.

Growing conditions and maintenance: Plant divisions of lemon grass in spring, spacing them 2 to 3 feet apart. Apply mulch both to conserve moisture in summer and to protect roots in winter. Where frost is a possibility, pot divisions in fall after cutting back to 3 inches and keep indoors over the winter, watering only sparingly to prevent root rot. Cut stems at ground level for fresh use, taking care when handling the leaf's sharp edges, and use the lower 3 to 4 inches for best flavor.

Dianthus
(dy-AN-thus)
PINK, CARNATION

Dianthus plumarius

Hardiness: *Zones 5-9*

Height: *4 to 20 inches*

Light: *full sun to light shade*

Soil: *moderately rich, well-drained, alkaline*

Plant type: *perennial*

Uses: *landscaping, arrangements, culinary*

Pinks' clove-scented flowers add fragrance to borders, beds, and rock gardens, where their evergreen foliage fills in among other plants or sprawls into ground-covering mats. Petals are often fringed, doubled, and shaded in tones of white to pink, red, purple, and yellow. The long-lasting flowers can also be dried for potpourri. Toss petals into salad or use to flavor vinegar, fruit syrup, or wine.

Selected species and varieties: *D.* x *allwoodii* (Allwood pink)—tufted blue-green foliage on 4- to 20-inch stems and 1- to 2-inch flowers. *D. caryophyllus* (carnation)—compact border varieties to 14 inches with blue-green leaves along woody stems and 2- to 3-inch flowers. *D. plumarius* (cottage pink, grass pink)—loose mats of gray-green foliage with 1½-inch flowers on 10- to 18-inch stems.

Growing conditions and maintenance: Sow seed in spring or propagate hybrids by summer cuttings or division in fall. Space plants 12 to 18 inches apart and mulch in cooler climates. Pinch to promote bushier plants, remove side buds for larger flowers, and deadhead to prolong the bloom.

Dictamnus
(dik-TAM-nus)
GAS PLANT

Dictamnus albus 'Purpureus'

Hardiness: *Zones 3-9*

Height: *2 to 3 feet*

Light: *full sun to light shade*

Soil: *moist, well-drained, slightly alkaline*

Plant type: *perennial*

Uses: *landscaping, arrangements*

As a border specimen, gas plant offers open mounds of lemon-scented glossy foliage crowned in late spring to early summer with tall flower spikes. The flowers, attractive in fresh bouquets, are followed by star-shaped seed capsules that add interest to dried arrangements. Gas plant once figured in herbal medicine, but all parts of the plant are now considered potentially toxic. The plant causes dermatitis in susceptible individuals.

Selected species and varieties: *D. albus* (gas plant, fraxinella, white dittany)—leathery oval leaflets with finely toothed edges in mounds to 3 feet high and as wide with spikes of 1-inch white flowers on erect stems; 'Purpureus' has mauve-purple blossoms veined deeper purple; 'Ruber', rose pink flowers.

Growing conditions and maintenance: Sow gas plant seeds in soil amended with organic matter. Space plants 3 to 4 feet apart; transplanting or dividing plants often kills them. Plants grown from seed take 2 to 3 years to produce blossoms.

Digitalis
(di-ji-TAL-us)
FOXGLOVE

Digitalis lanata

Hardiness: *hardy*

Height: *2 to 5 feet*

Light: *light shade to full sun*

Soil: *well-drained, acid*

Plant type: *biennial*

Uses: *landscaping, arrangements*

Foxglove's towering spikes of funnel-shaped flowers make a dramatic backdrop in shady borders, in combination with roses, or along the edge of woodland gardens. Flowers open in sequence from bottom to top along one side of erect stems. Foxgloves are the source of several important medicines but are highly toxic if ingested.

Selected species and varieties: *D. lanata* (Grecian foxglove, woolly foxglove)—a single stem to 3 feet tall lined with narrow, pointed, hairy leaves and tipped with cream to beige 1-inch flowers veined purple and brown. *D. purpurea* (common foxglove, purple foxglove)—clumps of stems to 5 feet tall lined with oval pointed leaves and flowers in multiple hues, often spotted and with contrasting throats; 'Alba' has white blossoms.

Growing conditions and maintenance: Sow foxglove seeds in spring to produce a rosette of leaves the first year, flowers the second year. Foxgloves self-sow freely; transplant self-sown seedlings in fall. Remove spent flower stalks to force a second, smaller bloom. Protect year-old plants with a winter mulch.

Eruca
(e-ROO-ka)
ROCKET, ARUGULA

Eruca vesicaria ssp. sativa

Hardiness: *hardy*

Height: *2 to 3 feet*

Light: *full sun to light shade*

Soil: *rich, moist*

Plant type: *annual*

Uses: *culinary*

Arugula's tangy young leaves add biting zest to mixed green salads. An essential ingredient in mesclun blends of salad greens, it can also be chopped to flavor sauces or steamed as a side dish. Use the flowers, which have a slightly milder flavor than the leaves, as a salad garnish.

Selected species and varieties: *E. vesicaria* ssp. *sativa* (arugula, rocket, Italian cress, roquette)—mustardlike leaves, rounded or arrowhead shaped at their tips, coarsely toothed along their midrib, and delicate purple-veined creamy late-summer-to-fall flowers followed by slender upright seedpods.

Growing conditions and maintenance: Make successive sowings of arugula seed from early spring through early summer, and thin plants to stand 6 to 8 inches apart. Leaves are ready to pick in 6 to 8 weeks. Plants develop their best flavor when they grow quickly in cool, moist soil; mature leaves or those grown in dry ground during hot weather become strong and bitter. Pull out maturing plants to make space for other sowings or allow a few plants to develop pods and self-sow for harvest the following spring.

Eucalyptus
(yew-ka-LIP-tus)
EUCALYPTUS

Eucalyptus citriodora

Hardiness: *Zones 9-11*

Height: *60 to 160 feet*

Light: *full sun*

Soil: *rich, organic*

Plant type: *tree*

Uses: *landscaping, houseplant, potpourri*

Eucalyptus is best known for its lemon-camphor-scented evergreen leaves, but the smooth bark on the bare, branching trunks also lends an architectural accent. The tree grows rapidly but can be pruned to remain a potted specimen for up to 6 years. Use dried leaves in potpourri, dried branches or seed capsules in arrangements. The oil derived from leaves, roots, and barks is toxic taken internally but has many medicinal uses as a respiratory aid and insect repellent.

Selected species and varieties: *E. citriodora* (lemon-scented gum)—white, sometimes pink to red, bark on trees up to 160 feet tall and spreading half as wide with 3- to 7-inch golden green narrow leaves and clusters of tiny white winter blooms followed by ⅜-inch seed capsules.

Growing conditions and maintenance: Sow eucalyptus seeds in spring or fall. Choose planting sites carefully, as roots secrete toxins that inhibit the growth of nearby plants. Trees grow 10 to 15 feet per year. Prune in spring to contain size, encourage more juvenile foliage, and develop thicker trunks. Avoid summer pruning, as excess sap attracts insects.

Eupatorium
(yew-pa-TOR-ee-um)
BONESET

Eupatorium perfoliatum

Hardiness: *Zones 3-10*

Height: *2 to 10 feet*

Light: *full sun to light shade*

Soil: *rich to average, moist*

Plant type: *perennial*

Uses: *landscaping, arrangements*

Boneset and Joe-Pye weed bear broad clusters of summer-to-fall flowers atop stiff stems lined with narrow, pointed leaves. The leaves are pleasantly aromatic when crushed, and the blossoms make long-lasting cut flowers. Use boneset and Joe-Pye weed in moist meadow gardens or at the back of perennial borders. Once widely used as an herbal medicine, boneset is now considered ineffective and possibly damaging to the liver and kidneys.

Selected species and varieties: *E. perfoliatum* (common boneset)—clusters of white flowers on 2- to 5-foot stems lined with pairs of 8-inch wrinkled vanilla-scented leaves dotted with yellow resin; Zones 3-8. *E. purpureum* (Joe-Pye weed) —clusters of rose pink flowers up to 12 inches across on 4- to 10-foot purplish stems lined with whorls of purple-veined vanilla-scented leaves; Zones 4-9.

Growing conditions and maintenance: Grow both species from seed sown in spring or from divisions transplanted in spring or early fall. Cut stems to the ground after flowering. The tough rhizomes can be invasive; spade around established clumps to control their spread.

Filipendula
(fil-i-PEN-dew-la)
MEADOWSWEET

Filipendula ulmaria

Hardiness: *Zones 3-9*

Height: *2 to 6 feet*

Light: *full sun to light shade*

Soil: *rich, moist*

Plant type: *perennial*

Uses: *landscaping, arrangements, potpourri*

Meadowsweet's billowy clusters of almond-scented flowers make long-lasting cut flowers especially prized in bridal bouquets. The feathery plumes open from summer through fall on erect stems lined with wintergreen-scented leaves. Meadowsweet grows well in moist meadows or along the edges of ponds and streams. Dry the leaves and flowers for potpourri. All parts of the plant yield various colors of dye, and the buds were the first recognized source of salicylic acid, the active ingredient in aspirin.

Selected species and varieties: *F. ulmaria* (queen-of-the-meadow)—cream-colored flowers on stems to 6 feet tall above oval, pointed, wrinkled leaves; 'Flore-Pleno' has double flowers on 2- to 4-foot stems; 'Variegata' produces leaves splashed yellow fading to cream on 2-foot plants.

Growing conditions and maintenance: Sow meadowsweet seeds in spring or divide roots in fall. Thin out seedlings or space transplants to stand 2 to 3 feet apart. Mulch to conserve moisture. Gather young leaves for drying before flowers appear. Cut flowers just as buds begin to open for fresh bouquets, or hang to dry.

Foeniculum
(fee-NIK-you-lum)
FENNEL

Foeniculum vulgare

Hardiness: *tender or Zones 9-10*

Height: *4 to 6 feet*

Light: *full sun*

Soil: *organic, well-drained*

Plant type: *perennial or annual*

Uses: *culinary, landscaping*

Fennel forms spreading clumps of succulent stems lined with feathery foliage. Flat summer-to-fall flower clusters are followed by oval seeds. Stems, leaves, and seeds all taste of anise. Substitute fresh stems for celery, or steam as a vegetable. Leaves complement seafood or garnish salads. Add seeds to baked goods, chew to freshen breath, or sprout for salads.

Selected species and varieties: *F. vulgare* (fennel, sweet anise)—branching stems to 6 feet lined with soft needlelike foliage and tipped with yellow flowers; 'Purpurascens' (copper fennel) has pink, copper, or bronze young foliage.

Growing conditions and maintenance: Fennel, though a tender perennial, is usually grown as an annual. Sow seeds successively from spring through summer for a continuous supply of leaves and stems. Left to form seed, fennel readily self-sows in fall for a spring harvest. Harvest stems as they thicken. Snip leaves anytime and use them fresh or frozen; they lose flavor on drying. Collect seed heads as they turn from yellow-green to brown and store in a paper bag until the seeds drop. Store in airtight containers.

Galium
(GAY-lee-um)
SWEET WOODRUFF

Galium odoratum

Hardiness: *Zones 4-8*

Height: *6 to 36 inches*

Light: *full shade to full sun*

Soil: *moist to dry*

Plant type: *perennial*

Uses: *landscaping, potpourri*

Sweet woodruff spreads into ground-covering mats with small clusters of white spring flowers above ruffs of leaves that become vanilla scented as they dry. Yellow bedstraw bears plumes of honey-scented yellow flowers from summer to fall. Weave fresh sweet woodruff stems into wreaths to dry or add dried leaves to potpourri. Use the dried flowers of yellow bedstraw to stuff herbal pillows.

Selected species and varieties: *G. odoratum* (sweet woodruff)—open clusters of ¼-inch flowers and shiny 1½-inch leaves on 6- to 8-inch stems. *G. verum* (yellow bedstraw, Our-Lady's bedstraw)—elongated clusters of ¼-inch flowers and needlelike leaves on 1- to 3-foot stems.

Growing conditions and maintenance: Sow woodruff seeds in late summer or divide roots after flowering, setting plants 6 to 9 inches apart in a shady, moist location enriched with organic matter. Sow bedstraw seeds or divide roots in spring, setting plants 9 to 12 inches apart in an average to dry location in sun or light shade; to control spread, set a can with the bottom removed in the soil; plant the seeds or divisions in the can.

Gaultheria
(gawl-THER-ee-a)
WINTERGREEN

Gaultheria procumbens

Hardiness: *Zones 3-10*

Height: *4 to 6 inches*

Light: *full to light shade*

Soil: *moist, organic, acid*

Plant type: *shrub*

Uses: *ground cover, culinary*

Wintergreen slowly creeps along to form low mats of glossy aromatic evergreen foliage ideal for ground cover and for use in rock gardens and wildflower gardens. Waxy summer flower bells dangle below the leaves, followed by fleshy red berries that remain on plants through the winter. Brew freshly chopped leaves or berries for a refreshing tea with hints of mint and camphor. Add a few berries to jams. Both yield an oil, now replaced by a synthetic formula, that was once used as a food flavoring and was applied externally to soothe sore muscles.

Selected species and varieties: *G. procumbens* (wintergreen, checkerberry, teaberry, ivry leaves)—leathery oval 2-inch leaves on short, erect stalks along trailing stems and ¼-inch white to pink flowers followed by edible red berries.

Growing conditions and maintenance: Propagate wintergreen from seeds sown or divisions made in spring, from rooted suckers in fall, or from cuttings taken in summer, and space plants 1 foot apart. Mulch with pine needles or leaf mold to conserve moisture. Harvest leaves anytime, berries when ripe.

Geranium
(jer-AY-nee-um)
CRANESBILL

Geranium maculatum

Hardiness: *hardy or Zones 3-8*

Height: *1 to 2½ feet*

Light: *full sun to light shade*

Soil: *organic, moist to well-drained*

Plant type: *perennial or annual*

Uses: *landscaping, potpourri*

Wild geranium forms loose clumps of deeply notched, hand-shaped leaves with spring flowers followed by long, beaked seed capsules. Herb Robert has finely divided lacy leaves along hairy red-tinged, somewhat malodorous, sprawling stems and paired flowers from summer through fall. Use both as border fillers or in a wild-flower garden. Add dried flowers of wild geranium to potpourri.

Selected species and varieties: *G. maculatum* (wild geranium, wild cranesbill, spotted cranesbill)—inch-wide pink to rose, sometimes lavender, flowers on stems to 2 feet and leaves up to 8 inches across; Zones 3-8. *G. robertianum* (herb Robert)—an annual with leaves to 4½-inches across and red-purple ¼-inch flowers.

Growing conditions and maintenance: Sow seeds of wild geranium or herb Robert in spring or fall or divide wild geranium's roots in fall. Both self-sow freely. Choose moist to wet sites for wild geranium; herb Robert prefers well-drained spots in the garden. Both will grow in light shade but are more compact or less sprawling in full sun. Remove spent flowers to prolong bloom period.

Glycyrrhiza
(gly-ki-RY-za)
LICORICE

Glycyrrhiza glabra

Hardiness: *Zones 5-9*

Height: *to 3 feet*

Light: *full sun to light shade*

Soil: *rich, moist*

Plant type: *perennial*

Uses: *landscaping, culinary*

Licorice spreads in broad clumps of erect branching stems lined with long leaves composed of paired 1- to 2-inch sticky yellow-green leaflets. In summer, short flower spikes appear in leaf axils. A branching taproot contains glycyrrhizin, a compound 50 times sweeter than sugar and a source of the food flavoring. Dry root pieces to chew, or boil dried roots to extract the flavoring. *Caution:* Some people are severely allergic to glycyrrhizin.

Selected species and varieties: *G. glabra* (licorice)—yellow-green leaflets and white to blue, sometimes violet, ½-inch flowers resembling tiny sweet peas on plants growing from a 4-foot or longer taproot branching into tangled mats.

Growing conditions and maintenance: Licorice grows very slowly from seed. More often, it is grown from division of the crowns, rooted suckers, or root cuttings at least 6 inches long with two to three eyes. Space plants 18 inches apart. Wait at least 3 years before harvesting roots; root pieces left behind will sprout the next year. Dry the roots in a shady location for up to 6 months and store in a cool location in airtight containers.

Hedeoma
(hed-ee-O-ma)
AMERICAN PENNYROYAL

Hedeoma pulegioides

Hardiness: *hardy*

Height: *4 to 12 inches*

Light: *full sun to light shade*

Soil: *rich, sandy*

Plant type: *annual*

Uses: *landscaping, potpourri*

With mint-scented leaves growing along erect, branching stems, American pennyroyal develops into low, bushy mounds. Tiny, insignificant flower clusters grow where leaves meet stems, emerging from summer through fall. Use American pennyroyal as an edging, ground cover, or filler plant in informal borders. Sow it into lawns for fragrance, or allow it to trail gracefully over the edges of hanging baskets. Add dried leaves and stems to herbal potpourri; they are widely used as an herbal repellent for fleas and weevils. Although it figures in herbal medicine, its oil can be toxic.

Selected species and varieties: *H. pulegioides* (American pennyroyal, mock pennyroyal)—1½-inch hairy oval leaves along square stems to 12 inches tall and ¼-inch blue to lavender flowers.

Growing conditions and maintenance: Start American pennyroyal seed indoors 6 weeks before the last frost or sow directly outdoors. Seed-grown plants take 2 years to reach flowering, but plants self-sow freely and seedlings transplant easily. To dry, pick stems while they are in flower and hang.

Helichrysum
(hel-i-KRY-sum)
EVERLASTING

Helichrysum angustifolium

Hardiness: *Zones 9-10*

Height: *12 to 18 inches*

Light: *full sun*

Soil: *rich, well-drained to dry*

Plant type: *perennial*

Uses: *landscaping, culinary, potpourri*

Curry plant's silvery needlelike evergreen foliage releases a sweet aroma reminiscent of curry spice when brushed or crushed, although it is not used in curry blends. Curry plants form tidy mounds ideal for formal edgings and can be grown in containers to bring indoors during winter in colder climates. Both the leaves and the small clusters of fragrant yellow gold summer flowers can be preserved for dried arrangements or added to potpourri.

Selected species and varieties: *H. angustifolium* [also classified as *H. italicum*] (curry plant, white-leaf everlasting)—woolly, erect stems to 18 inches long lined with narrow, inch-long leaves in compact mounds with flat flower clusters.

Growing conditions and maintenance: Grow curry plant from stem cuttings or divisions made in spring or fall. Space plants 12 to 18 inches apart. Protect plants from frost by burying in leaves or grow in containers to bring indoors when frost threatens. Pick leaves anytime, flowers as they mature.

Heuchera
(HEW-ker-a)
ALUMROOT

Heuchera americana

Hardiness: *Zones 4-9*

Height: *6 to 36 inches*

Light: *full to light shade*

Soil: *organic, well-drained*

Plant type: *perennial*

Uses: *landscaping, arrangements*

American alumroot forms neat clumps of evergreen foliage mottled gray-green or brown-green in spring, developing a reddish cast in summer through fall. Use it as edging or a ground cover in woodland gardens or under shrubs. In spring and summer, long stalks carry airy clusters of tiny flower bells, which make excellent fillers in fresh arrangements. The plant's roots have figured in herbal medicine.

Selected species and varieties: *H. americana* (American alumroot, rock geranium)—round or heart-shaped leathery leaves 2 to 5 inches across with finely toothed edges on long stalks, and plumy clusters of tiny green to white, sometimes pink, flower bells with protruding stamens on 2- to 3-foot stalks.

Growing conditions and maintenance: Sow American alumroot seed in spring or fall. Otherwise, divide plants in spring or fall and replant with crowns just at the soil surface. American alumroot tolerates full sun but grows best in somewhat dry soils in light shade.

Hibiscus
(hy-BIS-kus)
MALLOW, ROSE MALLOW

Hibiscus sabdariffa

Hardiness: *tender or Zones 7-11*

Height: *4 to 8 feet*

Light: *full sun*

Soil: *well-drained*

Plant type: *perennial or annual*

Uses: *landscaping, culinary*

Roselle develops round heads of broad leaves, sometimes deeply divided like the fingers on a hand, on woody stems. The dense foliage makes a handsome temporary screen. The showy flowers appearing in late summer through fall are surrounded by sepals that swell into succulent fleshy pseudofruits with a tart, acid flavor like that of cranberries. Fresh or cooked leaves taste like rhubarb. The fruits, which color dishes a deep burgundy, are used fresh or dried in herbal teas, jellies, jams, sauces, and curries. Steep leaves for tea, or roast the seeds for snacks.

Selected species and varieties: *H. sabdariffa* (roselle, sorrel, Jamaica sorrel, Indian sorrel, red sorrel)—leaves up to 6 inches across and 1½- to 2-inch-wide yellow flowers with red-purple throats on branching stems to 8 feet tall.

Growing conditions and maintenance: Sow roselle seeds outdoors after the soil warms in spring or start indoors 8 to 10 weeks before planting time. Space plants 1½ to 2 feet apart. Protect from frost, since blooms emerge only after the days begin to become shorter, and early frost will ruin fruits.

Hierochloë
(hi-er-OK-low-ee)
SWEET GRASS

Hierochloë odorata

Hardiness: *Zones 4-9*

Height: *10 to 24 inches*

Light: *full sun to light shade*

Soil: *moist, well-drained*

Plant type: *grass*

Uses: *landscaping, potpourri, crafts*

Sweet grass forms dense tufts of bright green leaves that gradually spread into wide mats. In spring, tall flowering stalks bear loose clusters of brown spikelets above the leaves. Use sweet grass as an informal edging or allow tufts to spread in a meadow garden. Its creeping runners form mats of roots that help hold soil in steep or difficult locations. Leaves develop a long-lasting aroma of vanilla or new-mown hay when dried for use in potpourri, bundled into closet sachets, or woven into baskets and mats.

Selected species and varieties: *H. odorata* (sweet grass, vanilla grass, holy grass, zubrovka)—thin, flat ¼-inch-wide leaves 10 to 20 inches long and pyramidal seed clusters on stalks to 2 feet.

Growing conditions and maintenance: Plant plugs or divisions of sweet grass in spring or fall, spacing them 15 to 24 inches apart. Sweet grass runners can be invasive; confine plants in pots with the bottoms removed to contain spread. Cut leaves at ground level and dry in bundles in a sunny location. For craft work, boil the harvested green grass 10 minutes, then dry in the sun for up to 1 week.

Humulus
(HEW-mew-lus)
HOP

Humulus lupulus 'Aureus'

Hardiness: *Zones 3-8*

Height: *10 to 25 feet*

Light: *full sun to light shade*

Soil: *rich, moist, well-drained*

Plant type: *perennial vine*

Uses: *landscaping, culinary, crafts*

Twining deciduous vines with coarse foliage like that of grapevines, hops quickly clamber over trellises to form dense, textured screens. In summer, female and male flowers appear on separate plants. Weave lengths of hopvine into garlands or wreaths for drying. Stuff dried female flowers, used as a bitter flavoring for beer, into herbal pillows to promote sleep. Blanch young leaves to remove bitterness and add to soups or sauces. Cook young side shoots like asparagus.

Selected species and varieties: *H. lupulus* (common hop, European hop, bine)—heart-shaped lobed leaves up to 6 inches across and female plants with paired yellow-green flowers ripening to papery scales layered in puffy cones; 'Aureus' has golden green leaves.

Growing conditions and maintenance: Because female plants are more desirable than male ones and the gender of plants grown from seed is unknown for 3 years, it is best to grow hops from tip cuttings taken from female plants, divide their roots, or remove their rooted suckers in spring. Space plants 1½ to 3 feet apart. Cut hops to the ground at season's end.

Hydrastis
(hy-DRAS-tis)
ORANGEROOT

Hydrastis canadensis

Hardiness: *Zones 3-8*

Height: *6 to 12 inches*

Light: *full to light shade*

Soil: *organic, moist, well-drained*

Plant type: *perennial*

Uses: *landscaping*

Goldenseal sends up solitary stems, each with a few broad, coarse leaves, and very slowly spreads into mats in woodland gardens. Tiny spring flowers develop into inedible fruits resembling raspberries in fall. Indians used goldenseal for body paint, as an insect repellent, and in various herbal medicines. Modern herbalists now consider it toxic, especially in large doses. In the past, inflated claims for its medicinal powers led to overcollecting in the wild, and goldenseal is now endangered in many places.

Selected species and varieties: *H. canadensis* (goldenseal, turmeric)—deeply lobed, hand-shaped leaves up to 8 inches across, a single leaf at the base of each stem and one or two at the top, growing from thick, yellow-fleshed rhizomes with a licorice odor and petal-less ½-inch green-white flowers with fluffy stamens.

Growing conditions and maintenance: Grow goldenseal from pieces of rhizomes with leaf buds collected in spring or fall. Set pieces ½ inch deep and space them 8 inches apart. Protect with a winter mulch. Propagation from seed is difficult, as seeds need 18 months to germinate.

Hypericum
(by-PER-i-kum)
ST.-JOHN'S-WORT

Hypericum perforatum

Hardiness: *Zones 5-9*

Height: *2 to 3 feet*

Light: *full sun to light shade*

Soil: *average to poor, dry, well-drained*

Plant type: *perennial*

Uses: *landscaping*

Aromatic St.-John's-wort's erect, branching stems lined with balsam-scented foliage are crowned in summer with flat, loose clusters of bright yellow lemon-scented flowers. Use St.-John's-wort as a fragrant filler in sunny borders or along the edges of woodland gardens. Flowers and stems provide both yellow and red dyes; petals exude a red pigment when pinched or crushed. Although once used in herbal medicine, St.-John's-wort in large amounts causes photosensitivity, with resulting sunburn and dermatitis.

Selected species and varieties: *H. perforatum* (common St.-John's-wort, perforate St.-John's-wort, Klamath weed)—pairs of inch-long oval leaves and inch-wide yellow flowers with black dots along their edges and fluffy golden stamens.

Growing conditions and maintenance: Start new plants from seeds in spring, from cuttings taken in midsummer, or from divisions in fall. Space plants 1 foot apart. Plants spread quickly by leafy runners but can be controlled by pulling unwanted stems.

Hyssopus
(hiss-O-pus)
HYSSOP

Hyssopus officinalis

Hardiness: *Zones 3-8*

Height: *18 to 36 inches*

Light: *full sun to light shade*

Soil: *well-drained to dry*

Plant type: *perennial*

Uses: *landscaping, culinary*

Hyssop's square stems are lined with camphor-scented narrow leaves and tipped with thick spikes of tubular flowers having flared lips favored by bees and hummingbirds. Grow them as bushy specimens or plant them closely for low hedges. Add the flowers to salads, use the sagelike leaves to flavor poultry or stuffings. Use dried flowers and leaves in herbal teas or potpourri.

Selected species and varieties: *H. officinalis* (common hyssop, European hyssop)—willowlike ¾- to 1¼-inch leaves and ½-inch blue-violet flowers on plants to 3 feet; 'Albus' [also called 'Alb'] (white hyssop) has white flowers; ssp. *aristatus* (rock hyssop) produces fine leaves on 18- to 24-inch plants.

Growing conditions and maintenance: Sow hyssop from seed to bloom its second year. Otherwise, grow from stem cuttings in midsummer or from divisions taken in spring or fall. Remove spent flowers to prolong bloom. Prune mature plants to the ground in spring. Shear into formal hedges for knot gardens or for use as edgings in formal gardens. Hyssop is sometimes evergreen in milder climates.

Inula
(IN-yew-la)
ELECAMPANE

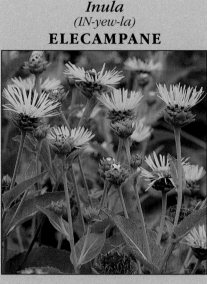

Inula belenium

Hardiness: *Zones 3-9*

Height: *4 to 6 feet*

Light: *partial shade to full sun*

Soil: *moist, well-drained*

Plant type: *perennial*

Uses: *landscaping, dried arrangements*

Elecampane's erect stems are lined with bold leaves and tipped with small clusters of sunflower-like blooms from summer through fall. The shaggy blossoms can be dried to add color to potpourri or allowed to form seed heads attractive in dried arrangements. Elecampane's sticky roots, with an aroma of bananas, were once sliced and crystallized for candies and also figured in herbal medicine.

Selected species and varieties: *I. belenium* (elecampane, wild sunflower)—grooved stems lined with pointed, elliptical leaves up to 18 inches long with downy gray hairs on their undersides and 3- to 4-inch-wide flowers with narrow yellow to orange petals arranged around prominent yellow centers that mature to brown.

Growing conditions and maintenance: Sow elecampane seeds or plant divided roots in spring or fall, spacing plants 2 to 3 feet apart. Plants self-sow. While elecampane is not fussy about light, constantly moist but well-drained soil is essential for it to thrive. Cut flowers for drying just after they open, and dry on screens in a shady location.

Iris
(EYE-ris)
FLAG, FLEUR-DE-LIS

Iris x germanica var. florentina

Hardiness: *Zones 3-10*

Height: *20 to 40 inches*

Light: *full sun*

Soil: *rich, well-drained or moist to wet*

Plant type: *perennial*

Uses: *landscaping, potpourri*

Growing on zigzag stems rising from tight fans of sword-shaped leaves, intricate iris flowers add drama to sunny borders with their arching petals, contrasting veining, and fuzzy beards. The thick roots of some species yield violet-scented orris, prized as a fixative in potpourri and sachets. Though irises once figured in herbal medicine, their fresh leaves and roots are now considered poisonous.

Selected species and varieties: *I.* x *germanica* var. *florentina* (orris)—pale blue or violet to iridescent white petals with prominent yellow beards on stems to 30 inches tall in spring; Zones 4-10. *I. versicolor* (blue flag, wild iris)—clusters of up to six yellow-veined beardless purple flowers on 20- to 40-inch stems in summer; Zones 3-8.

Growing conditions and maintenance: Divide irises after they flower, planting the divisions 1 to 2 feet apart, pointing the leafless end of the root in the direction the plant is to grow. Choose well-drained sites for orris; blue flag prefers moist to wet soil. To dry orris, dig roots that are at least 2 years old in fall, peel, and cut into chunks.

Isatis
(EYE-sat-is)
WOAD

Isatis tinctoria

Hardiness: *hardy or Zones 4-8*

Height: *2 to 4 feet*

Light: *full sun*

Soil: *rich, moist, well-drained*

Plant type: *biennial*

Uses: *landscaping, potpourri*

Before the discovery of indigo, weavers used fermented leaves of dyer's woad to produce blue hues. Now dyer's woad is enjoyed as a specimen or border backdrop, where the clouds of tiny yellow spring flowers produced on 2-year-old plants contrast attractively with the blue-green foliage. Dangling fiddle-shaped black seeds decorate the plants in fall. Dry the flowers to add color to potpourri. Woad is considered toxic.

Selected species and varieties: *I. tinctoria* (dyer's woad, asp-of-Jerusalem)—rosettes of oval leaves the first year followed by tall flowering stalks the second year tipped with large, airy clusters of ¼-inch four-petaled yellow flowers on sprawling to erect stems lined with narrow leaves.

Growing conditions and maintenance: Sow dyer's woad in late summer for flowering the following year. Space plants 6 inches apart in deep soil that can accommodate their long taproots. Pick flowers just after opening and dry on screens in a well-ventilated area. Left to form seed, plants self-sow freely; transplant seedlings in spring.

Laurus
(LAR-us)
LAUREL, SWEET BAY

Laurus nobilis

Hardiness: *Zones 8-10*

Height: *4 to 40 feet*

Light: *full sun to light shade*

Soil: *well-drained*

Plant type: *tree or shrub*

Uses: *culinary, landscaping, dried arrangements*

In warm climates, evergreen bay laurel grows as a multistemmed shrub or tree to 40 feet; in colder climates, it reaches 4 to 6 feet as a container-grown standard. The glossy, leathery, aromatic leaves with intense flavor are prized by cooks and essential in bouquets garnis. Add leaves to potpourri, or dry branches for bouquets or wreaths. Bay laurel is a traditional medicinal and insect-repellent herb.

Selected species and varieties: *L. nobilis* (bay laurel, bay, bay tree, true laurel)—narrow, oval 2- to 4-inch gray-green leaves; 'Angustifolia' (willow-leaved bay) has extremely narrow leaves; 'Aurea', tapered golden yellow leaves.

Growing conditions and maintenance: Plant balled-and-burlapped or container-grown specimens to harvest leaves the first season. Choose sites protected from winds. To grow as standards, train plants to a single stem and prune frequently; bring plants indoors before frost. Bay laurel can be propagated from seed or from hardwood cuttings but grows very slowly. Dry the leaves in a single layer in a warm, dark place; weigh down with a board to dry them flat. Store in airtight containers.

Lavandula
(lav-AN-dew-la)
LAVENDER

Lavandula angustifolia 'Hidcote'

Hardiness: *Zones 5-10*

Height: *1 to 5 feet*

Light: *full sun*

Soil: *dry, well-drained, sandy, alkaline*

Plant type: *perennial or small shrub*

Uses: *landscaping, culinary, arrangements*

Dense spikes of intensely fragrant blue to purple, sometimes white, ¼- to ½-inch flowers bloom throughout summer on leafless stalks above cushions of gray-green foliage. Mounds of lavender make fragrant border specimens or can be used as low hedges. Aromatic oils permeate all parts of the plant but are concentrated in flowers. Use fresh flowers to flavor jellies, vinegars, and sauces, toss with salads, or crystallize as a garnish. Use fresh or dried flower stalks in bouquets, dried flowers in sachets and potpourri. Some species are reputed to have medicinal and insect-repellent properties.

Selected species and varieties: *L. angustifolia* [also listed as *L. officinalis, L. spica, L. vera*] (English lavender)—broad, compact mounds of aromatic foliage; 'Hidcote' is slow growing to 16 inches with sweetly scented deep purple flowers above silvery foliage; 'Jean Davis' has prolific pale pink flowers on 18-inch mounds; 'Munstead', early large purple flowers on compact 14-inch plants; Zones 5-9. *L. dentata* var. *candicans* (French lavender, fringed lavender)—2- to 3-foot stalks of blue flowers

above pine-scented mounds of toothed leaves; Zones 9-10. *L.* x *intermedia* (lavandin)—robust, very fragrant hybrids ideal for landscaping; 'Alba' has white flower spikes on 3-foot stems; 'Dutch', very early dark violet flowers on 3-foot stems; 'Grosso', thick, 4- to 6-inch spikes of deep lavender flowers on 30-inch stems above compact 8-inch mounds of silvery foliage; 'Provence', very fragrant violet blossoms on 2-foot stems; 'Seal', pale violet flowers on vigorous plants to 5

Lavandula lanata

feet tall; Zones 6-8. *L. lanata* (woolly lavender)—deep purple flowers on 5-foot stems above mounds of white woolly foliage spreading to 4 feet; Zones 7-9. *L. pinnata*—an almost everblooming species in mild zones with lavender to deep purple blossoms on 30-inch stems above ferny foliage; Zones 8-10. *L. stoechas* (Spanish lavender)—extremely fragrant magenta-purple butterfly-shaped flowers on 18- to 24-inch stems; Zones 6-9.

Growing conditions and maintenance: Plant rooted lavender cuttings or divisions in spring, spacing them 12 inches apart for hedges, up to 6 feet apart in borders. Poor soil intensifies fragrance. Protect fringed lavender and *L. pinnata* from frost, or grow in containers that you can move indoors. Pinch flowers the first year to encourage wider mounds. Stems become woody their second season; prune woody stems in fall, or shear entire plant to 8 to 12 inches tall. Pick lavender before the flowers are fully open, cutting early in the day before the sun dries volatile oils. Hang in bunches to dry, or remove flowers from stems and spread on screens. Stored in airtight containers, lavender retains its fragrance over many months.

Levisticum
(le-VIS-ti-kum)
LOVAGE

Levisticum officinale

Hardiness: *Zones 3-8*

Height: *3 to 6 feet*

Light: *full sun to light shade*

Soil: *organic, moist, well-drained*

Plant type: *perennial*

Uses: *culinary, landscaping*

With divided leaflets resembling flat parsley, lovage develops into towering clumps of greenish red stalks useful as specimens or to shade lower-growing herbs. Lovage's hollow stems, wedge-shaped leaves, thick roots, and ridged seeds all share an intense celery flavor and aroma. Chop leaves and stems or grate roots to garnish salads or flavor soups, potatoes, poultry, and other dishes. Steam stems as a side dish. Toss seeds into stuffings, dressings, and baked goods. Steep leaves for herbal tea.

Selected species and varieties: *L. officinale* (lovage)—deep green leaflets with toothed edges on branching stems to 6 feet topped with a flat cluster of tiny yellow-green spring-to-summer flowers.

Growing conditions and maintenance: Sow lovage seeds in fall or divide roots in spring or fall, spacing plants 2 feet apart. Top-dress annually with compost or aged manure and keep well watered during dry spells. Harvest leaves two or three times a season. Deadhead to encourage greater leaf production, or allow flowers to ripen for seeds. Dry leaves in bundles, or blanch and freeze.

Lindera
(lin-DER-a)
SPICEBUSH

Lindera benzoin

Hardiness: *Zones 4-9*

Height: *6 to 15 feet*

Light: *light shade*

Soil: *moist, acid*

Plant type: *shrub*

Uses: *landscaping, culinary, potpourri*

A round, dense deciduous shrub with erect branches, spicebush offers three-season interest, fragrance, and flavor as a specimen or in a shrub border. Flowers bloom along bare branches of both male and female plants in early spring, followed by spicy-scented leaves. On female plants, leaves color and drop in fall to reveal bright red fruits. Steep young twigs and fresh or dried leaves and berries for herbal tea. Add dried leaves and berries to woodsy potpourri, or grind dried berries as a substitute for allspice.

Selected species and varieties: *L. benzoin* (spicebush, Benjamin bush)—fragrant, tiny yellow-green flowers in clusters emerge before the 2- to 5-inch pointed, oval leaves, which turn deep gold in fall, and ½-inch oval red fruits.

Growing conditions and maintenance: Sow ripe spicebush seed in the fall before it dries out, or hold at least 4 months in the refrigerator and sow in spring. Otherwise, start new shrubs from softwood cuttings taken in summer. Collect twigs in spring, leaves throughout the growing season, and berries in fall, and use either fresh or dried.

Lippia
(LIP-ee-a)
MEXICAN OREGANO

Lippia graveolens

Hardiness: *Zones 9-11*

Height: *3 to 6 feet*

Light: *full sun*

Soil: *organic, sandy, well-drained*

Plant type: *shrub*

Uses: *culinary, containers, landscaping*

Mexican oregano's upright branches are lined with intensely aromatic wrinkled leaves used fresh or dried to flavor tomato and other vegetable dishes as well as seafood, cheese dishes, and chili. Add them to salads and dressings, or steep them with other herbs for teas. In frost-free areas, Mexican oregano can be grown as a specimen plant or pruned into a hedge. Elsewhere, grow it as a container plant to move indoors for the winter.

Selected species and varieties: *L. graveolens* [also called *Poliomintha longiflora*] (Mexican oregano)—pointed, oval 1- to 2½-inch downy leaves and tiny yellow to white winter-to-spring flowers growing where leaves meet stems.

Growing conditions and maintenance: Sow Mexican oregano seeds anytime, or start new plants from softwood cuttings taken anytime. Keep plants slightly on the dry side. Remove deadwood in spring and prune severely to keep shrubs from sprawling. Pinch to promote branching and bushiness. Top prune, root prune, and repot container specimens as needed to maintain their size. Pick leaves anytime and dry in a single layer.

Marrubium
(ma-ROO-bee-um)
HOREHOUND

Marrubium vulgare

Hardiness: *Zones 4-9*

Height: *18 to 24 inches*

Light: *full sun*

Soil: *poor, sandy, well-drained to dry*

Plant type: *perennial*

Uses: *landscaping, containers, culinary*

Horehound's deeply puckered, aromatic gray-green leaves, woolly with white hairs, add texture and soft color as fillers or edgings. Horehound can also be pruned into container specimens. Flowers attract bees. Use the branching foliage as a filler in fresh or dried bouquets. Steep the fresh or dried leaves, which taste slightly of thyme and menthol, for a soothing tea or add seeds to cool drinks for flavor. Horehound is a staple for cough remedies in herbal medicine.

Selected species and varieties: *M. vulgare* (common horehound, white horehound)—pairs of 2-inch heart-shaped leaves with deeply scalloped edges along square stems, and whorls of tiny white spring-to-summer flowers.

Growing conditions and maintenance: Sow horehound seeds in spring, thinning seedlings to stand 1 foot apart. Horehound can also be grown from divisions in spring and from stem cuttings taken in summer. In addition, it self-sows so easily as to be invasive. Prune before or after flowering to keep edgings or container plants compact. Dry the leaves in a single layer and store in airtight containers.

Matricaria
(mat-ri-KAY-ree-a)
GERMAN CHAMOMILE

Matricaria recutita

Hardiness: *tender*

Height: *24 to 30 inches*

Light: *full sun*

Soil: *average to poor, well-drained*

Plant type: *annual*

Uses: *landscaping, culinary, arrangements*

German chamomile's erect stems lined with feathery, finely divided leaves are crowned with numerous daisylike, honey-scented flowers from late spring to early summer. The soft foliage is excellent as a filler, especially among plants reaching their maximum size in late summer, as German chamomile tends to disappear after flowering and setting seed. The plant makes an excellent filler in fresh or dried bouquets. Its flowers make a soothing tea with an aroma of apple or pineapple.

Selected species and varieties: *M. recutita* (German chamomile, sweet false chamomile, wild chamomile)—airy clumps of fine-textured leaves and inch-wide flowers with yellow centers fringed with drooping white petals.

Growing conditions and maintenance: Sow German chamomile in fall for early-spring flowers or in early spring for summer blossoms. Thin or transplant seedlings to stand 8 to 10 inches apart. Plants self-sow freely. Hang stems in bundles to dry. Flowers for tea are best if fresh or frozen, as they lose their flavorful oils on drying.

Melissa
(mel-ISS-a)
BALM

Melissa officinalis 'All Gold'

Hardiness: *Zones 4-9*

Height: *12 to 24 inches*

Light: *full sun to light shade*

Soil: *moist, well-drained*

Plant type: *perennial*

Uses: *landscaping, culinary, potpourri*

Lemon balm's highly aromatic foliage and small flowers growing where the paired leaves join the square stems attract bees and perfume the garden. Though the loosely branching plants can be somewhat floppy and coarse, cultivars with colorful foliage are often sheared as ground covers. The plant's fresh leaves add a citrusy tang to salads, poultry or fish dishes, marinades, and vinegar. Dried leaves and stems scent potpourri.

Selected species and varieties: *M. officinalis* (lemon balm, bee balm, sweet balm)—1- to 3-inch pointed, oval leaves puckered by deep veins and whorls of ½-inch white to yellow flowers in summer and fall; 'All Gold' has golden yellow foliage; 'Aurea', green-veined yellow leaves.

Growing conditions and maintenance: Sow lemon balm seeds or divide mature plants in spring or fall, spacing them 1 to 2 feet apart. Plant 'All Gold' in light shade to prevent leaf scorch, and shear 'Aurea' to prevent flower formation and greening of leaves. Lemon balm self-sows readily. Contain the creeping roots by planting in bottomless pots at least 10 inches deep. Dry the leaves on screens.

Mentha
(MEN-tha)
MINT

Mentha aquatica var. crispa

Hardiness: *Zones 3-10*

Height: *1 inch to 4 feet*

Light: *full sun to light shade*

Soil: *moist, well-drained*

Plant type: *perennial*

Uses: *landscaping, culinary, potpourri*

Paired mint leaves line the characteristic square stems and lend a sharp, peppery, sweet fragrance to borders, beds, and rock gardens. Tiny white, pink, lilac, purple, or blue summer flowers appear in spiky tufts at stem tips or in whorls where leaves join stems. Mints thrive in containers and can be potted for indoor use. Low-growing species make good ground covers for potted shrubs and quickly fill niches among paving stones; mow sturdy species into an aromatic carpet. Cooks prize the hundreds of mint varieties, which vary greatly in leaf shape, size, and fragrance. Fresh leaves are the most intensely flavored, but mint can also be frozen or dried. Use sprigs of fresh mint to flavor iced drinks and accent vegetable dishes. Mint sauces and jellies are a traditional accompaniment for meats; mint syrups dress up desserts; and crystallized mint leaves make an edible garnish. Steep fresh or dried leaves in boiling water for tea, or allow the infusion to cool into a refreshing facial splash. Add to bathwater for an aromatic soak. Mix dried leaves into herbal potpourri. Mints are a traditional herbal remedy, especially as a breath freshener and digestive aid. While pennyroyal enjoys a reputation for repelling insects, it can be toxic if ingested.

Selected species and varieties: *M. aquatica* (water mint)—heart-shaped 2-inch leaves on 1- to 2-foot stems; var. *crispa* (curly mint) has decoratively frilled leaf edges; Zones 5-10. *M. arvensis* var. *piperescens* [also spelled *piperascens*]

Mentha arvensis var. piperescens

(Japanese mint)—oval leaves with strong peppermint aroma; Zones 6-9. *M.* x *gracilis* (redmint, gingermint)—shiny red-tinged leaves and stems popular in Southeast Asian cuisine; Zones 3-9. *M. longifolia* (horsemint)—narrow, pointed, oval leaves; Zones 3-9. *M.* x *piperita* (peppermint)—characteristic 1- to 2-foot purple stems lined with intensely menthol-flavored deep green leaves yielding commercially important peppermint oil; var. *citrata* (bergamot mint, orange bergamot mint, lemon mint, eau de Cologne mint) has lemon fragrance and flavor; other varieties have aromatic overtones ranging from citrus to floral to chocolate; Zones 5-9. *M. pulegium* (pennyroyal)—round leaves to 1 inch long on 6- to 12-inch stems; 'Cunningham' (creeping pennyroyal) is a dwarf growing only 2 to 4 inches tall; Zones 6-9. *M. requienii* (Corsican mint, creme-de-menthe plant)—diminutive creeper only an inch tall forming mosslike mats of extremely aromatic ⅜-inch bright green leaves; Zones 7-9. *M.* x *smithiana* (red raripila mint)—narrow red-tinged leaves on 2- to 4-foot stems; Zones 7-9. *M. spicata* (spearmint)—wrinkled, oval, pointed leaves 2 inches long with a sweet taste and fragrance lining 1- to 3-foot stems; Zones 3-9. *M. suaveolens* (apple mint, woolly

mint)—hairy, wrinkled 2-inch leaves with a distinctly fruity aroma on 1- to 3-foot stems; 'Variegata' (pineapple mint, variegated apple mint) has creamy leaf edges and a pineapple scent; Zones 5-9.

Growing conditions and maintenance: Corsican mint and horsemint prefer very moist situations in partial shade. Give other mints a moist but well-drained location in full sun; they will grow in partial shade but they may be less fragrant. With the exception of pennyroyal, mints do not grow true from seed; plant divisions or rooted cuttings in spring or fall, setting them 8 to 12 inches apart. Provide Japanese mint, redmint, and apple mint with a protective winter mulch in colder zones. Restrain mint's aggressive spread by spading deeply around plants at least

Mentha x piperita

once annually or, more reliably, by confining plants in bottomless plastic or clay containers sunk with their rims projecting at least 2 inches above the soil and their sides at least 10 inches deep; pull out any stems that fall to the ground and root outside this barrier. Mints can also be restrained by growing them in patio containers. Established beds of pennyroyal, peppermint, horsemint, apple mint, and spearmint tolerate mowing. The leaves are most flavorful when cut before flowers appear; shear plants when buds first form to yield about 2 cups of leaves per plant, and continue to pinch or shear at 10-day intervals to prolong fresh leaf production. Dry the leaves flat on screens, or hang stems in bunches in a warm, well-ventilated area to dry, then rub the leaves from the stems. Crystallize leaves for garnishes by simmering gently in a heavy sugar syrup.

Monarda
(mo-NAR-da)
WILD BERGAMOT

Monarda fistulosa

Hardiness: *tender or Zones 4-10*

Height: *1 to 4 feet*

Light: *full sun to light shade*

Soil: *rich, moist or dry, slightly alkaline*

Plant type: *annual or perennial*

Uses: *landscaping, arrangements, culinary*

Monarda's tousled, spiky, fragrant flowers in a wide array of colors attract gardeners, bees, and hummingbirds alike. The spreading clumps of erect, square stems are ideal as border fillers or background plants; vegetable gardeners plant bee balm to attract the bees that pollinate their crops. The ragged whorls of tiny tubular flowers atop each stem make long-lasting cut flowers. Fresh blooms add color to salads; dried blossoms retain their fragrance well in potpourri. The pairs of fragrant, citrus-flavored gray-green leaves lining the stalks add their pungency to Earl Grey tea. Fresh leaves add flavor to fruit salads, preserves, fruit punches, and iced tea. Dried leaves are also used in tea and to scent potpourri.

Selected species and varieties: *M. citriodora* (lemon bergamot, lemon mint)—an annual to 2 feet with lemon-flavored leaves and showy purple to pink blossoms. *M. didyma* (bee balm, Oswego tea, red balm)—a perennial with deep scarlet blooms and bergamot-orange-scented leaves ideal for tea; 'Adam' grows especially prolific salmon red blossoms on 2- to 3-foot stems; 'Croftway Pink' has soft rose pink blooms on 2½- to 4- foot stems; 'Mahogany', deep red-bronze blooms on 2- to 3-foot stems; 'Violet Queen', lavender to deep violet flowers on 2- to 3-foot plants; 'Snow White', pure white flowers on stems to 3 feet; Zones 4-10. *M. fistulosa* (lavender wild bergamot)—a perennial with lemon-oregano-scented leaves and lavender flowers on 4-foot plants; Zones 4-9. *M. punctata* (spotted bee balm, dotted mint, dotted horsemint)—a

Monarda punctata

short-lived perennial with mint-thyme-scented leaves and purple-flecked yellow flowers on 1- to 3-foot stems; Zones 4-9.

Growing conditions and maintenance: Sow seed of annual or perennial monardas or set out divisions of perennials in spring, spacing or thinning to 2 feet; pinch flower heads from seed-grown perennials their first year to increase root vigor. Bee balm prefers moist, rich soil; plant other monardas in dry, well-drained sites. Monardas, particularly lavender wild bergamot, will fill in garden spaces quickly and can be invasive. Weed by hand to avoid damaging the shallow roots, and thin clumps to minimize powdery mildew. Cutting stems to within 2 inches of the soil just after the flowers bloom may force a second bloom. Harvest leaves as needed, stripping them from stems and drying in a single layer on screens in a shady, well-ventilated area. Cut plants back severely in fall, and provide a protective winter mulch. Propagate monardas from seed, by transplanting the self-sown seedlings of lavender wild bergamot, or by division every 3 or 4 years in early spring, discarding the inner portion of older, mature clumps.

Myrica
(mi-RYE-ka)
BAYBERRY

Myrica cerifera

Hardiness: *Zones 1-9*
Height: *2 to 35 feet*
Light: *full sun to light shade*
Soil: *poor, moist to dry*
Plant type: *shrub*
Uses: *landscaping, dried arrangements*

Southern wax myrtle and sweet gale have glossy leaves dotted underneath with fragrant resin. Both bear minute spring flowers in dangling catkins on separate male and female plants followed by waxy berries clinging to the stems of female plants. Boil berries to remove the waxy coating for candlemaking; one bushel of berries yields 4 pounds of wax. Allow berries to dry on branches for arranging.

Selected species and varieties: *M. cerifera* (southern wax myrtle, candleberry)—shrub to 35 feet high and as wide, with narrow 1½- to 3-inch evergreen leaves lining reddish stems and ⅛-inch fruits on previous season's growth; Zones 7-9. *M. gale* (sweet gale, bog myrtle)—oval 1½- to 2½-inch leaves on deciduous shrubs 2 to 4 feet tall and wide; Zones 1-9.

Growing conditions and maintenance: Sow seeds of both species in spring or fall or propagate from cuttings taken in summer. Plant southern wax myrtle 8 to 10 feet apart and shear into hedges or prune specimens as small trees. This salt-tolerant plant grows in poor, dry soil but does best in the moist, organically rich soil also preferred by sweet gale.

Myrrhis
(MIR-ris)
SWEET CICELY, MYRRH

Myrrhis odorata

Hardiness: *Zones 3-8*
Height: *2 to 3 feet*
Light: *partial shade to full sun*
Soil: *rich, moist, organic*
Plant type: *perennial*
Uses: *landscaping, culinary, crafts*

Sweet cicely's finely cut leaves perfume the garden with celery and anise when used as a filler. As flavorful as they are fragrant, the fresh leaves can be used as a sweetener for tart fruits to reduce the amount of sugar needed or to flavor salads, omelets, and soups. The spring-blooming flowers are followed by seeds that can be added either green or ripe to fruit dishes, salads, baked goods, and other dishes. The anise-scented taproot can be chopped into salads, served raw with dressing, or steamed as a vegetable.

Selected species and varieties: *M. odorata* (sweet cicely, myrrh)—fernlike leaflets along arching stems to 3 feet and flat clusters of tiny white flowers followed by ¾-inch upright, oblong, ridged green seeds ripening to brown-black.

Growing conditions and maintenance: Because sweet cicely germinates erratically, the most reliable way to grow it is to divide mature plants in fall and plant the divisions. Space seedlings or transplants 2 feet apart. Harvest fresh leaves anytime, seeds either green or ripe. Dry leaves lose their taste but can be used for crafts. Dig roots for culinary use in fall.

Myrtus
(MIR-tus)
MYRTLE

Myrtus communis 'Variegata'

Hardiness: *Zones 7-11*

Height: *5 to 20 feet*

Light: *full sun to light shade*

Soil: *average, well-drained*

Plant type: *shrub*

Uses: *landscaping, containers, culinary*

Myrtle's lustrous evergreen leaves, tiny flower buds, and white flowers with puffs of golden stamens share a spicy orange scent that has made the plant a favorite in wedding bouquets. Myrtle develops into upright specimens ideal for massing into hedges. Grown as container plants to move indoors when the weather turns cold, myrtle is often pruned into topiary. Weave fresh branches into wreaths. Toss fresh, peeled buds into salads. Use leaves and berries to flavor meats. Add dried flowers and leaves to potpourri.

Selected species and varieties: *M. communis* (sweet myrtle, Greek myrtle)—pairs of 2-inch pointed, oval glossy leaves and creamy white ¾-inch flowers followed by blue-black berries; 'Flore Pleno' has doubled petals; 'Microphylla' is a dwarf ideal for containers; 'Variegata' has leaves marbled gray-green and cream.

Growing conditions and maintenance: Start myrtle from seed sown in spring or from half-ripe cuttings taken in summer; plant in sites protected from drying winds. Myrtle will grow in light shade but prefers full sun. It tolerates severe pruning to maintain its size in containers.

Nepeta
(NEP-e-ta)
CATMINT

Nepeta x faassenii

Hardiness: *Zones 3-9*

Height: *12 to 36 inches*

Light: *full sun to light shade*

Soil: *well-drained, sandy*

Plant type: *perennial*

Uses: *landscaping, culinary*

Catmints form sprawling mounds of downy gray-green leaves along square stems tipped with spikes of tubular flowers attractive to bees. Catnip (*N. cataria*) is even more attractive to cats. Drawn by its musty, minty aroma, they go into ecstasies of rolling and rubbing. Use catmints as fillers or ground covers in an informal border. Steep dried leaves for tea or sew them into toys for a favored feline.

Selected species and varieties: *N. cataria* (catnip)—coarse 2- to 3-inch leaves and spikes of violet to white ¼- to ½-inch summer-to-fall flowers on 2- to 3-foot plants. *N. x faassenii* (Persian ground ivy)—sprawling 2-foot mounds of 1- to 1½-inch leaves and lavender-blue early summer flowers. *N. mussinii* 'Blue Wonder'—large 6-inch spikes of lavender-blue flowers that first emerge in spring on 12- to 18-inch plants.

Growing conditions and maintenance: Sow catmint seeds or divide mature plants in spring, spacing plants 12 to 18 inches apart. Shearing plants to remove dead flowers encourages a second bloom and keeps plants from becoming leggy. Catmint self-sows freely.

Nicotiana
(ni-ko-she-AN-a)
TOBACCO

Nicotiana rustica

Hardiness: *tender*

Height: *2 to 4 feet*

Light: *full sun*

Soil: *rich, organic*

Plant type: *annual*

Uses: *landscaping*

Indian tobacco's bold leaves alternating along sturdy stems and crowned with summer-to-fall flowers create a dramatic backdrop for borders large enough not to be overwhelmed by their size and coarse texture. Plants contain nicotine, a natural insecticide that is poisonous if taken internally or absorbed through the skin. Dry and powder the leaves for an insecticidal dust effective against both root- and leaf-chewing insects.

Selected species and varieties: *N. rustica* (Indian tobacco, wild tobacco)—pointed oval leaves 4 to 8 inches long and half as wide covered with sticky hairs, and hundreds of ½-inch yellow-green flowers.

Growing conditions and maintenance: Sow Indian tobacco outdoors in warm soil or start indoors 6 to 8 weeks before the last frost. Space seedlings 18 to 24 inches apart. Harvest wearing protective rubber gloves, picking leaves individually as they begin to yellow. Hang to dry, then crumble, remove stems, and store in airtight containers. Wearing protective clothing and equipment, grind the dried leaves to a powder and dust on plants at least 1 month before harvest.

Nigella
(nye-JELL-a)
FENNEL FLOWER

Nigella sativa

Hardiness: *tender*

Height: *12 to 18 inches*

Light: *full sun*

Soil: *well-drained, slightly alkaline*

Plant type: *annual*

Uses: *landscaping, culinary, potpourri*

Black cumin forms neat clumps of erect stems lined with finely cut leaves and crowned with intricate flowers whose spidery centers are surrounded by flat, broad petals. The inflated seedpods that follow are prized in dried arrangements and yield triangular seeds with a pepper-nutmeg flavor used in curries, breads, and cakes as a substitute for caraway or cumin. It is one of the four spices included in the *quatre épices* of classic French cuisine. Black cumin is particularly effective as a specimen or edging plant in a blue garden.

Selected species and varieties: *N. sativa* (black cumin, nutmeg flower, Roman coriander)—gray-green ferny leaves and 1½-inch-wide blue flowers in summer.

Growing conditions and maintenance: Sow black cumin in the garden in fall or spring and thin seedlings to stand 4 to 6 inches apart. Black cumin does not transplant well. Plants will grow in light shade, but with less intense flower color. Harvest seedpods on stems as they turn dark brown for dried arrangements. Crush pods open to collect seeds.

Ocimum
(OS-si-mum)
BASIL

Ocimum 'African Blue'

Hardiness: *tender*

Height: *6 inches to 3 feet*

Light: *full sun*

Soil: *rich, organic, well-drained*

Plant type: *annual*

Uses: *culinary, landscaping, potpourri*

Pointed, oval, slightly curved leaves with mixed scents of cinnamon, clove, anise, lemon, rose, orange, thyme, mint, or camphor make basil not only a classic culinary seasoning but also a choice fragrance planting. All species do well in containers, and most are ideal for window-sill pot culture throughout winter. Whorls of tiny flowers grow in spikes at the tips of stems from summer through fall. Add fresh or dried basil leaves to salads, sauces, soups, and vegetable dishes or steep them for tea. Use flowers as an edible garnish or in herbal bouquets. Add dried basil to herbal potpourri.

Selected species and varieties: *O.* 'African Blue'—resinous leaves tinged with purple-green on 3-foot stems tipped with purple flower spikes, valued as a border specimen and for fresh flowers. *O. basilicum* (common basil, sweet basil)—bushy 8- to 24-inch plants prized by cooks and ideal for garden edging, with fragrant 2- to 3-inch leaves lining stems tipped with white flowers; 'Anise' has purple-tinged licorice-scented leaves and pink flowers; 'Cinnamon', cinnamon-scented leaves especially good in tea;

'Dark Opal', deep purple leaves and pink flowers; 'Minimum' (bush basil, Greek basil) is a 6- to 12-inch dwarf with ½-inch leaves, ideal indoors; 'Minimum Purpurascens' (purple bush basil) has small purple leaves on 12-inch plants; 'Purple Ruffles', purple-black leaves whose edges are curled and frilled, excellent in pots. *O. sanctum* [also classified as *O. tenuiflorum*] (holy basil, clove basil, sri tulsi)—clove-scented 1½-inch leaves and branching spikes of tiny white flowers on stems 18 to 24 inches tall, primarily used in landscaping.

Growing conditions and maintenance: Sow basil indoors 8 to 12 weeks before the last frost or outdoors where it is to

Ocimum basilicum 'Dark Opal'

grow, spacing or thinning plants to 1 to 2 feet apart. Basil can be sown in pots for indoor culture year round. It can also be propagated from cuttings, which remain true to type. Basil needs soils 50° F or warmer to thrive. Provide mulch to keep roots from drying out and to keep leaves clean. Leaves are best picked before flowers appear; to delay flowering and encourage bushiness, pinch stems back to 4 sets of leaves as flower buds form. Avoid washing basil unless necessary as mold forms quickly on damp leaves. Preserve by blending fresh leaves into olive oil and refrigerating the oil or freezing it in small batches. Whole leaves can be layered in olive oil to preserve them, frozen flat on trays after first brushing both sides with olive oil, or layered in white vinegar; the leaves of purple bush basil give vinegar a burgundy tint. Basil can be difficult to dry successfully; lay the leaves in a single layer on trays between layers of paper towels to keep them from turning black.

Origanum
(o-RIG-a-num)
MARJORAM

Origanum majorana

Hardiness: *hardy or Zones 5-10*

Height: *6 to 24 inches*

Light: *full sun*

Soil: *rich, dry, well-drained*

Plant type: *perennial or half-hardy annual*

Uses: *culinary, landscaping, potpourri*

Fragrantly spicy small, oval leaves and branching clusters of tiny flowers on mounding or sprawling plants make marjorams useful in kitchen gardens, where leaves can be snipped to flavor meat, vegetable, cheese, and fish dishes. They can also be used as border edgings or ground covers. Tender perennial species grow as annuals in cooler climates; marjorams also do well in containers both indoors and out. Use fresh or dried marjoram leaves in cooking, dried leaves and flowers in teas and herbal potpourri.

Selected species and varieties: *O. dictamnus* (dittany-of-Crete)—tiny woolly white leaves and loose, nodding clusters of tiny pink summer-to-fall flowers on sprawling 1-foot-high plants ideal in rock gardens or hanging baskets; Zones 8-9. *O. majorana* (sweet marjoram)—spicy 1¼-inch leaves, an essential seasoning in Greek cuisine and more intensely flavored than those of *O. vulgare,* along 2-foot stems tipped with white to pink flowers; Zones 9-10. *O.* x *majoricum* (hardy marjoram, Italian oregano)—a hybrid similar to sweet marjoram but slightly hardier; Zones 7-10. *O. onites* (Greek oregano,

pot marjoram)—very mildly thyme-flavored medium-green leaves used in bouquets garnis or laid across charcoal to flavor grilled foods, and mauve to white flowers from summer to fall on 24-inch plants; Zones 8-10. *O. vulgare* (oregano, pot marjoram, wild marjoram, organy) —mildly pepper-thyme-flavored green leaves on sprawling 2-foot stems, not the same plant used in commercial dried oregano but used for flavoring and valued in landscaping for its branching clusters of white to red-purple summer flow-

Origanum vulgare 'Aureum'

ers, Zones 5-9; 'Aureum' has golden leaves, Zones 6-9; 'Aureum Crispum', round, wrinkled ½-inch golden leaves on 1-foot plants, Zones 7-9; 'Nanum' is an 8-inch dwarf with purple flowers, Zones 6-9; 'White Anniversary' has green leaves edged in white on 6- to 10-inch plants ideal for edging or containers; Zones 8-9.

Growing conditions and maintenance: Sow marjoram seeds or plant divisions in spring or fall, spacing or thinning plants to 12 to 18 inches apart. Give golden-leaved cultivars light shade to prevent leaf scorch. Pinch stems to promote bushiness and delay flowering. Cut perennial marjorams back to two-thirds of their height before winter to promote bushier growth the following season. *O. vulgare* can be invasive. Indoors, pot up divisions or sow seeds in pots where they are to grow. Propagate marjorams from seed, from early-summer stem cuttings, or by division in spring or fall. For best flavor, harvest leaves just as flower buds begin to open. Mash leaves in oil to preserve them, layer with vinegar, or freeze. Dry leaves or flowers in a single layer in a shady, well-ventilated area.

Panax
(PAN-ax)
GINSENG

Panax quinquefolius

Hardiness: *Zones 3-8*

Height: *6 to 36 inches*

Light: *light to full shade*

Soil: *organic, moist, well-drained*

Plant type: *perennial*

Uses: *landscaping, culinary*

Ginseng's thick roots send up a single thin stalk with leaves composed of several pointed leaflets arranged like the fingers on a hand. In late spring or summer, a short flower stalk carries a cluster of tiny yellow-green flowers above the foliage, followed by red berries. In woodland gardens, ginseng slowly spreads into a lacy ground cover. Ginseng's Greek name means "all ills," reflecting its root's fame as an herbal tonic in Oriental medicine. Roots are also used in herbal teas.

Selected species and varieties: *P. pseudoginseng* [also classified as *P. ginseng*]— stems 2 to 3 feet tall with two to six leaves composed of toothed leaflets growing from a carrotlike root. *P. quinquefolius* (American ginseng)—stems 6 to 20 inches tall with leaves composed of 6-inch leaflets growing from a cigar-shaped root.

Growing conditions and maintenance: You can sow ginseng seeds in spring or fall, but division and replanting of roots in spring is often more successful as the seeds take a year to germinate. Provide organic mulch annually. When roots are at least 6 years old, dig them up in fall to use fresh or dried for teas.

Papaver
(pa-PAY-ver)
POPPY

Papaver rhoeas

Hardiness: *tender*

Height: *8 to 36 inches*

Light: *full sun*

Soil: *well-drained*

Plant type: *annual*

Uses: *landscaping, culinary, dried arrangements*

Corn poppies decorate borders with brilliantly colored flower cups composed of crepey petals on slender stalks lined with hairy gray-green foliage. Mass them for showy display, then harvest their bulbous seedpods to collect the tiny blue-gray seeds. The seeds, which contain none of the narcotic alkaloids found in opium poppies, add a nutty flavor to breads and cakes. Add seed heads, with interesting flat caps, to dried arrangements.

Selected species and varieties: *P. rhoeas* (corn poppy, Flanders poppy, Shirley poppy)—branching stems lined with lobed leaves carrying red to reddish purple 2- to 4-inch blossoms, sometimes double petaled, with purplish filaments and dark throats; 'Shirley Single Mixed' has a single rim of petals in shades of red, pink, salmon, orange, white, or bicolors.

Growing conditions and maintenance: Sow corn poppies in spring or fall, just pressing the seeds into the soil. Thin plants to stand 12 inches apart. Make successive sowings and deadhead plants to prolong the blooming season. Pick seed heads just before fully ripe; allowed to ripen, poppies self-sow freely.

Pelargonium
(pel-ar-GO-nee-um)
GERANIUM, STORKSBILL

Pelargonium capitatum

Hardiness: *tender or Zone 10*

Height: *12 inches to 6 feet*

Light: *full sun to light shade*

Soil: *rich, moist, well-drained*

Plant type: *annual, perennial, or shrub*

Uses: *landscaping, culinary, potpourri*

When brushed or rubbed, the foliage of scented geraniums emits a citrusy, floral, minty, or resinous perfume depending on the species or cultivar. The kidney-shaped or broad, triangular leaves are wrinkled, lobed, frilled, or filigreed to add texture to the border. Loose, open clusters of small white, pink, mauve, or lilac flowers on branching stalks add color in spring or summer. Outdoors year round where they can be protected from frost, taller species grow as border specimens or background shrubs or can be pruned into standards; sprawling types can be used as ground covers or trained against trellises. Elsewhere, scented geraniums are treated like summer bedding plants or grown in containers or hanging baskets; they also do well year round as houseplants. Use fresh leaves of citrus, floral, or mint-scented geraniums in teas and to flavor baked goods, jam, jelly, vinegar, syrup, or sugar; use resinous leaves to flavor pâté and sausage. Toss flowers into salads for color. Add dried leaves to floral or herbal potpourri. Infuse leaves in warm water for an aromatic, mildly astringent facial splash.

Selected species and varieties: *P. capitatum* (wild rose geranium, rose-scented geranium)—a spreading plant 1 to 2 feet tall and up to 5 feet wide with crinkled, velvety 2-inch rose-scented leaves and mauve to pink summer flowers. *P. citronellum*—lemon-scented 3½-inch-wide leaves with pointed lobes and pink summer flowers streaked purple on upright shrubs to 6 feet tall and half as wide. *P. crispum* (lemon geranium)—strongly lemon-scented, kidney-shaped ½-inch leaves and pink to lavender flowers in spring and summer on plants 2 feet tall and half as wide, whose leaves are traditionally used in finger bowls; 'Variegatum' has cream-colored leaf edges. *P.* 'Fair Ellen'—finely textured lacy leaves with a balsam aroma and pale mauve summer flowers marked with pink on compact plants 1 to 2 feet tall and up to 3 feet wide. *P.* x *fragrans* 'Variegatum'

Pelargonium 'Fair Ellen'

(nutmeg geranium)—small, downy gray-green leaves smelling of nutmeg and pine, and white spring-to-summer flowers lined with red on compact plants 12 to 16 inches tall and as wide. *P. graveolens* (rose geranium)—filigreed, strongly rose-scented gray-green leaves and pale pink spring-to-summer flowers spotted purple on upright shrubs to 3 feet tall and as wide. *P.* 'Lady Plymouth'—lacy leaves with creamy edges and a rose-lemon scent with minty overtones on shrubs to 5 feet tall and as wide. *P. odoratissimum* (apple geranium)—a spreading plant 1 foot tall and twice as wide with small kidney-shaped, velvety, intensely apple-scented leaves and red-veined white spring and summer flowers on trailing flower stalks. *P.* 'Old Spice'—a compact mound 1½ to 2 feet tall and as wide with a piny aroma. *P. quercifolium* (oak-leaved geranium)—round, lobed 2- to 4-inch leaves with a resinous balsam odor and pink-purple spring-to-summer flowers on upright shrubs 1½ to 4 feet tall and up to 3 feet wide. *P.* 'Rober's Lemon Rose'—gray-green 2-inch leaves with an intense rose-lemon scent and pink summer flowers on shrubs to 5 feet tall and al-

Pelargonium 'Lady Plymouth'

most as wide. *P. tomentosum* (peppermint geranium)—a spreading plant to 3 feet tall and twice as wide with 4- to 5-inch peppermint-scented leaves and white spring-to-summer flowers.

Growing conditions and maintenance: Sow seeds of scented geraniums indoors 10 to 12 weeks before the last frost. While all scented geraniums do best in full sun, lemon geranium, apple geranium, and peppermint geranium will tolerate light shade. Too-rich soil tends to minimize fragrance. Remove faded flowers to encourage further blooming. In containers, scented geraniums do best when slightly potbound; repot only into the next larger size pot. Indoors, provide daytime temperatures of 65° to 70° F, about 10° cooler at night, with at least 5 hours of direct sunlight daily. Keep potted plants from becoming leggy by pruning them hard after blooming or in very early spring, then feeding with any complete houseplant fertilizer. To propagate scented geraniums, cut a branch tip at least 3 inches long just below a leaf node, dip into rooting hormone, and place in clean, moist sand to root; transplant into potting soil after 2 weeks. Pick scented geranium leaves for drying anytime and lay in a single layer on screens in a shady location.

Perilla
(per-RILL-a)
PERILLA

Perilla frutescens 'Atropurpurea'

Hardiness: *tender*

Height: *12 to 36 inches*

Light: *full sun to light shade*

Soil: *average to rich, sandy*

Plant type: *annual*

Uses: *landscaping, culinary, dried arrangements*

Perilla forms mounds of wrinkled burgundy leaves that contrast nicely when used as a filler among gray or white foliage in an herb garden or border. The leaves and seeds, with a fragrance and flavor blending mint with cinnamon and an oil 2,000 times sweeter than sugar, are staples in Japanese cuisine. Fresh or pickled, they are used to garnish sushi and to flavor bean curd. Spikes of flower buds are batter-fried for tempura. Leaves are used to color vinegar and fruit preserves. Add the dried seed heads to herbal wreaths.

Selected species and varieties: *P. frutescens* 'Atropurpurea' (black nettle)—pairs of wrinkled oval leaves up to 5 inches long on square stems tipped with spikes of tiny white summer flower in whorls, followed by brown nutlets.

Growing conditions and maintenance: Sow perilla seed in spring, and thin seedlings to stand 1 foot apart. Harvest leaves anytime, harvest flowers for tempura just as buds form. Pinch off spikes of flower buds to encourage bushier growth. Allowed to form seed, perilla self-sows freely.

Petroselinum
(pet-ro-se-LEE-num)
PARSLEY

Petroselinum crispum var. neapolitanum

Hardiness: *hardy or Zones 6-9*

Height: *12 to 24 inches*

Light: *full sun*

Soil: *rich, moist, well-drained*

Plant type: *biennial*

Uses: *culinary, landscaping, containers*

Bundled into a classic bouquet garni or chopped for use in sauces, eggs, vegetables, stuffings, and herb butters, parsley's deep green curly or flat leaves blend well with many flavors. Vitamin-rich parsley also freshens breath. Cooks consider flatleaf types more strongly flavored than curly varieties. A biennial flowering its second year, parsley is usually grown as an annual in an herb garden, as an edging plant, or in containers indoors or out.

Selected species and varieties: *P. crispum* var. *crispum* (curly parsley, French parsley)—highly frilled leaves on plants 12 to 18 inches tall. *P. crispum* var. *neapolitanum* (Italian parsley, flatleaf parsley)—flat, deeply lobed celery-like leaves on plants to 24 inches.

Growing conditions and maintenance: Soak parsley seed overnight to speed germination. Sow seed ¼ inch deep in soil warmed to at least 50° F. Thin seedlings to stand 4 to 6 inches apart. Begin harvesting leaves when plants are 6 inches tall. Dry Italian parsley in the shade, oven, or microwave. Chop curly parsley and freeze in ice cubes for best flavor.

Plectranthus
(plec-TRAN-thus)
INDIAN BORAGE

Plectranthus amboinicus 'Variegata'

Hardiness: *tender or Zones 10-11*

Height: *12 to 36 inches*

Light: *full sun to light shade*

Soil: *rich, well-drained*

Plant type: *annual*

Uses: *landscaping, culinary, containers*

The fleshy lemon-scented leaves of Indian borage have a flavor reminiscent of thyme, oregano, and savory. In tropical areas where those herbs fail to thrive, cooks grow the plant as an attractive ground cover. Elsewhere, grow it as a houseplant or a patio plant to move indoors when frost threatens. The leaves trail attractively from hanging baskets. Use fresh leaves to complement beans, meats, and other strong-flavored dishes.

Selected species and varieties: *P. amboinicus* (Indian borage, Spanish thyme, French thyme, soup mint, Mexican mint, Indian mint, country borage)—round gray-green leaves up to 4 inches across in pairs along thick stems, and whorls of tiny mintlike blue summer flowers in spikes up to 16 inches long; 'Variegata' has gray-green leaves edged in cream.

Growing conditions and maintenance: Start Indian borage from tip cuttings or divisions in spring or summer. Plants stop growing at temperatures below 50°F and are quickly killed by even light frost. Pinch tips to keep plants bushy and contain their spread. Cut leggy plants back in spring. Feed potted plants monthly.

Pogostemon
(po-go-STAY-mon)
PATCHOULI

Pogostemon cablin

Hardiness: *tender or Zones 10-11*

Height: *3 to 4 feet*

Light: *full sun to light shade*

Soil: *rich, moist*

Plant type: *perennial*

Uses: *landscaping, containers, potpourri*

Patchouli's hairy triangular leaves contain a minty, cedar-scented oil valued in the making of perfume. Dried leaves gradually develop the scent and retain it for long periods in potpourri. In tropical gardens, patchouli forms mounds of fragrant foliage; elsewhere it is grown in containers to bring indoors when frost threatens.

Selected species and varieties: *P. cablin* [also classified as *P. patchouli*] (patchouli)—lightly scalloped leaves up to 5 inches long and half as wide in pairs along square stems tipped with 5- to 6-inch spikes of violet-tinged white flowers with violet filaments in fall.

Growing conditions and maintenance: Patchouli rarely sets seed. Start new plants from tip cuttings or divisions in fall or spring. Outdoors where patchouli is not hardy, start tip cuttings to overwinter and treat plants as annuals, or grow in containers to move indoors. Feed potted plants weekly during spring and summer. Young leaves develop the best fragrance. Pinch plants two or three times each year to harvest young leaves and keep plants bushy. Dry leaves in a shady, well-ventilated area.

Polygonum
(po-LIG-o-num)
KNOTWEED

Polygonum odoratum

Hardiness: *Zones 8-9*

Height: *1 to 1½ feet*

Light: *light shade*

Soil: *moist*

Plant type: *perennial*

Uses: *culinary, containers, landscaping*

Vietnamese coriander's pointed dark green leaves have a lemony, cilantro-like aroma and flavor prized in Asian cuisine, particularly in poultry and meat dishes. Where short growing seasons prevent plants from blooming and setting seed, Vietnamese coriander can be grown as a fragrant, rambling annual ground cover. Elsewhere, it is grown in indoor or outdoor containers.

Selected species and varieties: *P. odoratum* (Vietnamese coriander, Vietnamese mint)—green leaves up to 3 inches long with darker green triangular blotches along jointed 1- to 1½-foot stems that root wherever they touch the ground and, rarely, small clusters of tiny pink flowers in fall.

Growing conditions and maintenance: Start new Vietnamese coriander plants from tip cuttings taken in summer and rooted in water. In cooler climates, grow as an annual and take cuttings to root overwinter as houseplants for the following year's planting outdoors. Keep plants well watered, even constantly moist, and provide winter protection where they remain outdoors year round.

Poterium
(po-TEER-ee-um)
SALAD BURNET

Poterium sanguisorba

Hardiness: *Zones 3-9*

Height: *12 to 36 inches*

Light: *full sun*

Soil: *well-drained*

Plant type: *perennial*

Uses: *landscaping, culinary*

Burnet forms round mounds of delicate blue-green foliage ideal for soft, colorful edgings. In summer, tall flower stalks carry thimble-shaped clusters of tiny flowers well above the hummocks of leaves. Add the slightly nutty, cucumber-flavored young leaves to salads, coleslaw, soups, vegetables, and cool summer drinks. Preserve them in vinegar for flavorful dressings.

Selected species and varieties: *P. sanguisorba* [also classified as *Sanguisorba minor*] (burnet, garden burnet, salad burnet)—¾-inch oval leaflets with deeply scalloped edges paired along the flexible leafstalks to 1 foot and dense ½-inch heads of minute greenish flowers tinged pink on stems to 3 feet.

Growing conditions and maintenance: Sow burnet seeds in spring or fall or divide young plants before taproots become well established. Space plants 8 to 12 inches apart. Established plants self-sow. Burnet is evergreen in milder climates; elsewhere, shear old foliage to the ground in late fall or early spring. Leaves are most flavorful when picked in early spring or late fall.

Primula
(PRIM-yew-la)
PRIMROSE

Primula veris

Hardiness: *Zones 3-8*

Height: *6 to 12 inches*

Light: *partial to full shade*

Soil: *organic, moist, well-drained*

Plant type: *perennial*

Uses: *landscaping, culinary, arrangements*

Cowslip and common primrose both produce fragrant, very early spring flowers above rosettes of oblong leaves. Use cowslip's nectar-rich flowers in jams or dry them for tea and potpourri; add the leaves to salads. Gather common primrose's flowers into posies, crystallize for decorations, add to salads, and dry for potpourri; boil the leaves as a vegetable, and add dried, powdered roots to potpourri. Both species make fine edging plants. Cowslip thrives as a houseplant.

Selected species and varieties: *P. veris* (cowslip)—clusters of tubular yellow 1- to 1½-inch-long flowers marked with orange on stalks to 12 inches above blue-green 2- to 8-inch leaves. *P. vulgaris* (common primrose)—single, flat-faced ½-inch-wide yellow, purple, or blue flowers with notched petals on 6-inch stems among 1- to 10-inch yellow-green leaves.

Growing conditions and maintenance: Sow seed when ripe in fall or divide plants after blooming, spacing them 6 to 12 inches apart. Where conditions are ideal, plants may rebloom in fall. Pick young leaves and flowers just after opening. Dig and dry roots in fall.

Prunella
(pru-NELL-a)
SELF-HEAL

Prunella vulgaris

Hardiness: *Zones 4-9*

Height: *12 to 20 inches*

Light: *light shade to full sun*

Soil: *average to dry, well-drained*

Plant type: *perennial*

Uses: *landscaping*

Common self-heal slowly creeps via underground runners and rooting stems into dense mats useful as ground covers, especially in difficult areas such as under shrubs. From summer through fall, small spikes of hooded flowers rise decoratively above the foliage, attracting bees and butterflies with their sweet nectar. Common self-heal's leaves and flowers have figured in herbal medicine.

Selected species and varieties: *P. vulgaris* (common self-heal, heal-all)—pairs of 1- to 2-inch oval or diamond-shaped leaves along square stems and dense 1- to 2-inch spikes of ½-inch-long purple to pale violet and sometimes pink flowers with flared upper lips overhanging lower ones like a small hood.

Growing conditions and maintenance: Sow common self-heal seeds in fall while ripe, or divide the underground runners in spring. Floppy stems root wherever they touch the ground, and plants self-sow freely. Common self-heal survives in dry, average soils but can be very invasive in moist, rich soils, particularly when planted at the edges of lawns.

Pulmonaria
(pul-mo-NAY-ree-a)
LUNGWORT

Pulmonaria saccharata 'Mrs. Moon'

Hardiness: *Zones 3-8*

Height: *6 to 18 inches*

Light: *light to full shade*

Soil: *moist, well-drained*

Plant type: *perennial*

Uses: *landscaping*

Lungworts produce low mounds of attractive silver-mottled hairy green leaves that remain evergreen in milder climates. In spring, clusters of flared tubular flowers bloom in soft pastel shades, then age to a second color. Use lungworts as foliage specimens or mass them as ground covers under deciduous trees and shrubs. As its name implies, lungwort once figured in herbal medicine but is now suspected to be toxic.

Selected species and varieties: *P. officinalis* (common lungwort, Jerusalem sage)—leaves up to 3 inches long and deep pink flowers aging to blue-purple; 'Sissinghurst White' has white blooms. *P. saccharata* (Bethlehem sage)—6-inch-long leaves in mounds 18 inches high and twice as wide; 'Mrs. Moon' has pink buds aging to blue; the vigorous 'Roy Davidson' has light blue flowers aging to pink.

Growing conditions and maintenance: Sow lungwort seeds in spring, or divide mature plants in late fall, spacing plants 1 to 1½ feet apart. Plants will grow in full sun, but foliage becomes unattractive by midsummer. Cut fading foliage back in fall in cooler climates.

Punica
(PEW-nik-a)
POMEGRANATE

Punica granatum var. nana

Hardiness: *Zones 7-10*

Height: *2 to 20 feet*

Light: *full sun*

Soil: *well-drained*

Plant type: *tree or shrub*

Uses: *landscaping, culinary, containers*

In spring, brilliantly colored fragrant blossoms with crepey pointed petals crown pomegranate's glossy deciduous foliage. In warm climates, plants produce shiny fruits filled with tangy-sweet juicy pulp and sour seeds. Pomegranate juice is used to flavor sorbets, fruit salad, and ice cream and to produce the cordial grenadine. Pulp and seeds can be boiled with sugar for a flavorful syrup. Pomegranates make excellent container specimens.

Selected species and varieties: *P. granatum* (pomegranate)—light green oval leaves turning yellow in fall along spiny branches with inch-wide red to red-orange blossoms and apple-sized yellow, orange, or red fruits with leathery skins; var. *nana* (dwarf pomegranate) is only 2 to 3 feet high with proportionally smaller foliage, making it ideal for containers or bonsai.

Growing conditions and maintenance: Sow pomegranate seeds in spring or root semiripe cuttings taken in summer. Fruits seldom develop except in warm climates with long summers. Remove root suckers that appear, or transplant them in fall for new plants.

Pycnanthemum
(pik-NAN-thee-mum)
MOUNTAIN MINT

Pycnanthemum virginianum

Hardiness: *Zones 4-8*

Height: *2 to 3 feet*

Light: *full sun to light shade*

Soil: *moist, well-drained*

Plant type: *perennial*

Uses: *landscaping, culinary, dried arrangements*

A sharp, peppery aroma fills gardens wherever Virginia mountain mint grows. The square stems lined with whorls of very narrow, pointed leaves branch into loose mounds. In summer, tufts of flowers growing at stem tips attract bees and butterflies where the plant grows in wildflower or meadow gardens. As intensely flavored as it is fragrant, Virginia mountain mint is an excellent culinary substitute for true mint. Dry the dense flower heads for arrangements, or add dried leaves and flowers to potpourri.

Selected species and varieties: *P. virginianum* (Virginia mountain mint, wild basil, prairie hyssop)—smooth or slightly toothed, pointed, very narrow 1- to 1½-inch leaves and tiny white to lilac flowers in very dense, flat heads.

Growing conditions and maintenance: Virginia mountain mint grows best from cuttings or divisions of mature plants. Set plants out in spring or fall, spacing them 8 to 12 inches apart. Restrain their spread by spading around plants annually or by planting them in bottomless tubs and removing branches that root outside this barrier.

Ricinus
(RISS-i-nus)
CASTOR BEAN

Ricinus communis 'Carmencita'

Hardiness: *tender*

Height: *4 to 15 feet*

Light: *full sun*

Soil: *organic, well-drained*

Plant type: *annual*

Uses: *landscaping, containers*

Castor bean grows rapidly into a coarse-textured border backdrop or temporary screen composed of glossy leaves up to 3 feet across. Each colorful leaf is composed of numerous toothed, pointed leaflets. Insignificant summer flower spikes precede seeds enclosed in burr-like cases. The source of medicinal castor oil, which is safe when extracted commercially, these seeds are extremely poisonous, as are all other parts of the plant.

Selected species and varieties: *R. communis* (castor bean)—purple-tinged young leaves maturing to gray-green or purple-green and white flowers on plants to 15 feet; 'Carmencita' has deep mahogany leaves and red flowers on plants to 5 feet; 'Impala', red-maroon young leaves and creamy yellow blooms on plants to 4 feet.

Growing conditions and maintenance: In tropical climates, castor bean grows as a tree to 40 feet; elsewhere, grow it as an annual. Sow seeds indoors 6 to 8 weeks before the last frost or outdoors after the last frost, spacing plants 4 feet apart. Mulch to conserve moisture. Castor beans can be grown as container plants, but pruning may kill them.

Rosa
(RO-za)
ROSE

Rosa canina

Hardiness: *Zones 2-10*

Height: *3 to 10 feet*

Light: *full sun*

Soil: *organic, well-drained*

Plant type: *shrub*

Uses: *landscaping, arrangements, potpourri*

Besides using roses in arrangements, try adding the petals to salads or crystallizing them as a garnish. Dry the buds and petals for potpourri. Use the fruit, or hips, for tea or jam.

Selected species and varieties: *R. canina* (dog rose, brier rose)—10-foot canes with white or pink 2-inch blooms, ¾-inch hips; Zones 4-9. *R. damascena* (damask rose)—very fragrant 3-inch blooms on 6-foot canes; 'Autumn Damask' is a double pink; 'Madame Hardy', a double white; Zones 5-9. *R. gallica* (French rose)—2- to 3-inch blooms on 3- to 4-foot plants; 'Officinalis' (apothecary rose) is a semidouble deep pink; 'Versicolor' (rosa mundi) is a semidouble pink- or red-striped white, red, or pink; Zones 4-10. *R. rugosa* (Japanese rose)—crimson 3½-inch blossoms and 1-inch hips; 'Alba' is white; 'Rubra', burgundy red; Zones 3-8.

Growing conditions and maintenance: Sow rose seeds, root hardwood cuttings, or plant commercial rootstock in fall. Mulch to conserve moisture. Prune dead or damaged wood in late winter, avoiding the previous season's growth, on which this season's flowers grow.

Rosmarinus
(rose-ma-RY-nus)
ROSEMARY

Rosmarinus officinalis 'Prostratus'

Hardiness: *Zones 7-10*

Height: *6 inches to 7 feet*

Light: *full sun*

Soil: *well-drained, alkaline*

Plant type: *perennial*

Uses: *landscaping, culinary, potpourri*

Rosemary's branching, stiff stems are lined with resinous, aromatic needlelike leaves. Small flowers cluster along the woody stems in winter. Grown as a ground cover or shrub in warm climates, rosemary is pot grown elsewhere. Use the piny leaves, fresh or dried, to flavor meats, sauces, vinegar, herb butter, and breads. Toss sprigs on coals for aromatic grilling or weave into wreaths. Add leaves to potpourri.

Selected species and varieties: *R. officinalis* (garden rosemary)—gray-green ⅓- to 1½-inch leaves along branches to 6 feet outdoors, 4 feet indoors, and ½-inch blue flowers; 'Arp' is very hardy, with lemon-scented leaves; 'Miss Jessup's Upright' has vertical branches; 'Prostratus' is almost everblooming, with twisting 6-inch-high, 36-inch-long branches; 'Tuscan Blue' is fast growing, with large deep blue leaves on branches to 7 feet.

Growing conditions and maintenance: Sow rosemary seed in spring, or start from summer cuttings, spacing plants 3 feet apart. Prune after flowering to encourage bushiness, removing no more than 20 percent of the plant at a time.

Rubia
(ROO-bee-a)
MADDER

Rubia tinctorum

Hardiness: *Zones 4-10*

Height: *10 to 36 inches*

Light: *full sun*

Soil: *rich, well-drained*

Plant type: *perennial*

Uses: *dyes*

Madder's jointed, prickly stems ramble along the ground or climb weakly over other plants. Leathery leaves grow in whorls at each joint, and in summer and fall a light froth of tiny pale flowers blooms among the foliage. Madder forms mats of pencil-thick, red-fleshed roots up to 3 feet long, which yield red dye valued by textile craftspeople or, with various mordants, shades of pink, lilac, brown, orange, or black.

Selected species and varieties: *R. tinctorum* (madder)—2-inch oblong, pointed leaves in whorls of four to eight and 1/10-inch pale yellow or white open flower bells in airy clusters on plants 3 years old or older, followed by 1/8-inch reddish brown fruits, which turn black.

Growing conditions and maintenance: Sow madder seeds while ripe in fall, divide plants anytime between spring and fall, or start new plants from cuttings. Plants root wherever joints touch the ground. Provide supports to control madder's spread and give plants structure. Dig roots of plants that are at least 3 years old in fall.

Rumex
(ROO-mex)
SORREL, DOCK

Rumex crispus

Hardiness: *Zones 3-8*

Height: *6 inches to 5 feet*

Light: *full sun to light shade*

Soil: *well-drained*

Plant type: *perennial*

Uses: *culinary, dried arrangements*

Sorrel's slightly sour, lemony, arrowhead-shaped leaves add zest to salads and accent soups and sauces. Use fresh leaves sparingly, as the high oxalic acid content can aggravate conditions such as gout. Boil leaves for a spinachlike vegetable, changing the water once to reduce the acid content. Birds love the tiny seeds produced at the tips of the stalks.

Selected species and varieties: *R. acetosa* (garden sorrel, sour dock)—narrow 5- to 8-inch leaves on clumps of 3-foot stems. *R. crispus* (curled dock)—extremely wavy, curly 12-inch leaves on plants 1 to 5 feet tall. *R. scutatus* (French sorrel)—thick, broad, shield-shaped leaves 1 to 2 inches long on trailing stems growing into mats 6 to 20 inches high and twice as wide.

Growing conditions and maintenance: Sow sorrel indoors 6 to 8 weeks before the last frost, outdoors after the last frost, or divide mature plants and space 8 inches apart. Leaves become bitter in hot weather, but flavor returns with cooler temperatures. Pinch out flowering stalks to encourage leaf production and control invasive self-sowing.

Ruta
(ROO-ta)
RUE

Ruta graveolens

Hardiness: *Zones 5-9*

Height: *12 to 36 inches*

Light: *full sun*

Soil: *well-drained*

Plant type: *perennial*

Uses: *landscaping, dried arrangements*

Common rue forms clumps of lacy, aromatic evergreen foliage that makes an attractive filler or low hedge in a perennial border. For several weeks in summer, frilly, spidery flowers bloom atop the foliage. The inflated lobed seed capsules that follow are attractive in dried arrangements. Once used in herbal medicine, rue is now considered poisonous. Sensitive individuals develop a blistering dermatitis after touching the leaves.

Selected species and varieties: *R. graveolens* (common rue)—upright stems lined with oblong leaflets and 1/2-inch yellow flowers in loose, open clusters; 'Jackman's Blue' is a compact, nonflowering cultivar with waxy blue foliage; 'Variegata' has leaves splashed with cream.

Growing conditions and maintenance: Start rue seeds indoors 8 to 10 weeks before the last frost, sow outdoors after the last frost, plant cuttings taken in summer, or divide mature plants in spring or fall. *R. graveolens* 'Variegata' comes true from seed, but 'Jackman's Blue' must be grown from cuttings or divisions. Wearing gloves, prune back hard to force new growth and to keep plants compact.

Salvia
(SAL-vee-a)
SAGE

Salvia officinalis 'Purpurea'

Hardiness: *hardy or Zones 4-11*
Height: *1 to 4 feet*
Light: *full sun*
Soil: *average to alkaline, dry, well-drained*
Plant type: *annual, biennial, perennial, or shrub*
Uses: *landscaping, culinary, potpourri*

Puckered by a network of pronounced veins and colored a distinct gray-green hue, sage leaves bring both interesting texture and an aroma reminiscent of pine or rosemary to the border or kitchen garden. The leaves, largest at the base of the stems, are of gradually diminished size toward the spikes of tiny white, blue, lilac, magenta, or pink flowers at the tips. There are sages useful as edgings or throughout the border, and many do well as container plants or houseplants. Those suitable only for mild winter climates are often grown as half-hardy annuals in cooler zones. Add sage leaves and flowers to salads, or steep them for tea. Use fresh or dried leaves to flavor meat, cheese, or vegetable dishes and sausages and stuffings; the dried herb is stronger than the fresh. Mix dried leaves into potpourri. Use sage in the water for a facial steam, add to the bath, or use an infusion of sage in water as a slightly astringent facial splash or aftershave or as a hair rinse. Sage is reputed to repel insects and also figures in herbal medicine; used in excess or for long periods, however, it can be toxic.

Selected species and varieties: *S. clevelandii* (blue sage, Jim sage)—an evergreen shrub with wrinkled 1-inch leaves on downy stems 2 to 3 feet tall and as wide tipped with violet or white spring-to-summer flowers, recommended for containers or as a houseplant; Zones 9-10. *S. coccinea* (Texas sage, scarlet sage)—a perennial or subshrub grown as an annual, with 2-inch heart-shaped leaves having wavy, indented edges on 3-foot stems tipped with branched spikes of red or white summer flowers that are valued in landscaping. *S. dorisiana* (fruit-scented sage)—an evergreen perennial with sweetly scented, velvety oval leaves 4 inches wide and up to 7 inches long on stems to 4 feet tall tipped with 6-inch

Salvia coccinea

spikes of 2-inch magenta to pink flowers in fall and winter; Zones 10-11. *S. elegans* (pineapple sage)—an evergreen perennial with fruit-scented, red-edged 3½-inch oval leaves lining 3- to 4-foot red stems tipped with late-summer red to pink 8-inch flower spikes used in cold drinks and fruit salads; Zones 8-10. *S. fruticosa* (Greek sage)—an evergreen shrub to 4½ feet with lavender-scented leaves and loose, 8-inch clusters of mauve to pink spring-to-summer flowers; Zones 8-9. *S. lavandulifolia* (Spanish sage, narrow-leaved sage)—a spreading evergreen shrub 12 to 20 inches tall with 1-inch white woolly leaves having a piny lavender aroma and red-violet summer flowers; Zones 7-9. *S. officinalis* (common sage, garden sage)—an evergreen shrub in mild climates with 2-inch velvety leaves on branching 2- to 3-foot stems tipped with edible violet to purple flower spikes in summer; 'Berggarten' is a compact 18-

inch cultivar with almost round leaves and blue-purple flowers; 'Icterina', a dwarf cultivar with yellow-splotched leaves; 'Nana', a compact cultivar with small, narrow leaves; 'Purpurea', an 18-inch plant with purple leaves; all are good for indoor winter pot culture; Zones 4-9.

Salvia sclarea var. turkestaniana

S. sclarea var. *turkestaniana* (clary sage)—a biennial producing rosettes of 6- to 9-inch oval leaves on pink stems its first year and branching 3- to 4-foot flower stalks the second year tipped with pink-and-white flowers used in tea and salads. *S. viridis* (bluebeard, painted sage)—an annual with narrow, pointed, oval leaves on erect 18-inch stems with inconspicuous summer flowers.

Growing conditions and maintenance: Sow sage seed in spring or set divisions out in spring or fall, spacing them 18 to 24 inches apart. Avoid hot, humid locations or those with too-rich soils. Provide a protective winter mulch in cooler climates. Prune sage heavily in spring to remove winter-killed stems and encourage bushy growth; cut back again immediately after flowering. Perennial sages are short-lived; renew plantings every 4 or 5 years. Propagate by division or by rooting 4-inch stem cuttings taken in summer to plant in fall. Seedlings or rooted cuttings take 2 years to reach maturity for picking. Fresh leaves can be harvested anytime but are most flavorful before flowers appear. Dry leaves slowly to prevent a musty odor, laying them in a single layer on a screen or cloth; refrigerate or freeze the dried leaves, as the aromatic oils become rancid easily. To make an infusion for an aftershave or a hair rinse, steep leaves in boiling water, cool, and strain.

Sanguinaria
(sang-gwi-NAR-ee-a)
BLOODROOT

Sanguinaria canadensis

Hardiness: *Zones 3-9*

Height: *3 to 8 inches*

Light: *partial to full shade*

Soil: *rich, moist, well-drained*

Plant type: *perennial*

Uses: *landscaping*

Bloodroot's very early spring flowers emerge tightly clasped within kidney-shaped leaves. The waxy leaves, with deep lobes and scalloped edges, slowly unfurl to reveal a single flower resembling a tiny water lily. Allow the creeping rhizomes to spread slowly in woodland and rock gardens or under the shade of shrubs. The red-orange juice flowing in stems and roots was once used in herbal medicine but is now thought to be toxic.

Selected species and varieties: *S. canadensis* (red puccoon)—grayish green leaves up to a foot across marked with radiating veins and 1½- to 2-inch flowers composed of a whorl of white waxy, pointed petals raised above leaves on 8-inch red stalks; 'Flore Pleno' [also called 'Multiplex'] has double whorls of petals.

Growing conditions and maintenance: Sow seeds of the species in spring or fall or divide roots immediately after flowering, spacing plants 6 to 8 inches apart and incorporating leaf mold into the soil. *S. canadensis* 'Flore Pleno' must be grown from divisions, as it does not come true from seed.

Santolina
(san-to-LEE-na)
LAVENDER COTTON

Santolina virens

Hardiness: *Zones 6-8*

Height: *1 to 2 feet*

Light: *full sun*

Soil: *well-drained*

Plant type: *subshrub*

Uses: *landscaping, dried arrangements*

Gray lavender cotton forms stiff cushions of aromatic gray-white finely divided foliage. A favorite in Victorian knot gardens, it is often sheared into low hedges, but its feathery light-colored foliage contrasts well with darker plants as a border specimen. Dry the musky leaves for potpourri or add the leaves and buttonlike flowers to dried arrangements. Herbalists consider lavender cotton a moth repellent.

Selected species and varieties: *S. chamaecyparissus* (gray lavender cotton)—dainty, hairy leaves only ⅟₁₆ inch wide and ½- to ¾-inch yellow summer flowers like felted domes. *S. virens* (green lavender cotton, green santolina)—spreading plants to 24 inches tall with fine-textured green leaves strongly scented of pine and ⅝-inch yellow summer flowers.

Growing conditions and maintenance: Sow santolina seeds in spring, start cuttings in spring, or divide in spring or fall, spacing plants 12 to 18 inches apart. Renew the brittle, woody stems by pruning back severely in early spring. Deadhead plants in fall, but do not prune. Pick leaves to dry anytime. Hang flowers to dry in midsummer.

Saponaria
(sap-o-NAR-ee-a)
SOAPWORT

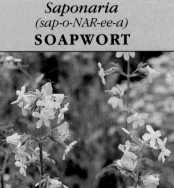

Saponaria officinalis 'Rubra Plena'

Hardiness: *Zones 3-8*

Height: *1 to 2 feet*

Light: *full sun to light shade*

Soil: *average to poor*

Plant type: *perennial*

Uses: *landscaping, potpourri*

Bouncing Bet bears clusters of raspberry-clove-scented summer flowers atop clumps of erect stems. The flowers resemble ruffled funnels during the day, then open fully at night into shaggy, open bells. Toss flowers into salads or dry them for potpourri. Leaves, stems, and roots boiled in rainwater produce a soapy liquid prized for cleaning antique textiles. Soapwort once figured in herbal medicine but is now considered toxic.

Selected species and varieties: *S. officinalis* (bouncing Bet)—pointed, oval leaves paired along sturdy stems and 1- to 1½-inch-wide pink flowers with single or double rows of petals; 'Rubra Plena' has double red petals that fade to pink.

Growing conditions and maintenance: Sow bouncing Bet in spring or fall, or divide mature plants in late fall or early spring. Avoid planting near ponds, as root secretions are toxic to fish. Plants self-sow invasively. Shear spent flowers to prevent seed formation and control spread. Shearing sometimes produces a second bloom. For liquid soap, boil sliced roots, stems, and leaves in lime-free water for 30 minutes and strain.

Satureja
(sat-yew-REE-jia)
SAVORY

Satureja hortensis

Hardiness: *hardy or Zones 5-9*

Height: *3 to 18 inches*

Light: *full sun*

Soil: *well-drained, slightly alkaline*

Plant type: *annual or perennial*

Uses: *landscaping, culinary*

Savory's aromatic needlelike leaves line erect stems tipped with whorls of tiny blossoms from summer through fall. Plant savories as border edgings, in kitchen or rock gardens, or in pots for the window sill. Use leaves fresh, dried, or frozen as fines herbes. Savory also figures in traditional herbal medicine.

Selected species and varieties: *S. hortensis* (summer savory)—a hardy annual to 18 inches tall with pink flowers. *S. montana* 'Nana' (pygmy winter savory)—6-inch plants with peppery leaves, white or lilac blooms; Zones 5-8. *S. spicigera* (creeping savory)—evergreen mats of 3-inch stems with white flowers; Zones 7-8. *S. thymbra* (goat thyme)—16-inch stems with pink blossoms; Zones 8-9.

Growing conditions and maintenance: Sow savory seeds outdoors in spring or transplant divisions of perennials in spring or fall. Pinch early growth to delay blooming, as fresh leaves are best picked before flowers emerge. For window sills, sow summer savory in fall or pot divisions of winter savory after cutting top growth back by half. Hang branches in bunches to dry, then rub leaves from stems.

Sesamum
(SES-am-um)
SESAME

Sesamum indicum

Hardiness: *tender*

Height: *18 to 36 inches*

Light: *full sun*

Soil: *well-drained*

Plant type: *perennial*

Uses: *culinary*

Each of sesame's bell-shaped flowers, which grow where leaves join the stem, produces an upright, pointed, oval capsule that bursts when ripe to release tiny nutty-tasting oily seeds, prized in Middle Eastern cuisines. The seeds are used whole in baked goods and candies and to garnish vegetables and salads. They can also be ground into dips, spreads, and sauces and pressed for cooking oil.

Selected species and varieties: *S. indicum* (sesame, benne, gingili)—square, sticky stems lined with oval, pointed 3- to 5-inch leaves and 1-inch white flowers tinged pink, yellow, or red.

Growing conditions and maintenance: Sow sesame seeds ¼-inch deep once nighttime low temperatures climb to 60° F, or start plants indoors 6 to 8 weeks in advance of this time. Space plants 6 to 8 inches apart. Plants need at least 120 days of hot weather to set seed. Harvest just as oldest pods begin to dry, cutting stems off at ground level, and hold them in a paper bag until pods dry and release seeds. Each seed that grows produces a single stem yielding approximately 1 tablespoon of seeds.

Solidago
(sol-i-DAY-go)
GOLDENROD

Solidago odora

Hardiness: *Zones 3-9*

Height: *3 to 4 feet*

Light: *full sun*

Soil: *average to poor, dry*

Plant type: *perennial*

Uses: *landscaping, culinary, arrangements*

From late summer into fall, sweet goldenrod produces enormous clusters of tiny yellow flowers. The plant will quickly spread through a meadow garden, or you can confine it in a container as a specimen. Although folk wisdom has long held its pollen to be allergenic—the troublemaker is actually *Ambrosia* (ragweed)—the flower clusters can safely be used in fresh or dried arrangements. Brew the fresh or dried anise-scented leaves for tea. The flowers yield yellow dye.

Selected species and varieties: *S. odora* (sweet goldenrod)—single stems lined with glossy, narrow 2- to 4-inch leaves and tipped with one-sided 8- to 12-inch plumes of ¼-inch yellow flower buttons.

Growing conditions and maintenance: Sow sweet goldenrod seeds or divide mature plants in early spring, spacing seedlings or divisions 12 to 15 inches apart. Plants begin blooming their second year and self-sow freely. Contain growth by planting in large containers or in the garden in bottomless pots, and remove spent flowers before they set seed. Shear plants to the ground in late winter or early spring, before new growth begins.

Stachys
(STAY-kis)
LAMB'S EARS, BETONY

Stachys officinalis

Hardiness: *Zones 4-8*

Height: *1 to 3 feet*

Light: *full sun to light shade*

Soil: *average, moist, well-drained*

Plant type: *perennial*

Uses: *landscaping, culinary*

Lamb's ears forms low rosettes of heart-shaped leaves with tall flower stems carrying short, dense spikes of small tubular flowers above them. A few sparser flowers often grow where leaves meet the square flower stems. Betony gradually spreads into low mats that provide a colorful filler in the perennial border when plants are blooming. Use the flowers in fresh bouquets. Steep the fresh or dried leaves for tea. Betony once figured prominently in herbal medicine but is now considered largely ineffective.

Selected species and varieties: *S. officinalis* (lamb's ears, common betony)—4- to 5-inch wrinkled, coarsely toothed basal leaves, with 1-inch leaves along flower stems, and whorls of ½- to ¾-inch purple, pink, or white flowers in 1- to 3-inch spikes.

Growing conditions and maintenance: Sow lamb's ears seed in early spring, and thin seedlings to stand 12 to 18 inches apart. Betony benefits from division every 3 or 4 years in early spring or late fall. Plants reseed themselves but are not invasive.

Symphytum
(SIM-fit-um)
COMFREY

Symphytum officinale

Hardiness: *Zones 3-9*

Height: *3 to 5 feet*

Light: *full sun to light shade*

Soil: *rich, moist*

Plant type: *perennial*

Uses: *landscaping, toiletries*

Comfrey forms bold clumps of coarse, hairy oval leaves useful as a backdrop in large borders or meadow gardens. From spring through fall, drooping clusters of funnel-shaped flowers decorate plants. Rich in nutrients, comfrey once figured prominently in herbal medicine but is now a suspected carcinogen and is recommended only for external use. Add dried and crumbled leaves to a bath as a skin softener. Steep leaves for liquid fertilizer, or add to the compost heap.

Selected species and varieties: *S. officinale* (common comfrey)—deep green rough-textured 10- to 20-inch basal leaves and ½-inch blue, white, purple, or rose tubular flowers. *S. x uplandicum* (Russian comfrey)—free-flowering with blue or purple blossoms; 'Variegatum' has leaves marbled cream and green.

Growing conditions and maintenance: Grow comfrey from root cuttings containing a growing tip, setting these divisions 6 to 8 inches deep and 2 to 3 feet apart. Choose sites carefully, as comfrey is difficult to eradicate once established. To control its spread, grow in large containers removed from other garden sites.

Tagetes
(ta-GEE-teez)
MARIGOLD

Tagetes patula

Hardiness: *tender or Zones 8-9*

Height: *6 to 36 inches*

Light: *full sun*

Soil: *organic, well-drained*

Plant type: *annual or perennial*

Uses: *landscaping, culinary, potpourri*

Primarily grown as bedding plants for their ferny, pungent foliage and clusters of flat flowers, marigolds are also valued for their root chemicals, which repel nematodes and inhibit weeds. Use leaves and flowers of some species as seasonings or to make tea; dried flower petals add color to potpourri.

Selected species and varieties: *T. lucida* (sweet mace)—a perennial to 30 inches tall with anise-scented leaves that can substitute for tarragon, and ½-inch yellow flowers; both leaves and flowers can be dried for tea; Zones 8-9. *T. minuta* (muster-John-Henry)—an annual to 3 feet with leaves lending an apple flavor; pale yellow flowers. *T. patula* (French marigold)—an annual 6 to 18 inches tall with yellow, orange, or brown flowers.

Growing conditions and maintenance: Sow annual marigold seeds indoors 4 to 6 weeks before the last frost or outdoors when the soil temperature reaches 60° F; transplant or thin to 12 inches. Deadhead to prolong bloom. Separate flower petals, and lay leaves flat to dry. Propagate sweet mace by division in spring in mild climates; grow as an annual elsewhere.

Tanacetum
(tan-a-SEE-tum)
TANSY

Tanacetum vulgare var. crispum

Hardiness: *Zones 4-9*

Height: *8 inches to 4 feet*

Light: *full sun to light shade*

Soil: *average to poor, dry, well-drained*

Plant type: *perennial*

Uses: *landscaping, potpourri, arrangements*

Tansy bears dainty flowers with conspicuous yellow button-shaped centers surrounded by a fringe of narrow, often inconspicuous white or yellow petals. Singly or in clusters, the flowers grow on branching stalks above pungent foliage that is semievergreen in milder climates. Smaller cultivars make informal border edgings, while others provide midborder fillers. Add the fresh flowers to rustic bouquets, or dry the branched flower stalks to accent dried arrangements. Insect-repellent properties are ascribed to all tanacetums, and some species are used in cosmetics and dyes. Traditional herbalists prescribed several species in medicines and teas, but these uses are no longer recommended, as the active chemicals can be toxic when eaten.

Selected species and varieties: *T. balsamita* [formerly classified as *Chrysanthemum balsamita*] (costmary)—pointed, oval, spearmint-scented leaves and clusters of tiny late-summer flowers on shrubby plants to 3 feet tall and 2 feet wide; Zones 4-8. *T. cinerariifolium* [formerly classified as *Pyrethrum cinerariifolium* and *Chrysanthemum cinerari-*

ifolium] (pyrethrum)—loose columns of foliage 18 to 24 inches tall and 12 inches wide with narrow filigreed leaves and almost petal-less summer-through-fall flowers borne singly or in sparse clusters that are the source of the relatively nontoxic insecticide pyrethrum; Zones 4-9. *T. parthenium* [formerly classified as *Pyrethrum parthenium* and *Chrysanthemum parthenium*] (feverfew)—cushions 1 to 3 feet tall and as wide of lacy leaves and clusters of ¾-inch summer flowers ideal for fresh or dried bouquets ; 'Aureum' (golden-feather) has golden green leaves on 12-inch mounds; 'Golden Ball', double rows of yellow petals on plants to 18 inches; 'White Bonnet', double-petaled white flowers on stems to 2

Tanacetum parthenium

feet; Zones 4-9. *T. vulgare* var. *crispum* (fern-leaved tansy)—leaves like small fern fronds in mounds to 4 feet high and flowers with yellow centers surrounded by insignificant petals; Zones 4-9.

Growing conditions and maintenance: Sow tanacetum seeds or transplant divisions in spring or fall, spacing them 1 to 4 feet apart. While tanacetums grow best in full sun, costmary and fern-leaved tansy tolerate partial shade. Rich soils produce floppy stems; trim plants back to prevent legginess. Provide a winter mulch in colder zones. Pick branching flower stalks just as blossoms open, and dry hanging upside down in bunches. Store dried tanacetums in tightly sealed containers to prevent their odor from penetrating other herbs. Propagate from seed, by vegetative cuttings taken in summer, or by division in spring or fall. All tanacetums self-sow, and feverfew and fern-leaved tansy can become invasive weeds.

Teucrium
(TEWK-ree-um)
GERMANDER

Teucrium chamaedrys

Hardiness: *Zones 5-9*

Height: *6 to 15 inches*

Light: *full sun to light shade*

Soil: *well-drained, slightly acid*

Plant type: *shrub*

Uses: *landscaping, dried arrangements*

Wall germander's spreading mounds of shiny evergreen foliage are covered from early to midsummer with spikes of small, lipped flowers. Allow a specimen to spread in a rock garden, or plant closely and clip into a low hedge resembling a miniature boxwood. The scalloped, oval leaves release a faintly garlicky odor when disturbed. Weave branches into dried wreaths. Wall germander once figured in herbal medicine but has fallen out of use.

Selected species and varieties: *T. chamaedrys* (wall germander)—square stems that trail, then turn up to stand 10 to 15 inches high lined with pairs of oval- to wedge-shaped ¼- to 1-inch leaves and tipped with whorls of ¾-inch white-dotted purple-pink flowers; 'Prostratum' has stems 6 to 8 inches tall spreading to 3 feet and pink flowers; 'Variegatum', green leaves splotched white, cream, or yellow.

Growing conditions and maintenance: Grow wall germander from seed, from spring cuttings, or by division, setting plants 1 foot part. Prune to shape in spring and deadhead to encourage bushiness. Provide protection from drying winter winds.

Thymus
(TY-mus)
THYME

Thymus x citriodorus 'Aureus'

Hardiness: *Zones 4-9*

Height: *2 to 18 inches*

Light: *full sun*

Soil: *average to poor, dry, well-drained, alkaline*

Plant type: *evergreen perennial or shrub*

Uses: *landscaping, culinary, potpourri*

Thyme adds pungent aroma, fine texture, and soft color to borders, rock gardens, and garden paths. Shrubby species with erect branches can be grown as specimens or low hedges. Creeping types fill niches among rocks or between paving stones, drape over walls, and sprawl into ground-covering mats. Thyme also grows well on window sills. Small clusters of ¼-inch nectar-filled summer-long flowers in a variety of shades are attractive to bees. Fresh or dried, the tiny ¼- to ½-inch narrow green to gray-green, sometimes variegated, leaves are used as a basic ingredient in bouquets garnis and fines herbes and are used to make tea. Both leaves and flowers are used in potpourris and toiletries. Herbalists use thyme as an insect repellent, medicinal plant, household disinfectant, and preservative.

Selected species and varieties: *T. caespititius* [formerly classified as *T. azoricus*] (tufted thyme, Azores thyme)—a subshrub forming 6-inch-high mats of twiggy branches lined with sticky, resinous leaves and tipped with white, pink, or lilac flowers; 'Aureus' has deep yellow-green leaves and pink flowers; Zones 8-9.

T. capitatus (conehead thyme)—upright bushy plants 10 inches tall and as wide with gray leaves and pink flowers crowded into cone-shaped tufts at the tips of branches; Zone 9. *T. cilicicus* (Cilician thyme)—deep green lemon-scented leaves and clusters of pale mauve to lilac blossoms on 6-inch stems; Zones 6-8. *T. x citriodorus* (lemon thyme)—forms a shrubby carpet up to 2 feet wide of foot-tall branches with tiny lemon-scented leaves; 'Aureus' (golden lemon thyme) has gold-edged leaves; 'Silver Queen', leaves marbled cream and silver gray; Zones 5-9. *T. herba-barona* (caraway thyme)—a fast-growing subshrub forming mats 4 inches tall and 2 feet across

Thymus herba-barona

with leaf flavors reminiscent of caraway, nutmeg, or lemon, and loose clusters of rose flowers; Zones 4-8. *T. mastichina* (mastic thyme)—an erect or sprawling shrub with 6- to 12-inch branches lined with gray-green eucalyptus-scented leaves; Zones 7-9. *T. praecox* ssp. *arcticus* [often sold under the name *T. serpyllum*] (creeping thyme, English wild thyme, nutmeg thyme)—2- to 3-inch-high carpets up to 18-inches wide with especially flavorful leaves and mauve to purple flowers; 'Coccineus' (crimson creeping thyme) has striking deep red blossoms; Zones 4-9. *T. pulegioides* [often sold under the name *T. serpyllum*] (broad-leaved thyme)—a shrub with large oval leaves lining 10-inch stems tipped with pink to purple flowers in broad mats; Zones 4-8. *T. serpyllum* (mother-of-thyme, wild thyme)—creeping stems only 2 to 3 inches tall in 3-foot-wide mats with cultivars in many shades of green or yellow, sometimes variegat-

ed; Zones 4-8. *T. vulgaris* (common thyme)—bushy shrubs 12 inches tall and as wide or wider with gray-green leaves used in cooking; 'Orange Balsam' has a scent recalling pine and citrus; Zones 4-8.

Growing conditions and maintenance: Plant thyme in spring, spacing transplants 12 to 24 inches apart. Select sites with average to poor soil and incorporate a small

Thymus praecox ssp. arcticus

amount of bone meal at planting time; rich or wet soils invite fungus and winter kill. To shape plants and encourage branching, prune hard in early spring before flowering or lightly after blooms appear. Remove green shoots of variegated cultivars to prevent them from reverting. Leaves are most pungent when picked while plants are in bloom and used while fresh; dried leaves are more flavorful than fresh winter leaves. Add leaves to meat dishes, stuffings, pâtés, salad dressings, vegetable dishes, herb butter, vinegars, and mayonnaise. To dry, hang bundles of branches upside down in a shady, warm, well-ventilated location, then crumble or strip fresh leaves from stems and dry on screens; store in airtight containers for use in cooking or sachets. An infusion of thyme made by boiling fresh leaves and flowers in water, then straining the liquid, creates a soothing facial rinse; add rosemary to the infusion for a hair rinse. To propagate thyme, root softwood cuttings taken in late spring or early summer or divide mature plants in early spring or late summer. Propagate from seed by sowing thickly in pots 6 to 8 weeks before the last frost, then set 4- to 6-inch seedlings out in clumps. Start thyme for a window-sill garden from seed, or pot divisions in late summer to bring indoors in late fall.

Tropaeolum
(tro-PEE-o-lum)
NASTURTIUM

Tropaeolum majus

Hardiness: *tender*

Height: *15 inches to 6 feet*

Light: *full sun to light shade*

Soil: *average, well-drained, sandy*

Plant type: *annual*

Uses: *landscaping, culinary, containers*

Nasturtiums bear funnel-like flowers with irregularly shaped petals from summer through frost. The flowers appear along mounding or trailing stems amid saucer-shaped leaves on twining stalks. Use dwarf, mounding nasturtiums as fillers, as houseplants, or among paving stones. Allow trailing or vining types to ramble as ground covers, cascade over walls, or trail from hanging baskets. Both the leaves and the flowers have a peppery flavor that adds zest to salads and sandwiches. Add flowers to vinegar. Substitute unripe seeds, fresh or pickled, for capers.

Selected species and varieties: *T. majus* (common nasturtium, Indian cress)—dwarf varieties to 15 inches tall, vining to 6 feet, with leaves to 6 inches across and 2½-inch flowers in yellow, orange, red, or mahogany; 'Empress of India' has vermilion blossoms amid blue-green foliage.

Growing conditions and maintenance: Sow nasturtium seeds ½ to ¾ inch deep in very early spring, spacing dwarf varieties 6 inches apart, vining types 12 inches apart. Plants growing in shade or rich soil produce more foliage and fewer flowers. Nasturtiums often self-sow.

Tulbaghia
(tul-BAJ-ee-a)
SOCIETY GARLIC

Tulbaghia violacea

Hardiness: *Zones 9-10*

Height: *1 to 2½ feet*

Light: *full sun to light shade*

Soil: *average, moist, well-drained*

Plant type: *bulb*

Uses: *landscaping, arrangements, culinary*

In summer, society garlic carries large clusters of starry flowers on tall stalks above clumps of grassy evergreen leaves. Use society garlic's neat mounds as a specimen in the perennial border, or grow the plant as an edging for garden beds or walkways. In cooler climates, society garlic grows well as a potted plant and can be wintered on a sunny window sill. Use the flowers in fresh bouquets. The leaves, with an onion or garlic aroma and a mild taste that does not linger on the breath, can be chopped and used like garlic chives as a garnish flavoring for salads, vegetables, and sauces.

Selected species and varieties: *T. violacea* (society garlic)—flat, grassy 8- to 12-inch leaves and ¾-inch white or violet flowers in clusters of eight to 16 blossoms on 1- to 2½-foot stalks; 'Silver Streak' has leaves striped cream and green.

Growing conditions and maintenance: Propagate society garlic by removing and replanting the small bulblets growing alongside mature bulbs in spring or fall. Space plants 1 foot apart. For indoor culture, plant one bulb per 6- to 8-inch pot.

Valeriana
(va-leer-ee-AY-na)
VALERIAN

Valeriana officinalis

Hardiness: *Zones 3-9*

Height: *3 to 5 feet*

Light: *full sun to light shade*

Soil: *average, moist, well-drained*

Plant type: *perennial*

Uses: *landscaping, arrangements, potpourri*

Valerian carries small flat-topped tufts of tiny flowers in summer in an open, branching cluster above a rosette of lacy leaves composed of narrow, paired leaflets. Both cats and butterflies find the plants attractive. The flowers, scented of honey and vanilla, are good in fresh bouquets. While some gardeners find the odor of the dried roots agreeable and add them to potpourri, others compare it to dirty socks. The roots yield a sedative compound used in herbal medicine. Add the mineral-rich leaves to compost.

Selected species and varieties: *V. officinalis* (common valerian, garden heliotrope)—erect, hairy stems lined with light green ferny leaves and flower stalks to 5 feet with tubular white, pink, red, or lavender-blue flowers in clusters up to 4 inches wide.

Growing conditions and maintenance: Sow common valerian seeds in spring, or divide the creeping roots in spring or fall. Space plants 2 feet apart, and mulch to conserve moisture. Valerian can be invasive; contain its spread by growing it in bottomless pots and removing flower heads before they form seed.

Verbascum
(ver-BAS-cum)
MULLEIN

Verbascum thapsus

Hardiness: *hardy or Zones 3-10*

Height: *4 to 6 feet*

Light: *full sun*

Soil: *dry, well-drained*

Plant type: *biennial*

Uses: *landscaping, arrangements, potpourri*

Mullein forms broad, low rosettes of gray-green velvety leaves its first year, followed by dramatic, tall flower spikes the second. Woolly leaves clasp each thick stalk, crowded at its tip with large green buds that open into small flowers with prominent stamens. Great mullein is one of the few gray plants that tolerate heat and humidity, making it a back-of-the-border specimen particularly well suited to warmer climates. Use the thick spikes in arrangements, or dry the honey-scented flowers, attractive to bees, for potpourri. Herbalists have used great mullein in medicines as well as for bandaging material. It has also been used for tinder, torches, and to reinforce shoe soles.

Selected species and varieties: *V. thapsus* (great mullein, common mullein, flannel plant, Aaron's rod)—thick, woolly leaves 6 to 18 inches long and spreading 3 feet wide, and ¾- to 1-inch-wide yellow flowers with orange stamens.

Growing conditions and maintenance: Sow great mullein seeds in fall or spring and space seedlings 2 to 2½ feet apart. Plants die after flowering but reseed themselves if flowers remain on plants.

Vetiveria
(vet-i-VERR-ee-a)
VETIVER

Vetiveria zizanioides

Hardiness: *Zones 9-10*

Height: *6 to 9 feet*

Light: *full sun*

Soil: *average to rich, moist to wet*

Plant type: *perennial grass*

Uses: *landscaping, potpourri*

Vetiver forms fountains of narrow, rough-edged leaves. Because its fibrous roots grow 10 feet deep, it is often planted to hold soil along the edges of streams and rivers. Flowers, when they occur, develop as flat spikelets in plumes on tall stems above the leaf clumps. The fragrant roots, with a woodsy, resinous scent overlaid by violets, can be dried to scent sachets. In the Far East, roots are woven into mats, screens, and baskets whose fragrance is renewed by dampening to scent rooms. Vetiver also yields an oil prized in expensive perfumes, soaps, and cosmetics.

Selected species and varieties: *V. zizanioides* (vetiver, khus-khus)—leaves ⅓-inch wide and up to 3 feet long and foot-long flowering spikes on stalks to 9 feet.

Growing conditions and maintenance: Vetiver grows best from divisions. Space plants 2 to 3 feet apart. The complex roots form dense sods that crowd out weeds. Harvest roots and renew plants by lifting and dividing every 3 to 4 years. Scrub the roots and spread on racks or screens to dry slowly. Use dried roots as weaving material or crumble for potpourri and sachets.

Viola
(vy-O-la)
VIOLET

Viola odorata

Hardiness: *Zones 3-10*

Height: *6 to 12 inches*

Light: *partial shade to full sun*

Soil: *moist, well-drained*

Plant type: *perennial or hardy annual*

Uses: *landscaping, culinary, potpourri*

Clumps of violets with five-petaled blossoms resembling tiny faces are a staple in old-fashioned gardens as fillers among taller perennials, as edgings for beds and walkways, or in containers. Available in a wide range of shades, the small blossoms add cheer and fragrance to nosegays of fresh flowers. Their soft colors and faintly wintergreen taste accent salads, jams, and jellies. Candied violets garnish cakes, puddings, and other desserts. Violet water enhances baked goods, ices, and chilled soups, and can be used as a mouthwash or facial rinse. Add dried blossoms to potpourri. Add the slightly tangy leaves, high in vitamins A and C, to salads, or use them to perfume water for a facial steam. The flowers, leaves, and roots all figure in herbal medicine.

Selected species and varieties: *V. odorata* (sweet violet, florist's violet, English violet)—a perennial with sweetly scented deep purple or white, sometimes yellow, 1- to 1½-inch blossoms having prominent yellow centers on 6- to 8-inch stems amid quilted heart-shaped leaves in late winter to early spring in mild climates, from late spring through summer elsewhere; 'Alba' bears quantities of snow white flowers; 'Royal Robe' has extremely fragrant deep purple blossoms on 8-inch stems; Parma violets produce double rows of petals; Zones 3-10 for most except Parma violets, which are hardy only to Zone 6. *V. tricolor* (Johnny-jump-up, miniature pansy, field pansy, European wild pansy, heartsease)—hardy annual or short-lived perennial producing small, inch-wide blossoms combining purple, white, and yellow petals on 6- to 8-inch stems amid clumps of scalloped leaves throughout spring and summer.

Viola tricolor

Growing conditions and maintenance: Sow violet seeds directly in the garden in late summer or early spring, or start indoors 8 to 12 weeks before the last frost. Sweet violet grows best in partial shade, Johnny-jump-up in full sun, but either tolerates less than ideal light. Johnny-jump-up self-sows readily and behaves like a perennial in locations that favor its growth; treat sweet violet as an annual in regions with mild winters. Provide sweet violets, which spread by underground runners, with a light winter mulch. For more prolific flowering, feed violets in very early spring and remove faded flowers; shear sweet violets in late fall and remove excess runners. Divide sweet violets in fall, and space transplants 6 to 12 inches apart. For fresh use, pick flowers early in the day, leaves while still young. Candy the blossoms by dipping them in a heavy sugar syrup, then laying them flat to dry. Pour 3 ounces of boiling water over 2 ounces of leaves and petals and allow to steep for use in baking or as a cosmetic. Dry blossoms slowly in a shaded location to retain their delicate color.

Vitex
(VY-tex)
CHASTE TREE

Vitex agnus-castus

Hardiness: *Zones 7-10*

Height: *6 to 15 feet*

Light: *full sun*

Soil: *average, moist to dry*

Plant type: *shrub or tree*

Uses: *landscaping*

Chaste tree's aromatic gray-green leaves are composed of narrow, pointed leaflets arranged like the fingers on a hand. Usually growing as a multitrunked shrub in a shrub border, it can be pruned as an umbrella-shaped tree to serve as a lawn specimen. In summer and sporadically in fall, chaste tree produces large flower spikes followed by fleshy fruits. The tiny fruits have a peppery flavor and are sometimes dried and ground as a condiment.

Selected species and varieties: *V. agnus-castus* (chaste tree, hemp tree)—shrubs up to 15 feet tall and as wide with lacy, fan-shaped leaves up to 6 inches across, dark green above and gray below, and 7-inch spikes of tiny lavender-blue flowers followed by red-black berries.

Growing conditions and maintenance: Sow chaste tree seed in spring or fall, or start new plants from softwood cuttings taken in spring or from semiripe cuttings taken in summer. Plants bloom on the current season's growth. Cut dead or damaged branches back to 2 inches in very early spring to renew older shrubs or those touched by frost. Collect and dry fruits in fall.

Zingiber
(ZIN-ji-ber)
GINGER

Zingiber officinale

Hardiness: *Zones 9-11*

Height: *3 to 4 feet*

Light: *light shade*

Soil: *rich, moist, well-drained*

Plant type: *perennial*

Uses: *containers, culinary*

Ginger's aromatic branching roots with a spicy, citrusy bite have been prized by cooks for centuries. Fresh grated or dried ground ginger flavors baked goods, marinades, curries, chutneys, beverages, syrups, vegetables, fruit dishes, and more. Grow ginger outdoors in hot, humid regions or as a container plant elsewhere.

Selected species and varieties: *Z. officinale* (common ginger)—2- to 4-foot flat leaves composed of pointed leaflets lining reedlike stems and, rarely, yellow-petaled summer flowers with yellow-streaked purple lips in conical spikes.

Growing conditions and maintenance: Purchase gingerroot from a nursery or grocery store. Pot a section with large growth buds just below the surface in equal parts of sand, loam, peat moss, and compost. Plants grow best in warm temperatures with constant humidity and soil moisture. After 8 to 10 months, harvest the roots, retaining a small section to replant. Refrigerated, roots keep 2 to 3 months wrapped in a damp towel and plastic film. Alternatively, peel the roots, slice into a jar of sherry, and refrigerate indefinitely.

Acknowledgments and Picture Credits

The editors wish to thank the following for their valuable assistance in the preparation of this volume:

Dr. Morgan Delaney, Alexandria, Virginia; Elise Felton, Southwest Harbor, Maine; Lydia Fontenot, Prairie Basse Nursery, Carencro, Louisiana; Cyrus Hyde, Well-Sweep Herb Farm, Port Murray, New Jersey; Michael and Susan McAdoo, Alexandria, Virginia; Arthur O. Tucker, Department of Agriculture and Natural Resources, Delaware State College, Dover; Washington Cathedral Greenhouse, Washington, D.C.

Bibliography

BOOKS:

Adams, James. *Landscaping with Herbs.* Portland, Ore.: Timber Press, 1987.

The American Horticultural Society Encyclopedia of Gardening. New York: Dorling Kindersley, 1994.

Ball, Jeff. *Rodale's Garden Problem Solver: Vegetables, Fruits, and Herbs.* Emmaus, Pa.: Rodale Press, 1988.

Bown, Deni. *The Herb Society of America Encyclopedia of Herbs and Their Uses.* New York: Dorling Kindersley, 1995.

Boxer, Arabella, and Philippa Back. *The Herb Book.* New York: Gallery Books (W. H. Smith), 1990.

Bradley, Fern Marshall (Ed.). *The Expert's Book of Garden Hints.* Emmaus, Pa.: Rodale Press, 1993.

Bremness, Lesley:
The Complete Book of Herbs. London: Guild Publishing, 1988.
Herbs (Eyewitness Handbooks). New York: Dorling Kindersley, 1994.

Buchanan, Rita. *A Weaver's Garden.* Loveland, Colo.: Interweave Press, 1987.

Clarke, Ethne. *Herb Garden Design.* New York: Macmillan, 1995.

Clarke, Graham, and Alan Toogood. *The Complete Book of Plant Propagation.* London: Ward Lock, 1992.

Clarkson, Rosetta E. *Magic Gardens: A Modern Chronicle of Herbs and Savory Seeds.* New York: Macmillan, 1939.

Clausen, Ruth Rogers, and Nicolas H. Ekstrom. *Perennials for American Gardens.* New York: Random House, 1989.

Courtier, Jane. *Gardening by Design: Herbs.* Topsfield, Mass.: Salem House, 1987.

DeBaggio, Thomas. *Growing Herbs from Seed, Cutting, and Root.* Loveland, Colo.: Interweave Press, 1994.

Dirr, Michael A. *Manual of Woody Landscape Plants* (4th ed.). Champaign, Ill.: Stipes Publishing, 1990.

Doole, Louise Evans. *Herbs for Health: How to Grow and Use Them.* North Hollywood, Calif.: Wilshire Book Company, 1972.

Downham, Fred. *Plant Propagation* (Ward Lock Master Gardener series). London: Ward Lock, 1993.

The Encyclopedia of Herbs, Spices, and Flavorings. New York: Dorling Kindersley, 1992.

Erler, Catriona Tudor. *Herb Gardens* (Better Homes and Gardens® Step-by-Step Successful Gardening series). Des Moines, Ia.: Meredith® Books, 1995.

Felton, Elise. *Artistically Cultivated Herbs.* Santa Barbara, Calif.: Woodbridge Press, 1990.

Ferguson, Nicola. *Right Plant, Right Place.* New York: Simon & Schuster, 1992.

Foster, Catharine Osgood. *Plants-a-Plenty.* Emmaus, Pa.: Rodale Press, 1977.

Foster, Gertrude B. *Herbs for Every Garden.* New York: E. P. Dutton, 1966.

Foster, Steven. *Herbal Renaissance.* Salt Lake City: Gibbs-Smith, 1993.

Foster, Steven, and James Duke. *Medicinal Plants* (Peterson Field Guides). Boston: Houghton Mifflin, 1977.

Garland, Sarah. *The Herb Garden.* New York: Penguin Books, 1984.

Gibbons, Euell. *Stalking the Healthful Herbs.* New York: David McKay, 1966.

Griffiths, Mark. *Index of Garden Plants.* Portland, Ore.: Timber Press, 1994.

Hill, Lewis. *Secrets of Plant Propagation* (Garden Way Publishing). Pownal, Vt.: Storey Communications, 1986.

Hill, Madalene, Gwen Barclay, and Jean Hardy. *Southern Herb Growing.* Fredericksburg, Tex.: Shearer Publishing, 1987.

Hopkinson, Patricia, et al. *Herb Gardening* (American Garden Guides). New York: Pantheon Books (Knopf), 1994.

Houdret, Jessica. *Herb Gardening* (Crowood Gardening Guides). Ramsbury, Wiltshire, U.K.: Crowood Press, 1992.

Jacobs, Betty E. M. *Growing and Using Herbs Successfully* (Garden Way Publishing). Pownal, Vt.: Storey Communications, 1995.

Kirkpatrick, Debra. *Using Herbs in the Landscape.* Harrisburg, Pa.: Stackpole Books, 1992.

Kowalchik, Claire, and William H. Hylton (Eds.). *Rodale's Illustrated Encyclopedia of Herbs.* Emmaus, Pa.: Rodale Press, 1987.

Lathrop, Norma Jean. *Herbs: How to Select, Grow, and Enjoy.* Tucson, Ariz.: HP Books, 1981.

McClure, Susan, and C. Colston Burrell. *Perennials* (Rodale's Successful Organic Gardening™ series). Emmaus, Pa.: Rodale Press, 1993.

Michalak, Patricia S. *Herbs* (Rodale's Successful Organic Gardening™ series). Emmaus, Pa.: Rodale Press, 1993.

Still, Steven M. *Manual of Herbaceous Ornamental Plants* (4th ed.). Champaign, Ill.: Stipes Publishing, 1994.

Strong, Roy. *Creating Formal Gardens.* Boston: Little, Brown, 1989.

Swanson, Faith H., and Virginia B. Rady. *Herb Garden Design.* Hanover, N.H.: University Press of New England, 1985.

Taylor's Guide to Herbs. Boston: Houghton Mifflin, 1995.

Webster, Helen Noyes. *Herbs: How to Grow Them and How to Use Them.* Newton, Mass.: Charles T. Branford, 1942.

Westcott, Cynthia. *The Gardener's Bug Book* (4th ed.). Garden City, N.Y.: Doubleday, 1973.

Westcott's Plant Disease Handbook (4th ed.). Revised by R. Kenneth Horst. New York: Van Nostrand Reinhold, 1979.

Western Garden Book (rev.). Menlo Park, Calif.: Sunset Publishing, 1995.

Wilder, Louise Beebe. *The Fragrant Garden.* New York: Dover Publications, 1974.

Wilson, Jim. *Landscaping with Herbs.* Boston: Houghton Mifflin, 1994.

Wrensch, Ruth D. *The Essence of Herbs.* Jackson: University Press of Mississippi, 1992.

Wyman, Donald. *Wyman's Gardening Encyclopedia* (2d ed.). New York: Macmillan, 1986.

Zabar, Abbie. *The Potted Herb.* New York: Stewart, Tabori & Chang, 1988.

PERIODICALS:

Buchanan, Rita. "Herbal Lawns." *Herb Companion,* June/July 1993.

Cook, Adrienne:
"Chef's Special: Planting Herbs on a Windowsill to Harvest in Winter." *Washington Post,* September 28, 1995.
"A Tea-Riffic Idea: Planting a Garden of Herbs to Provide Cupfuls of Comfort All Winter." *Washington Post,* October 5, 1995.
"Tending to Rosemary: Caring for the Herb through Winter." *Washington Post,* December 15, 1994.

DeFeo, Dale. "Indoor Gardens." *Capital Gardener,* Winter 1995.

England, Yvonne. "Herbs Find a Home in an Ornamental Garden." *Fine Gardening,* August 1994.

Erler, Catriona Tudor. "Garden Guide: Conserving Water in Container Plants." *San Diego Home/Garden,* May 1983.

Gardner, Jo Ann. "Flowering Herbs." *Horticulture,* February 1993.

Hälvä, S., et al.: "Growth and Essential Oil in Dill (*Anethum graveolens* L.) in Response to Temperature and Photoperiod." *Journal of Herbs, Spices, and Medicinal Plants,* Vol. 1, no. 3, 1993. "Light Quality, Growth, and Essential Oil in Dill (*Anethum graveolens* L.)." *Journal of Herbs, Spices, and Medicinal Plants,* Vol. 1, no. 1/2, 1992.

Letchamo, W. "Effect of Storage Temperatures and Duration on the Essential Oil and Flavonoids of Chamomile." *Journal of Herbs, Spices, and Medicinal Plants,* Vol. 1, no. 3, 1993.

Proctor, Rob. "Every Nook and Cranny." *Herb Companion,* August/September 1995.

Randhawa, G. S., and B. S. Gill. "Transplanting Dates, Harvesting Stage, and Yields of French Basil (*Ocimum basilicum* L.)." *Journal of Herbs, Spices, and Medicinal Plants,* Vol. 3, no. 1, 1993.

Shaudys, Phyllis V. "Herb Chart." *Potpourri from Herbal Acres,* Pine Row Publications, Washington Crossing, Pa., 1995.

Worthington, Frances. "Oregano! . . . Or Is It?" *Carolina Gardener,* October 1995.

Index

Numerals in italics indicate an illustration of the subject mentioned.

156

TIME ®
LIFE
BOOKS